Legal Aspects of Consent

Legal Aspects of Consent

Second edition

BJN monograph
Legal Aspects of Health Care series

Bridgit Dimond

MA, LLB, DSA, AHSM, Barrister-at-law,
Emeritus Professor of the University of Glamorgan

QUAY
BOOKS

A division of MA Healthcare Ltd

Quay Books Division, MA Healthcare Ltd, St Jude's Church, Dulwich Road, London
SE24 0PB

British Library Cataloguing-in-Publication Data
A catalogue record is available for this book

© MA Healthcare Limited 2009

ISBN-10: 1 85642 384 0
ISBN-13: 978 1 85642 384 7

Printed by CLE, Huntingdon, Cambridgeshire

Contents

Contents

Foreword to the first edition

We lawyers are unpopular people and that is not surprising. We come along after the event and tell people what they should have done (or not done). This is particularly annoying for conscientious professionals who have to take sensitive and difficult decisions – about what to tell a patient, whether the patient is able to agree to or refuse treatment, whether he or she has in fact done so – in the heat of the moment. Much better if they have a clear idea of the legal principles and sensible guidance about how to apply them in advance. That is what Bridgit Dimond has set out to give you in this book.

But it goes further than that. The health care professions, the Department of Health and the NHS service providers are developing models of 'good professional practice' in this area. If there is clear professional guidance about what is good practice on a particular point, then a professional may have to justify departing from it in an individual case. It is harder to say that it was regarded as acceptable by a 'responsible body of medical opinion' (in the well known test laid down in *Bolam* v. *Friern Hospital Management Committee* [1957]). So the responsible professional needs to know what the guidance says as well as what the law says.

And on top of all that is the Human Rights Act 1998. The very essence of the European Convention on Human Rights is respect for human dignity and human freedom, as the European Court of Human Rights said in the case of Diane Pretty (the motor neurone disease sufferer who wanted her husband to be allowed to help her to commit suicide). The court also said that the notion of personal autonomy is an important principle underlying the right to respect for private life in Article 8. This does not mean that the patient's wishes always prevail. But you need a book like this to tell you when they do and when they don't.

Brenda Hale
December 2002

Preface to the first edition

Like the first book in this series, the law relating to patient confidentiality, this monograph follows the publication of a series of articles in the *British Journal of Nursing* on consent. The advantages of a book for health professionals setting out the law and practice on consent led to Quay Books agreeing that the articles, updated and revised, could form the basis of a concise publication covering the main concerns which arise in respecting the law relating to consent. Like the other books in this series, this is intended for all health professionals, health service managers and patient groups and their representatives. It aims to use a style which avoids legal jargon and by the use of illustrating situations or cases provides an easy guide to the law relating to consent. Since by far the majority of health professionals are women, *she* rather than *he* and *her* rather than *his* has been used for the registered practitioners whose role is considered in the following pages.

Many readers may not be acquainted with basic facts of the legal system and so these are briefly set out in the first chapter. It is hoped that this book, like the others in this series, will provide a succinct, useful basis from which practitioners and others can extend their knowledge of the law for the protection of their patients, their colleagues and themselves.

Bridgit Dimond
October 2002

Preface to the second edition

Since 2002, when the first edition of this book was published, there have been significant changes in the law relating to consent. The most important is the enactment and implementation of the Mental Capacity Act 2005, which provided a statutory framework for decision making on behalf of those adults lacking the requisite mental capacity to make specific decisions. This Act, along with other statutory changes, decided cases and new guidance from the DH and professional bodies, has led to major amendments to the first edition. It is hoped that this new edition will continue to provide a useful foundation on which health professionals can build their understanding of the laws relating to consent.

Bridgit Dimond
May 2009

Acknowledgements

I should like to thank all those many practitioners with whom I have come into contact through conferences and teaching who have raised with me the questions and issues which form the basis of this book. I am also indebted to the constant support and encouragement of my family and Bette, who once again prepared the index and tables of cases and statutes. Finally, I would like to acknowledge the advice, assistance and encouragement of Tessa Shellens over many years, and it is to Tessa that this book is dedicated.

CHAPTER I

Sources of law and guidance

Introduction

This first chapter sets out the legal basis from which our laws of consent derive, and it also explains the provisions of the Human Rights Act 1998 and the legal system of the UK. The information is of necessity brief and readers may be interested in reading more detailed works set out in Further reading on page 267.

Source of law

Our laws derive from two principal sources: Acts of Parliament/statutory instruments (known as a statute or legislation) and decided cases. (See the Glossary – page 269 – for further explanations of legal terms.)

Legislation

Legislation, as well as consisting of Acts of Parliament (approval by the Houses of Commons and Lords and the Queen's signature) would also include directives and regulations emanating from the European Community, which the UK as a member state is required to implement and obey (see below).

Legislation can be primary or secondary. Primary legislation consists of Acts of Parliament, known as Statutes, which come into force at a date set either in the initial Act of Parliament or a date subsequently fixed by order of a Minister (i.e. by Statutory Instrument). The date of enforcement is often later than the date on which it is passed by the two Houses of Parliament and signed by the Crown. The statute sometimes gives power to a Minister to enact more detailed laws, and these regulations are known as secondary legislation. Statutory Instruments which are quoted in the text are an example of this secondary legislation. Devolution has given to the different parts of the UK (Scotland, Wales and Northern Ireland) varying powers of lawmaking, and increasingly different statutory provisions are coming into force in these parts of the UK.

Common law, judge made law, case law

The other main source of law is the decisions of the courts. This source is known as case law, or judge made law or the common law. The courts form a hierarchy and the highest court in this country is the House of Lords. The courts lay down principles which must be followed by courts below that level, unless the decision can be distinguished on the basis that it is not relevant to the case before it. Thus if the House of Lords sets out a specific principle, known as a precedent, then this is binding on all courts in the country except itself (i.e. the House of Lords does not have to follow its own precedents).

In the case of Diane Pretty (*R. (On the application of Pretty) v. DPP* [2001]), the House of Lords decided that her application (that her husband should be given an advanced immunity against any possible proceedings under the Suicide Act 1961 if he were to aid and abet her suicide), could not be granted. They did not find that her human rights as set out in the European Convention on Human Rights (see below) were breached by the Suicide Act 1961. She then applied to the European Court of Human Rights alleging a breach of her human rights but failed in her application (*Pretty* v. *United Kingdom* (2002)). (The case is discussed further in Chapter 19.)

The decisions of the courts are reported so that lawyers and judges can refer to a specific case and the principles established by it. These principles are known as the *ratio decidendi* and can be applied to any matters in dispute. Judges might also make statements about wider matters that are not directly the subject of the case before them, and these statements are known as *obiter dicta*. These may be of persuasive authority and interest in subsequent cases, but they are not binding as precedents. If there is a dispute between a case and a statute the latter would take priority: judges have to follow an Act of Parliament. Thus in the Diane Pretty case, had the House of Lords thought that the Suicide Act 1961 was contrary to the European Convention on Human Rights (see below), then it could have referred this statute back to Parliament for review. (In practice, however, the House of Lords did not consider that there was any clash between the Suicide Act 1961 and the articles in the European Convention on Human Rights.) Parliament can enact legislation which would overrule a principle established in the courts.

Human Rights Act 1998

This came into force in England, Wales and Northern Ireland on 2 October 2000 and on devolution in Scotland. It incorporates the articles of the European Convention on Human Rights (contained in Schedule 1 to the Act) into the UK's laws. (Schedule 1 can be found in Appendix 1 to this book.) The Act:

- requires all public authorities to implement the articles of the European Convention on Human Rights,
- gives a right to anyone who alleges that a public authority has failed to respect those rights to bring an action in the courts of this country and
- enables judges who consider that legislation is incompatible with the Articles of the Convention to refer that legislation back to Parliament.

Whilst there are no specific articles which expressly consider the law on consent, Article 2 on the right to life, Article 3 on the right not to be subjected to torture or to inhuman or degrading treatment or punishment, Article 5 on the right to liberty and security of person and Article 8 on the right to respect for privacy, family and correspondence all relate to some of the issues which arise in the laws on consent and will be considered in subsequent chapters. In a case concerning Siamese twins, the Court of Appeal had to decide if it was lawful to allow an operation to proceed which would automatically lead to the death of the one child who was dependent upon her sister's heart and lungs for survival. There was evidence that the dependent child Mary was killing her sister Jodie. Whilst both children had a right to life under Article 2 of the European Convention on Human Rights, the Court of Appeal held that the best interests of the twin who had the heart and lungs should prevail over the other and that the operation should go ahead. (In re A (Minors) 2000.)

Effect of the European Community

Since the UK signed the Treaty of Rome in 1972 it has been one of the member states of the European Community. The effect of this is that the UK is now subject to the laws made by the Council of Ministers and the European Commission. In addition, secondary legislation of the European Community in the form of regulations is binding on the member states. Directives of the Community must be incorporated by Act of Parliament into the law of each member state. Appeals from UK courts on EC laws can be made to the European Court of Justice in Luxembourg, which gives interpretations of the European laws. Their decisions are binding on the courts of member states.

Criminal and civil law

Issues relating to consent arise in both the criminal law and civil law. Criminal offences, which may be defined by both statutes and the common law, can be prosecuted in the criminal courts of this country. A public prosecution is brought in the name of the Crown and the prosecution has to establish that the offence has been committed beyond reasonable doubt. (It is also possible to bring a private prosecution, but this can be costly and is often difficult to secure a conviction.) The offence of assault is a criminal offence under the Offences Against the Person Act 1861; battery is an offence at common law. An absence of consent to treatment could therefore lead to criminal prosecution against the perpetrator. If an operation is performed which is totally contrary to reasonable professional practice, even with the consent of the patient, this consent may not be sufficient to defend the surgeon against criminal proceedings, nor against causing grievous bodily harm. (See Chapter 22 on consent to the amputation of healthy limbs.)

In addition, the same acts could constitute a civil wrong and therefore be actionable by the victim in the civil courts. The civil courts can award compensation and can issue other orders such as an order for specific performance, an injunction, or a declaration. The claimant must establish his or her case on a balance of probabilities, which, in contrast to the standard of proof in the criminal courts, is a lighter burden.

Law and ethics

There is considerable overlap between the law and ethics. One's ethics or moral standards derive from a variety of sources: religion, upbringing and personal experience all lead to a person's ethical values. In any democratic society one would hope that there would be a strong reciprocal relationship between the law and ethics. Therefore many civil and criminal wrongs would also be regarded as ethically wrong. All registered health professionals are required to obey a code of professional conduct which contains ethical principles. There may be ethical views which are not part of the law. In this book we are concerned with the law and therefore there can be little discussion of ethical issues. However, in many of the situations we discuss there is also a moral or ethical perspective and the reader is referred to the reading list for sources on ethics in healthcare for further discussion of this.

Department of Health guidance

The Department of Health (DoH) has published a Guide to Consent for Examination or Treatment (DoH, 2001a). This is a comprehensive document covering a wide range of situations. The appendices include the principles to be followed in applications to court when there is doubt as to the patient's capacity to consent, as well as further reading and legal references. Forms which can be used as evidence that consent has been given have been published and were implemented from April 2002 (DoH, 2001b).

The DoH has also provided, as part of the Reference Guide, additional guides for relatives and carers, parents, adults, children and young people and people with learning difficulties (with helpful pictures). It also provides a single sheet entitled '12 key points on consent: the law in England' which could be put on the noticeboards of wards or departmental offices in England. All those involved in obtaining consent should ensure that they have easy access to this information and that it is updated at regular intervals. It is the Department of Health's intention that the Reference Guide should be revised on a regular basis. It can be accessed via the Department of Health's web site (DoH, 2002c). Since the implementation of the Mental Capacity Act 2005 guidance has been issued by the Department of Health, the Ministry of Justice and the Office of Public Guardian on decision making on behalf of mentally incapacitated adults. Guidance can be down loaded from their websites.

Kennedy Report

An inquiry was set up to investigate the circumstances leading to the deaths of several children who underwent cardiac surgery in Bristol and was chaired by Professor Kennedy. His report was published in 2001 (Kennedy, 2001) and made extensive and radical recommendations for reform within the NHS, including issues relating to consent. The recommendations will be referred to in several chapters in this book.

Professional advice

Many of the registered practitioners who are involved in consent issues with their patients have guidance from their professional bodies on the law and professional practice relating to consent to treatment. For example the Nursing and Midwifery Council (NMC) (NMC, 2008) in its Code of Professional Conduct states:

> Ensure you gain consent
> - You must ensure that you gain consent before you begin any treatment or care
> - You must respect and support people's rights to accept or decline treatment and care
> - You must uphold people's rights to be fully involved in decisions about their care
> - You must be aware of the legislation regarding mental capacity, ensuring that people who lack capacity remain at the centre of decision making and are fully safeguarded
> - You must be able to demonstrate that you have acted in someone's best interests if you have provided care in an emergency

The General Medical Council (GMC) (2008) has also issued guidance on consent for its registered medical practitioners. Failure to comply with the codes of professional practice and other guidance issued by a registration body could result in a practitioner facing professional conduct proceedings, with the ultimate threat of being struck off from the register.

Employment law

Most health professionals are employees who have a contract of employment with their employers. This contract may spell out explicitly duties in relation to the care of the patient, the observation of a duty of confidentiality and duties in relation to health and safety. In addition, the law implies certain terms into the contract of employment. For example, under these implied terms an employee would be expected to obey the reasonable orders of the employer, to act with reasonable care and skill and to recognise the duty of confidentiality. There is an implied duty that an employer will take reasonable care of the health and safety at work of the employee. Failure to obey express or implied terms could result in an employee facing disciplinary action, with the ultimate sanction of dismissal from her post. Following a dismissal, an employee with the requisite length of service could apply to an employment tribunal for a declaration that the dismissal was unfair and for compensation and/or reinstatement.

Thus any employee who failed to follow the legal principles relating to consent to treatment could face criminal, civil, professional conduct and disciplinary proceedings.

References

Dimond, B. (2008) *Legal Aspects of Nursing*, 5th edn. Pearson Education, Harlow.

Department of Health (2001a) *Reference Guide to Consent for Examination or Treatment*. DoH, London.

Department of Health (2001b) *Good Practice in Consent Implementation Guide: Consent to Examination and Treatment*. DoH, London.

Department of Health (2002c) web site: http://www.doh.gov.uk/consenttotreatment/.

General Medical Council (2008) *Consent: Patients and Doctors Making Decisions Together*. GMC, London.

Kennedy Report (2001) *Bristol Royal Infirmary Inquiry. Learning from Bristol: the Report of the Public Inquiry Into Children's Heart Surgery at the Bristol Royal Infirmary 1984–1995*. Command paper CM 5207 Stationery Office London.

Re A (Minors) (Conjoined twins: Surgical Separation) *The Times Law Report* 10 October 2000; [2001] Fam.147 CA.

Nursing and Midwifery Council (2008) *Code of Professional Conduct: Standards for Conduct, Performance and Ethics*. NMC, London.

R (On the application of Pretty) v. *DPP* [2001] UKHL 61 [2001] 3 WLR 1598.

Pretty v. *United Kingdom* [2002] 35 EHRR 1; [2002] 2 F.L.R. 45.

CHAPTER 2

The mentally competent adult

Box 2.1 Case scenario

Following a road accident, Ralph, a 25-year-old man, has been told that his hand has been so badly injured that it cannot be saved and he therefore needs to have it amputated. He says that he would prefer to die than have an artificial 'hook'. The ward sister arranges for him to be visited by a young woman who has had a similar amputation following injury and has learnt to use a prosthesis. Ralph still refuses. He is visited by a psychologist who considers that he has the necessary mental capacity to make his own decisions. His family and girlfriend plead with the surgeons to carry on regardless of his refusal, since he is too young and immature to understand the implications of his decision. He repeats to the nursing staff that he knows he will probably die without surgery, but he has made up his mind.

Introduction

Before treatment commences, the law requires that the health professional obtains the consent of a mentally competent person. Simple though this principle seems, many additional questions and problems arise: what if a person lacks mental competence? What about children? What about the way in which consent should be given? And what about the rights of relatives? This chapter examines the principle relating to the right of refusal by a mentally competent adult.

Without the consent of a mentally competent adult, any treatment or care which involves touching the person could be considered a trespass to the person, a civil wrong and in some circumstances a criminal assault. The fact that consent has been given is the most important defence in facing any such action. The burden is upon the claimant (i.e. the person bringing any claim, who used to be known as the plaintiff) to prove that a valid consent was not given.

Trespass to the person

An action for trespass (which belongs to a group of civil wrongs known as 'torts') is one of the oldest remedies in law (known as a right of action in law); it includes an assault and a battery. An action for assault arises where the employee of the defendant (in this context it is normally the employer of the health professional who would be sued because of its vicarious liability for the actions of the employee) causes a claimant reasonable apprehension of the infliction of a battery upon him or her; a battery arises where there is intentional and direct application of force to another person.

Assault and battery are also used to describe possible criminal actions, but when we are using the terms in relation to a trespass to the person we are referring to a civil action brought in the civil courts (i.e. County Court, High Court) for compensation by a claimant.

Unlike an action for negligence, harm does not have to be proved. The mere fact that a trespass has occurred is sufficient to bring an action. The action is known as actionable *per se*, i.e. actionable without proof of harm having been suffered. Trespass can also exist in relation to land and to goods. The mere touching of another person's property or possessions can constitute in law an actionable trespass. Clearly, however, an exception to trespass exists for the ordinary social contact of everyday life. For example, a person could not enter the London Underground at rush hour and say: 'Don't touch me or I'll sue for trespass to the person'. However, any deliberate touching of another person may constitute an assault or battery (see Box 2.2). An action can still constitute a trespass even when it is performed in the best interests of a person who is mentally capable but has not given consent.

In the case scenario (Box 2.1), Ralph appears to be mentally capable. He has even been visited by a psychologist who has declared that he is mentally competent for the purposes of making the decision about whether or not to have his hand amputated. (The determination of competence is considered in Chapter 6.) He is over 18 years and therefore an adult. Ralph is entitled to refuse to give consent for a good reason, a bad reason or no reason at all (*Re MB (Adult Medical Treatment)* [1997]; see Chapter 12). There can be no question of overruling his refusal. His right of autonomy permits him to make such decisions, even if death is the likely outcome.

Operating without consent

Let us imagine the following outcome. Ralph's family and girlfriend know that Ralph is a health fanatic and is in training for a place in the national gym-

Box 2.2 The case of Re F (*Re F (A mental patient: sterilisation)* [1990])

In this case, Lord Goff said:

A prank that gets out of hand, an over-friendly slap on the back, these things may transcend the bounds of lawfulness, without being characterised as hostile... Any touching of another's body is, in the absence of lawful excuse, capable of amounting to a battery and a trespass. Furthermore, in the case of medical treatment, we have to bear well in mind the libertarian principle of self-determination, which, to adopt the words of Cardozo J [an American Judge], recognises that:

> Every human being of adult years and sound mind has a right to determine what shall be done with his own body; and a surgeon who performs an operation without his patient's consent commits an assault for which he is liable in damages (*Schloendorff* v. *Society of New York Hospital* 211 NY 125 (1914).

nastics team. They consider that because of the trauma of the accident, he is, at this point, incapable of accepting such a reversal to his lifestyle and to his future ambitions and, therefore, in the short term, cannot cope with the situation. They discuss the situation with the ward staff and surgeons and ask that the operation should go ahead because they know that once it is performed Ralph will accept the situation and then learn to adapt to a new way of life and adopt new interests and hobbies. They suggest that the doctors should take Ralph down for surgery, telling him that only conservative action would be taken. In other words, his refusal should be overruled. They point out that had the amputation taken place when Ralph was brought into the hospital unconscious, he would have been faced with a *fait accompli*. They say that they are prepared to sign any consent form for the operation on Ralph.

On the basis of this agreement, Ralph is taken to theatre. He does not sign any form. He understands that he is being operated on for his hand to be saved if possible and no amputation is to take place. When he returns from theatre, he is told that the operation has taken place and that unfortunately his hand could not be saved and an amputation has taken place. He is extremely upset. Instead of accepting the situation and learning to adjust to it, he wishes to take legal action against those who carried out the surgery without his consent and he brings an action for trespass to the person. The lawyers to the trust suggest that the action should be defended as the doctors at all times acted in the best

Table 2.1 Reasons why Ralph would be successful in any court action if his hand was amputated without his consent

- He did not give consent to the operation and therefore the operation constituted a trespass to his person.

- He had the mental capacity to know what was being intended, to retain the information and make a decision upon it. He knew the likely consequences of his refusal and was mentally competent to make the decision.

- The fact that he has not suffered harm, but in fact has benefited from the operation, is irrelevant to the fact that it was a trespass to the person.

- The fact that the relatives gave consent is irrelevant. In law relatives do not have the power to give consent to treatment on behalf of patients who are over 18 years old if the patients possess the requisite mental capacity to make their own decisions; and here of course, Ralf has the requisite mental capacity. (The situation where an adult lacks capacity is considered in Chapter 7.)

interests of Ralph. The outcome is likely to be a successful action for Ralph (Table 2.1).

Valid consent

To be valid, consent must be given by a person who has the necessary mental capacity. This could include a child of 16 or 17 who has a statutory right to give consent, or a child under 16 years who has a right recognised at common law (i.e. judge made law) to give consent, provided the child is 'Gillick competent' (see Chapters 8 and 9). There is a presumption that a person over 16 years has the requisite mental capacity to give consent (Section 1(2) Mental Capacity Act (MCA) 2005), but this presumption can be rebutted (removed) if there is evidence to the contrary. Such a rebuttal would be tested on a balance of probabilities (Section 2(4) MCA). Consent must be given voluntarily – there must be no coercion, deceit or fraud.

Sufficient information must be given to the person so that he or she understands the basics of what is proposed. There are advantages in ensuring that the consent is evidenced in writing, but the writing is not the consent; the consent is the actual agreement by the person that what is proposed can go ahead.

Consent can be given in general terms to a particular procedure without every single aspect being explained to the patient, but failure to warn of the significant risks of substantial harm could constitute an action for breach of the duty of care to inform (this will be considered in Chapters 4 and 5).

Miss B case

In the case of *Re B* (2002), the President of the Family Division stated that a mentally competent patient could ask for her ventilator to be switched off and that it was a trespass to her person to treat her without her consent. The facts are shown in Box 2.3.

Box 2.3 Facts of *Re B* (2002)

Ms B suffered a ruptured blood vessel in her neck which damaged her spinal cord. As a consequence she was paralysed from the neck down and was on a ventilator. She was of sound mind and knew that there was no cure for her condition. She asked for the ventilator to be switched off. Her doctors wished her to try out some special rehabilitation to improve the standard of her care and felt that an intensive care ward was not a suitable location for such a decision to be made. They were reluctant to perform such an action as switching off the ventilator without the court's approval. Ms B applied to court for a declaration to be made that the ventilator could be switched off.

The main issue in the case was the mental competence of Ms B. If she were held to be mentally competent, then she could refuse to have life-saving treatment for a good reason, a bad reason or no reason at all. She was interviewed by two psychiatrists who gave evidence to the court that she was mentally competent. The judge therefore held that she was entitled to refuse to be ventilated. The judge, Dame Elizabeth Butler-Sloss, President of the Family Division, held that Ms B possessed the requisite mental capacity to make decisions regarding her treatment and thus the administration of artificial respiration by the trust against her wishes amounted to an unlawful trespass. It was reported on 29 April 2002 that Ms B had died peacefully in her sleep after the ventilator had been switched off. The decision was made before the Mental Capacity Act 2005 came into force, but the same outcome would have followed.

Withdrawal of consent

Just as a mentally competent adult can give a valid consent, so can this consent be withdrawn at any time, unless it has been given under contractual arrangements which limit the withdrawing of consent. Another exception would be where the patient has ceased to be mentally competent and the withdrawal of consent would be contrary to his or her best interests. For example a mentally competent patient may agree to have a termination of pregnancy which is to be undertaken in two stages, first the taking of medication, then admission to hospital for the termination to be clinically supervised. If a woman has taken the medication which is to induce a miscarriage, but then goes on a drinking spree which leads to her being mentally incapable of making her decisions, she would not be able to withdraw her consent to the abortion, firstly because it is already in process, and secondly because she lacks the mental capacity to make an effective withdrawal of the original consent. A case where a husband withdrew consent to the posthumous use of his sperm is considered in Chapter 24 (*Centre for Reproductive Medicine* v. *U* [2002]).

Guidance on consent to treatment

The Department of Health (DoH) (2001a) published a Reference Guide to consent to treatment which it is intended will be regularly updated with changes in statute and case law. It also prepared practical guidance for the NHS with new forms (DoH, 2001b) which were to be used from April 2002. These are considered in Chapter 3.

The recommendations of the Kennedy Report (2001) on paediatric heart surgery in Bristol also emphasise the importance of respect and honesty being at the centre of the relationship between health professional and patient.

Some of the specific recommendations made in the Kennedy Report (2001) are shown in Box 2.4. Other recommendations are set out in Chapters 4 (Box 4.2) and 5 (Table 5.1).

Jehovah's Witnesses

One of the most frequent examples of patients refusing life-saving treatment is when Jehovah's Witnesses refuse to have a blood transfusion. As mentally

---

Box 2.4 Recommendations of the Kennedy Report on Consent

In a patient-centred healthcare service patients must be involved, wherever possible, in decisions about their treatment and care.

5. Information should be tailored to the needs, circumstances and wishes of the individual.

23. We note and endorse the recent statement on consent produced by the DoH 'Reference guide to consent for examination and treatment', 2001. It should inform the practice of all healthcare professionals in the NHS and be introduced into practice in all trusts.

24. The process of informing the patient, and obtaining consent to a course of treatment, should be regarded as a process and not a one-off event consisting of obtaining a patient's signature on a form.

25. The process of consent should apply not only to surgical procedures but also to all clinical procedures and examinations which involve any form of touching. This must not mean more forms: it means more communication.

---

competent adults their right to refuse such treatment must be respected and the Royal College of Surgeons drew up a Code of Practice for the Surgical Management of Jehovah's Witnesses in 1996. It emphasises that 'if the patient is able to give an informed and rational opinion or if an applicable advance direction [see Chapter 16 of this book] exists, then this should be acted upon. If they are not the clinical judgment of the doctor should take precedence over the opinion of relatives and associates'. In the case of *Re T* [1992] a pregnant woman signed a form, under the influence of her mother, a Jehovah's Witness, that she would not wish to have a blood transfusion, at a time when such treatment seemed extremely unlikely. The Court of Appeal held that there is a rebuttable presumption that adults have capacity to consent to or refuse treatment and in this case this presumption could be rebutted since there was evidence that the patient was under the influence of her mother and a blood transfusion was in the patient's best interests. The existence of a rebuttable presumption in favour of mental capacity has now been placed on a statutory basis by the Mental Capacity Act 2005.

Exceptions to the right of self-determination of the mentally competent adult

Whilst the general principle is that a mentally competent adult has the right to give or withhold consent to treatment, there are exceptions as a result of public health legislation. Section 37 of the Public Health (Control of Diseases) Act 1984 enables a Justice of the Peace, on the application of the local authority, if satisfied that a person is suffering from a notifiable disease and it is necessary in order to prevent the spread of infection, to remove the person to suitable accommodation. The Public Health (Infectious Diseases) regulations 1988 S. I. 1988 No.1546 enable section 37 to be applied to those suffering from AIDS as though it were a notifiable disease.

In addition, the House of Lords (*R* v. *Brown* [1993]) has held that consent to sado-masochistic acts is not a valid defence to the criminal charge of inflicting violence upon oneself or others. This case and the amputation of healthy limbs are considered in Chapter 22.

There are also statutory powers to compel those persons suffering from mental disorder who are detained under the Mental Health Act 1983 (as amended by the Mental Health Act 2007) to receive treatment. These are discussed in Chapter 25.

Conclusion

Recognising that Ralph has the right to determine his own life and treatment is difficult for relatives and professionals. Only if there is clear evidence that he lacks the mental capacity to make that decision could his refusal be overruled and action taken in his best interests. Paternalistic action cannot be a defence against an action for trespass brought by a mentally competent adult. In the next chapter we will consider the form that any consent should take and when writing is required. However, as emphasised in the Kennedy Report, obtaining consent is a process of communication, not simply the signing of a form.

References

Re B (Consent to treatment: capacity) *The Times Law Report* 26 March 2002 [2002] 2 All ER 449.

Centre for Reproductive Medicine v. *U* [2002] EWCA Civ 565, *The Independent* 1 May 2002 CA.

Department of Health (2001a) *Department of Health Reference Guide to Consent for Examination or Treatment*, DoH, London; http//www.doh.gov.uk/consent/.

Department of Health (2001b) *Good Practice in Consent Implementation Guide*. DoH, London.

Re F (A mental patient: sterilisation) [1990] 2 AC 1.

Kennedy Report (2001) *Bristol Royal Infirmary Inquiry. Learning from Bristol: the Report of the Public Inquiry Into Children's Heart Surgery at the Bristol Royal Infirmary 1984–1995*. Command paper CM 5207, Stationery Office, London.

Re MB (Adult Medical Treatment) [1997] 2 FLR 426.

R v. *Brown* [1993] 2 All ER 75.

Royal College of Surgeons (1996) *Code of Practice for the Surgical Management of Jehovah's Witnesses*. RCS, London.

Schloendorff v. *Society of New York Hospital* 211 NY 125 (1914).

Re T [1992] 4 All ER 647.

CHAPTER 3

The different forms of consent

Box 3.1 Case scenario

Mary, following preoperative medication, was taken to theatre for a biopsy for possible breast cancer. When the theatre staff went through their check list they could not find a consent form. The consultant surgeon said that he had seen her in the outpatients' department two weeks before and she had given a clear consent, not only for the biopsy but also for a radical mastectomy should the results show that to be necessary. He said that he had no problems with continuing the operation. The theatre sister was unsure of the legal position.

Introduction

Consent is the agreement by a mentally competent person, voluntarily and without deceit or fraud, to an action which without that consent would be a trespass to the person. (See Chapter 2 for discussion of trespass to the person). Evidence of the fact that consent has been given could be a signed document, the spoken words of the patient or the non-verbal actions of the patient implying consent. All these different forms of showing that consent is being given are equally valid in law, but clearly vary considerably in evidential terms.

Consent in writing

This is by far the best form of providing evidence that consent has been given. The document is not the actual consent, but evidence that the patient agreed to the procedure. The Department of Health (DoH, 2001b) has recommended various forms which can be used to record the fact that consent has been given. They include forms for completion by the adult patient, by a child and parent of a child, and also a form where a person lacks the mental competence to give consent, which will be considered in Chapter 7. It was recommended that these forms should be used from April 2002. Any health professional can make use of the forms, since unlike the earlier forms issued in 1992 they do not just relate to treatment by doctors and dentists. There are therefore considerable advantages for other health professionals, such as nurses, midwives, physiotherapists and therapeutic radiographers in making use of the forms. The forms can also be adapted to cover consent for specific procedures. There are advantages in obtaining evidence in writing that consent has been given, when the treatment involves any risks or where there could be a subsequent dispute over whether consent was given.

Consent form 1 is the form to be used by mentally competent adults, and many NHS Trusts have taken the basic format suggested by the Department of Health and adapted it for specific types of treatment. The basic outline ensures that all the steps which are required in securing a valid consent are taken. Relatives do not have a right to give consent on behalf of another mentally competent adult (see Chapter 2). Consent form 2 can be used where the patient does not lose consciousness. The topic of consent and the mentally incapacitated adult is considered in Chapter 7.

What is covered by the written consent

The explanation of the intended treatment should include details of what is actually proposed together with information about the significant risks of substantial harm (see Chapter 5 for further discussion of this). However, it is not a requirement that every single aspect of the procedures would have to be mentioned to secure a valid consent. What if a patient after surgery discovered that he had been given a painkiller administered by a pessary? Could he maintain that that was a trespass to his person, since he had not given specific consent to administration of medicines in that format? The answer is probably 'No', since provided that he had given a consent to the overall treatment to be given, his consent to each and every procedure within that heading would not be required (*Sidaway* v. *Bethlem Royal Hospital Governors* [1985]). However, if it becomes known that certain types of administration of medicines or other procedures cause disquiet to patients, then there would be justification for ensuring that the patient was aware of these in advance, to prevent subsequent complaints.

Consent by word of mouth

On a day-to-day basis, most health professionals work on consent by word of mouth as the basis for performing regular routine care and treatment. 'Are you ready to have your injection?', if responded to by a clear 'Yes', is an example of consent by word of mouth. It would be a ridiculous requirement of bureaucracy if written consent were required for every item of care or procedure. Normally there would be no problems, but if subsequently the patient stated that consent had not been given to such a procedure, unless another person overheard the patient's agreement it would be one person's word against another.

Non-verbal consent

Sometimes known as implied consent, this relates to the behaviour of the patient which indicates to the health professional that the patient is agreeing to the proposed treatment. For example, instead of responding by saying 'Yes' to the question 'Are you ready to have your injection?', the patient might nod his or her head in agreement. No word is spoken by the patient. There is no consent by word of mouth, but the nodding conveys to the nurse that the patient is agreeing to the injection. The nurse could, therefore, proceed to give the patient the injection, knowing that consent was given. However, if subsequently a patient denies that he agreed to the injection, and merely moved his head because his neck was aching, it would not be easy for the nurse to dispute the fact that consent was not given. The nurse could point to other non-verbal communication such as the patient holding out his arm and rolling up a sleeve, as all such actions would suggest non-verbal agreement. Also, failure on the patient's part to stop the injection would also indicate that there was agreement. However, the nurse is clearly in a more vulnerable position than if he or she had consent in writing.

The term 'implied consent' is sometimes incorrectly used. For example, it is sometimes suggested that by coming into hospital the patient has given an implied consent to the treatment and care provided. However, it would be dangerous to rely upon such an assumption because there are so many choices in treatment and care that it would be difficult to show that the patient had given consent to one particular form of treatment rather than another. It has also been suggested that when a patient is unconscious and brought into hospital following a road accident, then he or she is implying consent to being treated (*Mohr* v. *Williams*, 1905). A preferable view to take is that where a patient is unconscious, without any advance statement of directions, he implies nothing, and health professionals act on a different basis in law: the statutory duty set out in the Mental Capacity Act 2005 to act in the best interests of a mentally incapacitated person. The statutory duty replaced the duty recognised at common law to act out of necessity in the best interests of a mentally incapacitated adult (*F* v. *West Berkshire Health Authority and another* [1989]; this is considered in Chapter 7).

Consent to screening

The same principles which apply to consent to treatment also apply to patient participation in screening or in agreeing to undergo tests. When blood is taken to be tested, the mentally competent patient must give consent to that blood being taken and also be given information about the use which will be made of that sample. Difficulties have arisen with testing for HIV. In practice, a distinction has been made between anonymous testing when the test result is not linked back to a specific patient and testing where the individual patient is told the result. In the latter case the patient should receive counselling before giving consent to his or her blood being tested for HIV antibodies. The Public Health Laboratory Service commenced a programme of anonymous HIV antibody testing, using blood left over from other tests authorised by the patient. A UKCC Registrar's letter (12/93) dated 6 April 1993 sets guidelines for practitioners involved in such testing and implicitly supported such testing provided that it was on an anonymous basis for epidemiological purposes.

In December 1998 the Government launched a campaign to encourage all pregnant women to have an HIV test. The press release stated that only 30 per cent of women who are HIV-positive are aware that they are infected. If a pregnant woman is known to be HIV-positive, then the risk of passing on HIV to the foetus can be reduced by arranging for delivery to be by Caesarean section. Avoiding breast feeding also removes the risk of passing on the virus through the milk. However, the law has not been changed and a test for HIV still requires the consent of the woman. The Government set a national target to achieve an 80 per cent reduction by December 2002 in the number of children who acquire HIV from their mothers (HSC 1999/183).

In the HIV/AIDS Services 2000/2001 allocation and strategy, NHS organisations were instructed that part of the HIV prevention budget was to be used to support antenatal services in recommending an HIV test to all pregnant women. A research project to estimate the cost effectiveness of a universal, voluntary HIV screening programme has suggested that it is effective and should be implemented in the London area, with other areas being considered for screening (Postma MJ and others, 1999).

DNA fingerprints

There had been controversy over whether the police were entitled to keep fingerprint and DNA information about individuals who have been acquitted or ceased to be suspected of criminal offences. The Court of Appeal ruled on 12 September 2002 that police could keep DNA and fingerprints from unconvicted suspects. It held that the present procedure complied with the European Convention on Human Rights. The case eventually came before the European Court of Human Rights. Two men from Sheffield, Michael Marper and S, brought the case because they were arrested in 2001 and had their fingerprints and DNA samples taken. They were not convicted of any crime and argued that the samples should have been destroyed and not kept on the National DNA database. Their case was rejected by the British courts and in February 2008 the European Court of Human Rights gave permission for the case to proceed (*Marper* v. *UK* 2007 and 2008). In December 2008 the ECHR held that storage of DNA profiles of suspects who were not convicted was a breach of Article 8 and constituted a disproportionate interference with the applicants' right to privacy (*Marper* v. *UK* [2007]).

There were concerns that if the men were to succeed in their claim it would lead to more than half a million samples being removed from the database (O'Neill, 2008) and there have been calls for an independent national database to be set up, rather than one held by the police.

It is a criminal offence under section 45 of the Human Tissue Act 2004 to analyse a DNA sample without the consent of the patient, unless the circumstances specified in the Act exist.

Case scenario (Box 3.1)

Mary's consultant is correct in that if Mary has given him, in the outpatients' consultation, consent to have a biopsy and, if necessary, to follow the biopsy with a radical mastectomy, then that is valid in law. It is assumed that Mary had the necessary mental capacity, that there was no compulsion, and that she was clearly informed about the biopsy and when a radical mastectomy might be the preferred treatment. If the consultant is correct in his recollection, then there has been consent by Mary to both the biopsy and the radical mastectomy. It has to be assumed that Mary has not withdrawn the consent which she gave by word of mouth and it is reasonable to rely upon it. However, the consultant is in a vulnerable position if, having undertaken a radical mastectomy, Mary denies that she had agreed to the full operation. She may say that she had only agreed to come into hospital for the biopsy. She had planned, if there was malignancy, to have chemotherapy and radiotherapy and to avoid any major surgery. It may be that a nurse in the outpatient department recollected the conversation or the consultant may have recorded in his medical records that Mary was to have a biopsy and, if necessary, a radical mastectomy. However, if Mary denies that she ever gave consent, and is adamant that she intended to pursue other courses of treatment, then it would be very difficult for the consultant to refute her evidence. He would be in a much stronger position if he had the written consent by Mary to both the biopsy and, should it prove necessary, the radical mastectomy.

While the surgeon might be prepared to take the risk of proceeding on his recollection of what was said in outpatients, the theatre sister would be very wise to insist that the surgeon should not proceed and postpone the surgery for later that day. It might be suggested that if Mary has only had the preoperative medication, and has not been anaesthetised, then she could sign the consent form there and then. However, this ignores the fact that Mary, as a result of that medication, may not have the mental capacity to understand what may happen and to give a clear consent. It would be much wiser not to rely on any written consent which is signed after the preoperative medication has been given.

While this may subsequently infuriate Mary, the wisest course of action is for the surgeon and nurses to accept that they need to have Mary's consent in writing to what is proposed and to ask for her to be returned to the ward. When she has recovered from the preoperative injection she must be told about what is intended and given the opportunity to sign the consent form.

Clearly apologies and explanations would have to be given to Mary as to why she was brought back from theatre, but it is a lesson to the ward staff that they should not have given Mary the preoperative medication until they had checked that a valid consent in writing was present among the records. Hopefully, Mary's fury and the inconvenience to ward and theatre staff would prevent such a reoccurrence and ensure that an appropriate procedure was implemented in future.

Conclusions

This chapter has considered the documentation which should evidence that consent has been given. In the next chapter we consider how much information should be given to patients or parents.

References

Department of Health (2001a) *Department of Health Reference Guide to Consent for Examination or Treatment*. DoH, London; http://www.doh.gov.uk/consent/.

Department of Health (2001b) *Good Practice in Consent Implementation Guide*. DoH, London.

F v. *West Berkshire Health Authority and another* [1989] 2 All ER 545; *Re F (mental patient: sterilization)* [1990] 2 AC 1.

Marper v. *UK* [2007] Application Nos. 30562/04 and 30566/04; [2008] EHCR 178, *The Times* 8 December 2008.

Mohr v. *Williams* (1905) 104 NW (Sup Ct Minn) Judge Brown.

O'Neill, S. (2008) DNA database under threat from the European Court, warns police chief. *The Times*, 7 June, p. 34.

Postma, M. J. and others (1999) Universal HIV screening of pregnant women in England: cost effectiveness analysis. *British Medical Journal*, **318**, 1656–60.

Sidaway v. *Bethlem Royal Hospital Governors* [1985] 1 All ER 643 [1985] AC 871.

UKCC Registrar's letter (12/93) dated 6 April 1993.

CHAPTER 4

The duty of care to inform

> ### Box 4.1 Case scenario
>
> Mrs Pearce was expecting her sixth child. The expected date of delivery was 13 November 1991. On 27 November, when she saw the consultant, the baby had still not arrived. She begged the doctor to induce her or to carry out a Caesarean. He preferred to let nature take its course, and explained to her the risks of induction and a Caesarean section. The baby died *in utero* some time between 2 and 3 December. The delivery of a stillborn baby was induced on 4 December. She brought an action alleging that the consultant should have advised her of the increased risk of stillbirth as a result of the delay in delivery between 13 November and 27 November (*Pearce v. United Bristol Healthcare NHS Trust*, 1998).

In this chapter, we consider the law and cases relating to the duty of care to inform. The next chapter will consider some of the problems in implementing this duty.

The duty of care

If a valid consent by a mentally competent person has been given for a particular procedure, then that will be a defence against a possible action for trespass to the person. The patient may, however, allege that he or she was not told about specific risks associated with the procedure. If these risks subsequently occur and harm is caused and the patient can show that he or she would have hesitated to agree to the procedure had he or she known of these risks, then the patient may succeed in an action for negligence against the professional or the professional's employer. The latter is vicariously liable for any negligence by its employees committed in the course of their employment. Unlike an action for trespass to the person, where harm does not have to be established, an action for negligence will only succeed if harm can be shown. As in any other action for negligence, there are four elements which the claimant will have to establish:

- A duty of care is owed by the defendant (or the defendant's employee), including the duty to inform
- There has been a breach of this duty of care by a failure to follow the reasonable standard of care, as defined in the Bolam Test (*Bolam* v. *Friern Barnet Management Committee* [1957])
- A reasonably foreseeable consequence of this breach of duty is that
- Harm has occurred.

All four elements must be established by the claimant on a balance of probabilities. These elements in an action for negligence will be considered in relation to the giving of information to the patient.

Withholding information

The other question which arises is: in what circumstances, if any, could information be withheld from the patient? This is considered below on page 40.

Chatterton v. Gerson

A case where the clear distinction was drawn between an action for trespass to the person and an action for breach of the duty of care to inform was the case of *Chatterton* v. *Gerson* [1981]. In this case, Judge Bristow said:

> In my judgment once the patient is informed in broad terms of the nature of the procedure which is intended, and gives her consent, that consent is real, and the cause of the action on which to base a claim for failure to go into risks and implications is negligence, not trespass.

The duty of care

The duty of care to diagnose, advise and treat also includes the duty to inform the patient. The courts have held that the duty of care is not divisible: it includes all the above components (*Sidaway* v. *Bethlem Royal Hospital Governors* [1985]).

The standard of care

How much information are doctors, nurses and other health professionals expected to give the patient? In America, there is a concept of informed consent, and it is a requirement that any relevant information in the knowledge of the health professionals should be given to a patient before consent is given to a particular procedure.

In the Sidaway case (*Sidaway* v. *Bethlem Royal Hospital Governors* [1985]), the House of Lords held that the English courts do not recognise a concept of informed consent. The facts of this case were that Amy Sidaway agreed to undergo an operation to relieve pain in her neck. She was informed about the possibility of disturbing a root nerve, but not about the risk of damage to the spinal cord. Unfortunately, the latter occurred and she became severely disabled. She sued for negligence on the basis that there was a breach of the duty of care to inform her about the possibility of such a risk.

The trial judge held that the surgeon had told her about the possibility of damage to the nerve root, and that he had not told her of the danger of damage to the spinal cord (the aggregate risk of damage to the nerve root or spinal cord occurring was estimated at between one and two per cent), nor did he tell her that it was an operation of choice rather than necessity.

However, in refraining from informing her of these facts, he was following a practice at that time (1974) which would have been accepted as proper by a responsible body of skilled and experienced neurosurgeons. The judge thus applied what has become known as the Bolam Test (*Bolam* v. *Friern Barnet Management Committee* [1957]) to the case. In the Bolam case Judge McNair stated that:

> The standard of care was that of the ordinary skilled man exercising and professing to have that special skill... A doctor was not guilty of negligence if he acted in accordance with the practice accepted at that time as proper by a responsible body of medical opinion, notwithstanding that other doctors adopted different practices.

As a consequence, Amy Sidaway lost her case in the High Court and appealed to the Court of Appeal unsuccessfully and thence to the House of Lords. The judges in the House of Lords all had different bases for their views, but they agreed that in general she had failed in her action. Lord Diplock applied the

Bolam Test to the duty of care to inform. Lord Bridge distinguished between two extremes: warning the patient of all possible risks once the treatment has been decided upon in the patient's best interests, and not warning the patient of any risks in order to not alarm the patient. Between these two extremes, Lord Bridge suggested that the Bolam Test should be applied, but this did not mean handing over to the medical profession the entire question of the scope of the duty of disclosure. There will be circumstances where the judge could come to the conclusion that disclosure of a particular risk was so obviously necessary to an informed choice on the part of the patient that no reasonably prudent medical person would fail to make it.

Lord Templeman stated that:

> In my opinion if a patient knows that a major operation may entail serious consequences, the patient cannot complain of lack of information unless the patient asks in vain for more information or unless there is some danger which by its nature or magnitude or for some other reason required to be separately taken into account by the patient in order to reach a balanced judgment in deciding whether or not to submit to the operation.

Lord Scarman supported a 'prudent patient test', a concept derived from an American case, *Canterbury* v. *Spence* 464 F 2d 772 (DC, 1972). In this case, it was recognised that there were four principles, as listed in Table 4.1.

Table 4.1 The four principles of the *Canterbury* v. *Spence* 464 F 2d 772 (DC, 1972) case.

1. Every human being of adult years and of sound mind has a right to determine what shall be done with his/her own body.

2. The consent is the informed exercise of a choice, and that entails an opportunity to evaluate knowledgeably the options available and the risks attendant on each.

3. The doctor must therefore disclose all 'material risks'. What risks are 'material' is determined by the 'prudent patient' test, which is as follows:

   a risk is... material when a reasonable person, in what the physician knows or should know to be the patient's position, would be likely to attach significance to the risk or cluster of risks in deciding whether or not to forgo the proposed therapy

4. The doctor has, however, a therapeutic privilege. This exception is that a reasonable medical assessment of the patient would have indicated to the doctor that disclosure would have posed a serious threat of psychological detriment to the patient.

Bolam Test

The Bolam Test does not assume that there is only one way to inform patients or to carry out treatment procedures. As McNair said, a doctor was not guilty of negligence if he acted in accordance with the practice accepted at that time as proper by a responsible body of medical opinion, notwithstanding that other doctors adopted different practices. This conforms with the ruling given by the House of Lords in the Maynard case (*Maynard* v. *W Midlands Regional Health Authority HL* 1985), where the House of Lords emphasised that:

> It was not sufficient to establish negligence for the plaintiff [i.e. claim-ant] to show that there was a body of competent professional opinion that considered the decision was wrong, if there was also a body of equally competent professional opinion that supported the decision as having been reasonable in the circumstances.

However, the House of Lords (*Bolitho* v. *City and Hackney HA*) has urged that experts must give responsible and reasonable evidence (see below). In the case of *Smith* v. *Tunbridge Wells Health Authority* it was held that even though some surgeons were not providing warnings of the risk of a rectal prolapse, it was not reasonable nor responsible for the surgeon in that particular case, who was therefore held to be in breach of the duty of care to inform.

Gold v. Haringey Health Authority [1988]

The principles set by the House of Lords in the Sidaway case were followed in *Gold* v. *Haringey*. In this case, following a sterilisation, the patient became pregnant with her fourth child. She sued for negligence alleging that she should have been warned of the failure rate of female sterilisations, and had she been told, her husband would have had a vasectomy. Evidence was given that at that time (1979) a competent body of professional opinion would not have given a warning. The judge, however, held that this test only applied to advice in a therapeutic context and not to a warning in a contraceptive situation, and found for the claimant. The Court of Appeal held that there was no distinction in law between advice given in a therapeutic context and a non-therapeutic context and the Bolam Test applied to diagnosis, treatment and the giving of advice.

The Pearce case

The situation set out in the case scenario (Box 4.1) is an actual situation and a decided case (*Pearce* v. *United Bristol Healthcare NHS Trust*, 1998). The trial judge dismissed Mrs Pearce's claim, holding that there had been no negligence on the part of the consultant in not advising Mrs Pearce of the small risk attached to waiting for natural labour to begin.

The Court of Appeal held that the experts had agreed that the risk of the child being stillborn was not a significant risk – possibly 0.1–0.2 per cent. The Court of Appeal stated that it would not interfere with the clinical opinion of the expert medical man responsible for treating Mrs Pearce. It accepted that there would be occasions in which the courts could decide that the expert opinion is not acceptable to the court.

In this, the court was reiterating the ruling in the Bolitho case (*Bolitho* v. *City and Hackney HA* [1997]), where the House of Lords held that there would be occasions where the courts could find that expert opinion presented to it was not acceptable. The House of Lords held that:

> The use of the adjectives 'responsible, reasonable and respectable' [in the Bolam case] all showed that the court had to be satisfied that the exponents of the body of opinion relied upon could demonstrate that such opinion had a logical basis.

Overruling experts was seen, however, as an extreme situation:

> It would seldom be right for a judge to reach the conclusion that views held by a competent medical expert were unreasonable.

Failure to give information

What does a claimant have to prove to succeed in a case of failure to give information. It was once considered necessary for a claimant to establish that had they known about the risks of a particular treatment, then they would not have given consent. However this was extremely difficult to prove when they had not been given the information. The House of Lords considered this issue in the case of *Chester* v. *Afshar* (2002 and 2004) which is discussed in the next chapter.

Future developments

There would appear to be a development in favour of greater openness between professional and patient, with the presumption in favour of the patient having all relevant information. Whilst the UK courts have not accepted that a doctrine of informed consent is recognised in law, ethical practice is placing more emphasis on the rights of the patient to be given as much information as possible. It may be that in the future there will be statutory provisions over what the patient should be told. For example, explanatory leaflets must be provided by pharmaceutical companies as a result of a European Directive (92/27/EEC). It may be an area where the recommendations of the National Institute for Health

Box 4.2 Recommendations on information giving in the Kennedy Report

4. Information about treatment and care should be given in a variety of forms, be given in stages and be reinforced over time.
5. Information should be tailored to the needs, circumstances and wishes of the individual.
6. Information should be based on the current available evidence and include a summary of the evidence and data, in a form which is comprehensible to patients.
7. Various modes of conveying information, whether leaflets, tapes, videos or CDs, should be regularly updated and developed and piloted with the help of patients.
8. The NHS Modernisation Agency should make the improvement of the quality of information for patients a priority. In relation to the consent and dissemination of information for patients, the Agency should identify and promote good practice throughout the NHS. It should establish a system for accrediting materials intended to inform patients.
9. The public should receive guidance on those sources of information about health and health care on the Internet which are reliable and of good quality: a kitemarking system should be developed.
26. As part of the process of obtaining consent, except when they have indicated otherwise, patients should be given sufficient information about what is to take place, the risks, uncertainties, and possible negative consequences of the proposed treatment, about any alternatives and about the likely outcome, to enable them to make a choice about how to proceed.

and Clinical Excellence cover the information given to patients. The Kennedy Report (2001) made clear recommendations on the giving of information to patients. These are shown in Box 4.2 (see also Box 2.4 and Table 5.1).

Conclusion

Although the judges in the House of Lords in the Sidaway case all had different reasons for their decision to dismiss Mrs Sidaway's appeal, it is possible to make the following statement in the light of the more recent House of Lords decision in the Bolitho case.

The courts have the right to decide if they consider that the expert opinion on the standard of disclosure is acceptable to the courts. They will require a patient to be informed of significant risks according to the reasonable standard of medical practice (i.e. Bolam), but that this will be subject to the duty to ensure that the patient is notified of any serious risk which a prudent patient would be expected to want to know.

The implications of this will be considered in the next chapter when these legal rulings will be applied to practical questions frequently faced by health professionals.

References

Bolam v. *Friern Barnet Management Committee* [1957] 1 WLR 582.

Bolitho v. *City and Hackney HA* [1997] 4 All ER 771.

Canterbury v. *Spence* 464 F 2d 772 (DC, 1972).

Chatterton v. *Gerson* [1981] QB 432.

Chester v. *Afshar* [2002] *The Times Law Report*, 13 June 2002; [2002] 3 All ER 552 CA; *The Times Law Report* 19 October, 2004 HL; [2004] UKHL 41; [2004] 3 W.L.R. 927 European Directive 92/27/EEC (L113/8).

Kennedy Report (2001) *Bristol Royal Infirmary Inquiry. Learning from Bristol: the Report of the Public Inquiry Into Children's Heart Surgery at the Bristol Royal Infirmary 1984–1995*. Command paper CM 5207, Stationery Office, London.

Gold v. *Haringey Health Authority* [1988] 1 QB 481.

Maynard v. *W Midlands Regional Health Authority HL* [1985] 1 All ER 635.

Pearce v. *United Bristol Healthcare NHS Trust* (1998) n48 MLR 118 CA; [1999] PIQR P53 CA.

Sidaway v. *Bethlem Royal Hospital Governors* [1985] 1 All ER 643 [1985] AC 871.

Smith v. *Tunbridge Wells Health Authority* [1994] 5 Med LR 334.

CHAPTER 5

Duty to inform patients of risks

> ## Box 5.1 Case scenario – scared stiff
>
> Fred has suffered for many years with a hernia and has been placed on the waiting list for surgery. He is finally admitted, but is extremely frightened, never having had any contact with hospitals before. He keeps asking about what will happen to him. Nurses discover that his mother died when he was only 8 following an operation for the removal of gall stones. He is afraid that the same thing will happen to him.

In the last chapter we considered the cases which set down the principles which apply to the duty to inform the patient, noting that a modified Bolam Test (*Bolam* v. *Friern Barnet Management Committee* [1957]) was now the basic principle, i.e. that health professionals should inform patients according to the reasonable standards recognised by the accepted practice, but that this was subject to oversight by the courts. Patients should be notified of significant risks that are likely to cause substantial harm. However, practitioners could withhold information if disclosure poses a serious threat of psychological detriment to the patient.

The House of Lords has considered how much information should be given to the patient in a recent case. The facts are shown in Box 5.2.

The Court of Appeal held that the purpose of the rule requiring doctors to give appropriate information to their patients was to enable the patient to exercise her right to choose whether or not to have the particular operation to which she was asked to give her consent. The patient had the right to choose what would and would not be done with her body and the doctor should take the care expected of a reasonable doctor in the circumstances in giving her the information relevant to that choice. The law was designed to require doctors properly to inform their patients of the risk attendant on their treatment and to answer questions put to them as to that treatment and its dangers, such answers to be judged in the context of good professional practice, which had tended to a greater degree of frankness over the years, with more respect being given to patient autonomy.

Box 5.2 *Chester* v. *Afshar* (2002 and 2004)

The patient suffered from severe back pain and gave consent to an operation for the removal of three intra-vertebral discs. The neurosurgeon failed to give a warning to her about the slight risk of post-operative paralysis which the patient suffered following the operation. The trial judge held that the doctor was not negligent in his conduct of the operation, but was negligent in failing to warn her of the slight risk of paralysis which she suffered and gave judgment for damages to be assessed. The defendant appealed against this finding of failing to give the appropriate information to the Court of Appeal.

The object was to enable the patient to decide whether or not to run the risks of having that operation at that time. If the doctor's failure to take care resulted in her consenting to an operation to which she would not otherwise have given her consent, the purpose of that rule would be thwarted if he were not to be held responsible when the very risk about which he failed to warn her materialised and caused her an injury. The Court of Appeal rejected the surgeon's appeal. The surgeon appealed to the House of Lords, which by a majority verdict dismissed his appeal. The House of Lords held that the claimant had shown that had she been notified of the risk, which in fact occurred, she would have had to think further about undergoing the surgery, and therefore she had established a causal link between the breach of duty to inform and the injury she had sustained, and the defendant was liable in damages.

Case of *Chinchen* v. *University Hospital of Wales Healthcare NHS Trust* 2002

In this case a patient underwent surgery for revision decompression of his spine. The facts are shown in Box 5.3. He claimed that he was not given proper advice before the decompression procedure. Had he received proper advice, he would not have consented to that procedure. The judge found in favour of C. The reasons for the judge's decision are shown in Box 5.4. The case shows the importance of which side can prove what was actually said before the patient agreed to undergo the operation.

Box 5.3 *Chinchen v. University Hospital of Wales Healthcare NHS Trust 2002 (facts)*

In April 1996 C underwent surgery for a revision decompression of his spine. A consultant orthopaedic surgeon carried out the procedure. Four days later, C suffered loss of spinal fluid from the operation wound and was readmitted to hospital. In May a posterior exploration of C's lower lumbar spine was carried out. The dura was inspected and there was no obvious leak. A muscle patch was applied to the dura and C was later discharged home. C suffered constant and debilitating pain and an inability to return to work after the procedures and claimed that he was not given proper advice before the decompression procedure. Had he received proper advice, he would not have consented to that procedure.

Box 5.4 *Chinchen v. University Hospital of Wales Healthcare NHS Trust 2002 (reasons)*

The judge preferred C's recollections of the pre-operative discussion. Both C and his wife's version were the same: they were convincing witnesses, and they had the benefit of consulting solicitors no later than a year after the operation and so events were fresh in their minds. The surgeon's evidence had changed and he had been in a difficult position, as he had not had to try to recall the events until four years after the operation. On the evidence C had not been advised of alternative procedures, nor had he been warned of the possible risks consequent upon undergoing revision surgery. The surgeon had conveyed assurances that it would be fine and C had not been told that the surgery was urgent. The advice given did not satisfy the minimal standards of professional competence. There should have been a clear warning of the higher incidence of problems arising from revision surgery and other options should have been discussed. The surgeon admitted that he had not explained to C that any course of action was available other than surgery. In the instant circumstances, had C received the appropriate advice he would not have agreed to undergo the operation. The judge found that there was a causal and temporal connection between the surgery and the symptoms, which were different and worse very soon after the surgery. The two operations had occurred within a short period on a site previously operated upon and had caused damage resulting in C's operation. The symptoms were much worse than they would have been without the surgery.

Common questions

How much do I tell the patient?

Any health practitioner who is caring for a patient should ensure that the patient is aware of any significant risks of substantial harm. For example, a nurse may be asked by the patient what is going to happen, even though the patient has signed the consent form. The patient's question would appear to suggest that the patient has not had a clear explanation of the proposed procedure. The nurse may be able to answer the question herself, but only if she has kept up to date with research and the treatment proposed. If she does not have the knowledge to answer the patient's questions she should ask the doctor or other health professional concerned to return and give the patient the information required. Where possible, the health professional should attempt to ensure that information for the patient is put in writing as well as being given to the patient by word of mouth. This gives the patient the opportunity to look over the information sheet at leisure and also has the additional advantage of providing some evidence that the patient was informed of specific risks described in the leaflet.

When is a risk significant?

A risk is significant if it is the kind of information which a reasonable patient would want to know before agreeing to a particular treatment. The courts have been reluctant to rely on risk percentages and have not laid down any principle, e.g. that all risks higher than 10 per cent should be notified to the patient. When assessing the significance of a risk it has to be linked with the extent of the harm. Clearly, even a small risk of a devastating disability will be more material to the decision-making processes of the patient than a large risk of minimal harm. For example, a 1 per cent risk of paralysis will be of more concern than a 50 per cent risk of a temporary headache.

What if the patient asks questions?

Lord Bridge suggested in the Sidaway case (*Sidaway* v. *Bethlem Royal Hospital Governors* [1985]) that if the patient asked questions, then the doctor has a duty to answer these truthfully and as fully as the questions require. Lord Diplock stated:

> No doubt if the patient in fact manifested this attitude (i.e. wanted to decide for themselves what should be done to them) by means of questioning, the doctor would tell him whatever it was the patient wanted to know.

What if the patient does not ask questions?

If the patient does not appear to want more information, provided that the health professional has informed the patient of the basic information according to the Bolam Test, there would appear to be no duty to continue to provide all the additional information which may be sought by a particularly informed and interested patient. Many health professionals are familiar with patients who say 'whatever you recommend nurse, doctor, etc.' and who appear not to want to have much information about their condition, treatment or prognosis. However, patients should be given any available leaflet, whether they are likely to read it or not, so that the health professional can fulfil his or her duty to inform.

In the Blyth case (*Blyth* v. *Bloomsbury HA* [1993]), in the Court of Appeal, Lord Justice Kerr held that:

> The question of what a plaintiff should be told in answer to a general enquiry cannot be divorced from the Bolam Test, any more than when no such enquiry is made. In both cases, the answer must depend upon the circumstances, the nature of the enquiry, the nature of the information which is available, its reliability, relevance, the condition of the patient, and so forth. Any medical evidence directed to what would be the proper answer in the light of responsible medical opinion and practice – that is to say, the Bolam Test – must in my view equally be placed in the balance in cases where the patient makes some enquiry, in order to decide whether the response was negligent or not.

When can I withhold information?

In the case scenario (Box 5.1), it is clear that Fred is very nervous. Although his hernia repair operation may be attended by very little risk, it may be that notifying him of any risks will deter him from having the operation. The fact that his mother died during an operation should be taken into account in assessing Fred's suitability for surgery and all necessary tests should be undertaken. For example, it may be that his mother died because of an allergic response to the anaesthetic, and this could be a hereditary condition. If so, it is essential that Fred is tested for any such allergy before the operation. Such additional precautions may assist in reassuring Fred about the dangers of the operation so that he is able to give consent. However, he may still ask questions about the possibility of different kinds of risks. A professional judgment then has to be made as to whether such information is counterproductive and should be withheld from Fred.

In a sense this is paternalistic practice, but there is a substantial legal justification for such withholding of information (*Sidaway* v. *Bethlem Royal Hospital Governors* [1985]).

Also, legislation such as the Data Protection Act 1998 and the regulations for access to health records made under it recognises that access to records can be withheld where such access would cause serious harm to the physical or mental condition of the patient. The patient does not have an absolute right to access his or her health records or to obtain information.

However, any withholdings should be the exception rather than the rule and should be clearly defensible. It is also highly recommended that the fact and reasons for the withholding should be clearly documented, so that, in the event of a patient challenging the fact that this information was not given, the reasons for this are clearly recorded.

What if more information is available because of research being conducted locally?

This question was raised in *Blyth* v. *Bloomsbury HA* [1993]. Mrs Blyth brought an action against the health authority on the grounds that she had been given negligent advice and information. She had been administered the contraceptive drug Depo-Provera by injection and claimed that she had suffered unpleasant side-effects. She alleged that had she been informed about the possible side-effects more fully, she would not have agreed to have the injection. The trial judge held that there was an obligation to give the plaintiff all the information available to the hospital, including information in the files of a consultant who had studied the subject. This, however, was overruled by the Court of Appeal, which held that there was no such obligation.

Case scenario: Box 5.2

Fred presents a difficult case. His fear should not be used to justify withholding information about significant risks of substantial harm. If he is a mentally competent person, and on the facts given here it would appear that there is no suggestion to the contrary, he needs to be questioned about what happened to his mother to ensure that he is not at risk from a genetic defect and encouraged to undergo all the necessary tests to check out reasonably foreseeable risks. His questions must be answered fully and truthfully and he should be given all the information with which similar patients are provided, and if possible, in writing. Health professionals should ensure that they have followed the reasonable standard of care in informing Fred about the operation and its after effects. Documentation should record such discussions and the handing out of leaflets giving details of the treatment and risks associated with it.

Guidance

Determining how much information to give to patients is a difficult area and health professionals should be aware of the guidance which is available not only from their own professional registration bodies, but also from professional associations. In addition, standards on the giving of information to patients before the consent is signed have been laid down by the Clinical Negligence Scheme for Trusts (CNST). The standards will be monitored as part of the CNST's administration of the pool for paying out claims arising from clinical negligence. The Department of Health has issued a reference guide on consent to treatment (DoH, 2001a) together with practical guidance on the implementation of the principles (DoH, 2001b) which has been noted in earlier chapters. The DoH forms could be adapted for recording consent to specific procedures and set out information relating to serious risks of substantial harm from these interventions. The Kennedy Report (2001) has made significant recommendations on communications with patients. Some of its recommendations on information giving are shown in Box 4.2. Table 5.1 sets out the Kennedy recommendations on communication with patients.

Table 5.1 Recommendations of Kennedy Report on communications with patients (see also Box 2.4 and Box 4.2).

10. Tape-recording facilities should be provided by the NHS to enable patients, should they so wish, to make a tape recording of a discussion with a healthcare professional when a diagnosis, course of treatment, or prognosis is being discussed.

11. Patients should always be given the opportunity and time to ask questions about what they are told, to seek clarification and to ask for more information. It must be the responsibility of employers in the NHS to ensure that the working arrangements of healthcare professionals allow for this, not least that they have the necessary time.

12. Patients must be given such information as enables them to participate in their care.

13. Before embarking on any procedure, patients should be given an explanation of what is going to happen and, after the procedure, should have the opportunity to review what has happened.

14. Patients should be supported in dealing with the additional anxiety sometimes created by greater knowledge

15. Patients should be told that they may have another person of their choosing present when receiving information about a diagnosis or a procedure.

16. Patients should be given the sense of freedom to indicate when they do not want any (or more) information: this requires skill and understanding from healthcare professionals.

17. Patients should receive a copy of any letter written about their care or treatment by one healthcare professional to another.

19. Healthcare professionals responsible for the care of any particular patient must communicate effectively with each other. The aim must be to avoid giving the patient conflicting advice and information.

20. The provision of counselling and support should be regarded as an integral part of a patient's care. All hospital trusts should have a well-developed system and a well-trained group of professionals whose task it is to provide this type of support and to make links to various other forms of support (such as that provided by voluntary or social services) which patients may need.

33. A duty of candour, meaning a duty to tell a patient if adverse events have occurred, must be recognised as owed by all those working in the NHS to patients.

34. When things go wrong, patients are entitled to receive an acknowledgement, an explanation and an apology.

Conclusions

Honesty and respect are at the heart of a good system of communications with patients, and any withholding of information should be based on sound justification and clearly documented. The recommendations of the Bristol Inquiry shown in Table 5.1 have significant resource and training implications. However, it is essential that trusts work to this high standard of communication with patients. The presumption is in favour of ensuring that the mentally competent patient is fully informed of the proposed treatment and care, and its risks and side-effects. Account must be taken of the differing abilities of patients in understanding the information and use made of a wide variety of types of communication. In the next chapter we consider the question of assessing mental capacity.

References

Blyth v. *Bloomsbury HA* [1993] 4 Med LR 151 CA.

Bolam v. *Friern Barnet Management Committee* [1957] 1 WLR 582.

Chester v. *Afshar* (2002) *The Times Law Report* 13 June 2002; [2002] 3 All ER 552 CA; [2004] UKHL 41; [2004] 3 W.L.R. 927.

Chinchen v. *University Hospital of Wales Healthcare NHS Trust* 8 November 2001 (*Current Law* 340 April 2002).

Department of Health (2001a) *Department of Health Reference Guide to Consent for Examination or Treatment*. DoH, London; http://www.doh.gov.uk/consent/.

Department of Health (2001b) *Good Practice in Consent Implementation Guide*. DoH, London.

Kennedy Report (2001) *Bristol Royal Infirmary Inquiry. Learning from Bristol: the Report of the Public Inquiry Into Children's Heart Surgery at the Bristol Royal Infirmary 1984–1995*. Command paper CM 5207. Stationery Office, London.

Sidaway v. *Bethlem Royal Hospital Governors* [1985] 1 All ER 643 [1985] AC 871.

CHAPTER 6

The determination of mental capacity

Box 6.1 Case scenario 1

Doctors advised a patient (C) from Broadmoor Special Hospital, who was suffering from chronic paranoid schizophrenia, that he had gangrene in his foot. He was transferred to Heatherwood Hospital, where the doctor diagnosed a grossly infected right leg with a necrotic ulcer covering the whole of the dorsum. The consultant vascular surgeon considered that C would die imminently unless he had a below-knee amputation. His chances of survival were assessed as being no better than 15 per cent if he just had conservative treatment. C stated that he would prefer to die with two feet than live with one. He therefore refused to give consent to the operation and he sought an injunction from the High Court to stop the amputation from going ahead (*Re C (adult: refusal of medical treatment)* [1994]).

In Chapter 2 it was stated that in order to be valid, consent must be given by a person who has the necessary mental capacity. This chapter seeks to explore what is meant by 'capacity' and how this can be determined in individual circumstances.

Presumption of mental capacity

One of the five principles set out in the Mental Capacity Act (MCA) states that:

> A person must be assumed to have capacity unless it is established that he lacks capacity (Section 1(2) MCA).

This presumption that a person over 16 years has the mental capacity to make a valid decision and therefore the right of self-determination is therefore the starting point in determining whether an individual's refusal is binding upon health professionals. Evidence can be brought to refute this presumption. The MCA states that:

> In proceedings under this Act or any other enactment, any question whether a person lacks capacity within the meaning of this Act must be decided on the balance of probabilities. (S.2(4) MCA)

Mental Capacity Act 2005

This Act came fully into force in October 2007. Its enactment followed a long process of debate and discussion over more than 15 years. In 1995 the Law Commission (an independent body which reviews UK laws) published its report *Mental Incapacity* (Law Commission Mental Capacity, 1995) which followed five years of consultation and consultation papers on all aspects of mentally incapacitated adults. In 1997 Lord Chancellor's Office published *Who Decides?* (Lord Chancellor's Office, 1997) It set out the issues which had been considered by the Law Commission between 1991 and 1995 and was followed by a white paper *Making Decisions* in October 1999 (Lord Chancellor's Office, 1999). Subsequently the Department of Health published a draft Mental Incapacity Bill in 2003 which was subjected to scrutiny by a joint committee of the House of Commons and House of Lords. The joint committee published its report in November 2003 and made almost 100 recommendations on changes to the draft bill including the change of title to Mental Capacity Bill. After considerable debate, the Bill was signed by the Queen in April 2005 and brought into force between April and October 2007. The Act sets out five principles which are to apply where decisions relating to mental capacity have to be made (see Chapter 7), defines mental capacity (discussed in this chapter) and sets out how the best interests of a person should be determined (see Chapter 7). The Act also creates a new Court of Protection and a new Office of Public Protection, introduces a lasting power of attorney (see Chapter 11) and recognises advance decisions refusing treatment (see Chapter 16). Further information on the Act can be found in the author's work (Dimond, 2008).

Case scenario

In Case scenario 1 (Box 6.1), the sole issue before Judge Thorpe was did C have the requisite capacity to give a valid refusal, i.e. was his right of self-determination to be upheld? If the answer to the question was 'yes', then he had the right in law to refuse any treatment, 'for a good reason, a bad reason or for no reason at all' (words used by the Court of Appeal in *Re MB (an adult: medical treatment)* (1997)). On the other hand, if the effect of his chronic paranoid schizophrenia was to render him incapable of making a valid decision, then action could be taken in his best interests and his refusal overruled.

Judge Thorpe stated that there were three stages in determining whether the requisite mental capacity existed:

- Could the patient comprehend and retain the necessary information?
- Was he able to believe it?
- Was he able to weigh the information, balancing risks and needs, so as to arrive at a choice?

Mental Capacity Act 2005 and the statutory definition of mental capacity

The common law rulings relating to the definition of capacity have now been replaced by a statutory definition set out in sections 2 and 3 of the MCA. This imposes a two-stage test: Is the patient suffering from a mental impairment or a impairment of, or a disturbance in the functioning of, his mind or brain? If the answer to this question is 'Yes', then the second test is: Does this impairment or disturbance cause him to be unable to make a decision for himself in relation to the specific matter which has arisen? These two issues will be considered separately.

Impairment or disturbance in the functioning of the mind or brain

The Code of Practice on the Mental Capacity Act (Ministry of Justice, 2007), which can be accessed on its web site (http://www.justice.gov.uk/) provides guidance on the interpretation and implementation of the Act. Chapter 4 explains what the Act means by 'capacity' and 'lack of capacity'. It provides guidance on how to assess whether someone has the capacity to make a decision, and suggests when professionals should be involved in the assessment. Paragraph 4.12 gives the following examples of an impairment or disturbance in the functioning of the mind or brain:

- conditions associated with some forms of mental illness
- dementia
- significant learning disabilities
- the long-term effects of brain damage
- physical or medical conditions that cause confusion, drowsiness or loss of consciousness
- delirium
- concussion following a head injury
- the symptoms of alcohol or drug use

These are of course only examples, there may be other causes of an impairment or disturbance in the mind or its functioning.

Section 2(2) of the MCA states that it does not matter whether the impairment or disturbance is permanent or temporary. A person must have the requisite mental capacity at the time the decision has to be made. Mental capacity is decision specific. A person may have the mental capacity to make one type of decision but not another. For example, a person with severe learning disabilities may have the mental capacity to decide what clothes to wear or what food to eat, but not to decide whether to have major surgery.

Paragraph 4.2 of the Code of Practice states that:

A person can lack capacity to make a decision at the time it needs to be made even if:
- the loss of capacity is partial
- the loss of capacity is temporary
- their capacity changes over time.

A lack of capacity cannot be established merely by reference to:

(a) a person's age or appearance, or
(b) a condition of his, or an aspect of his behaviour, which might lead others to make unjustified assumptions about his capacity. (S.2(3) MCA)

Thus superficial judgements about a person's capacity should not be made: there must be a proper assessment without any assumptions being made.

Does the impairment or disturbance in the functioning of the mind or brain cause an inability to make decisions?

Section 3 of the MCA defines what is meant by 'inability to make decisions'. A person is unable to make a decision for himself if he is unable:

(a) to understand the information relevant to the decision,
(b) to retain that information,
(c) to use or weigh that information as part of the process of making the decision, or
(d) to communicate his decision (whether by talking, using sign language or any other means).

This is very similar to the definition of mentally incapacitated used by the judge in the Broadmoor case (Box 6.1).

The MCA also says (S.3(2)) that a person is not to be regarded as unable to understand the information relevant to a decision if he is able to understand an explanation of it given to him in a way that is appropriate to his circumstances (using simple language, visual aids or any other means). This places a responsibility upon the person making the assessment to ensure that all practical means are used to ensure that effective communication can take place.

The relevant information is further defined (S.3(4) MCA) as including information about the reasonably foreseeable consequences of:

(a) deciding one way or another, or
(b) failing to make the decision.

The Code of Practice (Paragraph 4.16) gives examples of the kind of information which may be relevant to decision making. Relevant information includes:

- the nature of the decision
- the reason why the decision is needed, and
- the likely effects of deciding one way or another, or making no decision at all.

The fact that a person is able to retain the information relevant to a decision for a short period only does not prevent him from being regarded as able to make the decision (S.3(3) MCA). The Code of Practice (Paragraph 4.27) emphasises that:

As in any other situation, an assessment must only examine a person's capacity to make a particular decision when it needs to be made. It may be possible to put off the decision until the person has the capacity to make it.

Temporary incapacity may where possible lead to a postponement of the decision making.

Non-supportable or irrational decisions

Principle 3 set out in the MCA (see Chapter 7) states that:

A person is not to be treated as unable to make a decision merely because he makes an unwise decision

None of the factors used in determining mental capacity include agreeing with the patient's choice. The fact that others might disagree with the person's decision or the person is not necessarily acting in their own best interests is not a determinant of mental capacity. If a requisite of the decision-making process was that the patient made a decision that health professionals agreed with, then those who are Jehovah's Witnesses would find that they could not refuse blood. Self-determination is the opposite of paternalism. Health professionals may find it difficult to accept when a mentally competent patient refuses life-saving treatment, but that is the patient's right in law. It follows therefore that provided the patient is defined as having the mental capacity to make a decision, according to the approved tests, the fact that the decision is irrational or unwise or contrary to the best interests of the patient, is not relevant. This is the ruling of the case of *Re MB (an adult: medical treatment)* (1997) (see below and also Chapter 12) and also of the recent case of *Re B (Consent to treatment: capacity)* 2002 (see below).

The capacity must relate to the decision to be made

There are different levels of decision making, e.g. from deciding what clothes to wear, to deciding whether to have an operation or donate bone marrow. Those patients who suffer from learning disabilities may be able to make decisions on day-to-day matters, but may not have the capacity to be able to weigh the information, balancing risks and needs, so as to arrive at a choice for the more critical decisions.

Whether or not a patient has the capacity to make specific decisions is part of the risk assessment process which any treatment plan should include. Obviously, clear documentation of the analysis and the reasons for any decision on mental capacity should be kept.

Who determines capacity?

> ### Box 6.2 Case scenario 2
>
> Fred has suffered for many years with a hernia and has been placed on the waiting list for surgery. He is finally admitted, but is extremely frightened, never having had any contact with hospitals before. He keeps asking what will happen to him. Nurses discover that his mother died when he was only 8 years old following an operation for the removal of gallstones. He is afraid that the same thing will happen to him.

Case scenario 2 appeared in the previous chapter. Let us assume that after all the tests had been conducted and all the information and reassurance given to Fred, he still decided that he would not have the operation. Should this refusal be overruled? The question then arises as to Fred's mental capacity to make a valid refusal.

There are considerable advantages in bringing in a specialist outside the clinical team caring for Fred. Preferably, this would be a psychologist whose training includes the determination of mental capacity. If the psychologist were to say that Fred's fear of the operation because of the death of his mother is such that it makes it impossible for him to make a valid decision, i.e. his fear renders him mentally incapable, then it could be argued that his refusal is invalid and he could be treated as a mentally incapacitated adult and action taken in his best interests. In one case the Court of Appeal agreed with the High Court's decision that a fear of needles meant that the patient was mentally incapable of making a decision and a Caesarean section could be performed in her best interests (*Re MB (an adult: medical treatment)* (1997)).

It does not, however, follow that the operation must therefore proceed. In Fred's case the operation is elective. It does not appear, on the facts, to be a life-saving necessity, so it is possible that an invalid refusal could prevail and Fred's refusal be accepted. There would certainly seem to be strong reasons not to compel Fred to undergo surgery, but instead to accept his refusal and, if subsequently surgical intervention did become a life-saving necessity, to reconsider the whole issue. (The question of the care of the person lacking mental capacity is considered in the next chapter.)

Could a member of the clinical team determine competence?

In practice, this happens in day-to-day matters. Every health practitioner is regularly deciding whether a person's presumption of self-determination is valid. Unfortunately, there is a tendency, particularly in the care of psychiatric patients, to assume that a passive acceptance of what is proposed by the health professionals indicates mental capacity, but when there is refusal to accept recommended treatment, then the capacity of the individual to refuse is questioned.

Clearly, if the situation is a life and death matter, as in the Broadmoor case of *Re C*, then there are strong legal arguments why an expert should be brought in to examine the patient and determine his or her mental capacity. If the case does come before the Court of Protection, this may be the sole point at issue between the parties and evidence of the alleged incapacity will be required by the court.

The Ms B case

In Chapter 2 we considered the case of Ms B (*Re B* 2002), who asked for her ventilator to be switched off. (The facts of the case are set out in Chapter 2.) The sole issue before the Family court was whether Ms B had the mental capacity to refuse life-saving treatment and care. The President of the Family Division, Dame Elizabeth Butler-Sloss, restated the principles which had been laid down by the Court of Appeal in the case of St George's Healthcare Trust (1998):

- There was a presumption that a patient had the mental capacity to make decisions whether to consent to or refuse medical or surgical treatment offered.
- If mental capacity was not an issue and the patient, having been given the relevant information and offered the available option, chose to refuse that treatment, that decision had to be respected by the doctors, considerations of what the best interests of the patient would involve were irrelevant.
- Concern or doubts about the patient's mental capacity should be resolved as soon as possible by the doctors within the hospital or during other normal medical procedures.

- Meanwhile, the patient must be cared for in accordance with the judgment of the doctors as to the patient's best interests.
- It was most important that those considering the issue should not confuse the question of mental capacity with the nature of the decision made by the patient, however grave the consequences. Since the view of the patient might reflect a difference in values rather than an absence of competence the assessment of capacity should be approached with that in mind, and doctors should not allow an emotional reaction to, or strong disagreement with, the patient's decision to cloud their judgment in answering the primary question of capacity.
- Where disagreement still existed about competence, it was of the utmost importance that the patient be fully informed, involved and engaged in the process (which could involve obtaining independent outside help) of resolving the disagreement, since the patient's involvement could be crucial to a good outcome.
- If the hospital was faced with a dilemma which doctors did not know how to resolve that must be recognised and further steps taken as a matter of priority. Those in charge must not allow a situation of deadlock or drift to occur.
- If there was no disagreement about competence, but the doctors were for any reason unable to carry out the patient's wishes it was their duty to find other doctors who would do so.
- If all appropriate steps to seek independent assistance from medical experts outside the hospital had failed the hospital should not hesitate to make an application to the High Court or seek the advice of the Official Solicitor.
- The treating clinicians and the hospital should always have in mind that a seriously physically disabled patient who was mentally competent had the same right to personal autonomy and to make decisions as any other person with mental capacity.

Whilst the case of MS B was decided before the Mental Capacity Act 2005 came into force, the rulings by the President of the Family Division accord with the principles set out in the MCA. From October 2007 a similar dispute would be heard in the Court of Protection.

Conclusion

When Judge Thorpe applied the three-stage test to *Re C*, it was decided that C did have the mental capacity to refuse to give consent to the amputation and an injunction was issued forbidding any person to amputate his leg without his consent. This case shows that a person may suffer from a specific form of mental disorder, yet may still have the requisite mental capacity to give or refuse consent. The same principles apply since the implementation of the Mental Capacity Act 2005.

References

Dimond, B. C. (2008) *Legal Aspects of Mental Capacity.* Blackwell Publishing, Oxford.

Law Commission Mental Incapacity (1995) Report No 231. Stationery Office, London.

Lord Chancellor's Office (1997) *Who Decides?* Stationery Office, London.

Lord Chancellor's Office (1999) *Making Decisions: the Government's Proposals for Making Decisions on Behalf of Mentally Incapacitated Adults.* Stationery Office, London.

Ministry of Justice (2007) *Code of Practice on the Mental Capacity Act 2005.* Stationery Office, London.

Re B (Consent to treatment: capacity) (2002) *The Times Law Report* 26 March 2002; [2002] 2 All ER 449.

Re C (adult: refusal of medical treatment) [1994] 1 WLR 290.

Re MB (an adult: medical treatment) (1997) 38 BMLR 175 CA.

St George's Healthcare NHS Trust v. *S. The Times*, 8 May 1998 [1999] Fam 26.

CHAPTER 7

The Mental Capacity Act 2005

Box 7.1 Case scenario

Bob Davies, aged 75 years, was admitted to hospital with what was thought to be an ulcerated hiatus hernia. The surgeon advised June, his only child, that with surgery he had a 60–70 per cent chance of a reasonable prognosis. However, without an operation he was unlikely to survive because he was haemorrhaging badly. He asked June if she was prepared to give consent and sign the form.

Introduction

In the last chapter, the statutory definition of mental capacity as set out in the Mental Capacity Act 2005 was discussed. This chapter considers the law which relates to the care of a person who lacks the necessary mental capacity to make a valid decision. If an adult lacks the mental capacity to make his or her decisions, then under the Mental Capacity Act 2005 decisions must be made in the best interests of the patient. The vacuum in law which had been filled by the common law has been filled by statutory provision.

Common law powers pre the Mental Capacity Act 2005

Prior to the introduction of statutory provision for decision making on behalf of mentally incapacitated adults, the courts filled the vacuum and laid down the principles which applied. These are illustrated in the leading case of *Re F* (Box 7.2).

> ## Box 7.2 Sterilisation of a mentally incapacitated adult (*Re F (mental patient: sterilisation)* [1990])
>
> F was 36 years old and had severe learning disabilities, with the mental age of a small child. She lived in a mental hospital and had formed a sexual relationship with a male patient. The hospital staff considered that she would be unable to cope with a pregnancy and recommended that she should be sterilised, considering that other forms of contraception were unsuitable. Her mother supported the idea of a sterilisation operation, but because F was over 18 years did not have the right in law to give consent on her behalf. The mother therefore applied to court for a declaration that an operation for sterilisation was in her best interests and should be declared lawful.

In this case, the judge granted the declaration sought by F's mother. The official solicitor (who acted on behalf of the mentally incapacitated adult) appealed against the declaration to the Court of Appeal, which upheld the judge's order. The official solicitor then appealed to the House of Lords. The House of Lords held that there was at common law (i.e. judge made law or case law) the power for a person to act in the best interests of a mentally incapacitated adult. This power was derived from the principle of necessity.

Statutory provision for mental incapacity: Scotland

In Scotland, the Adults with Incapacity (Scotland) Act 2000 enables decisions to be made on behalf of mentally incapacitated adults. It covers both the making of medical decisions and also decisions relating to property and finance. The bulk of the provisions came into force in April 2002. The Act introduces a new regime of intervention and guardianship orders and reforms the law on powers of attorney. Former powers under the Mental Health (Scotland) Act 1984 are repealed. A new court jurisdiction is set up. The first section sets out the principles which are to apply, including the principle that 'there shall be no intervention in the affairs of an adult, unless the person responsible for authorising or effecting the intervention is satisfied that the intervention will benefit the adult and that such benefit cannot reasonably be achieved without the intervention'.

Statutory provision for mental incapacity: England and Wales

The Mental Capacity Act 2005, which came fully into force by October 2007, replaces the common law principles for decision making on behalf of those who lack the mental capacity to make their own decisions. It also, as we have seen in Chapter 6, sets a statutory definition for determining mental capacity. This chapter considers the stages which are taken in determining the best interests of a person lacking mental capacity and the other provisions of the Mental Capacity Act 2005.

Principles set by the Mental Capacity Act 2005

The Act sets out the principles which must be followed. They are:

1. A person must be assumed to have capacity unless it is established that he lacks capacity.
2. A person is not to be treated as unable to make a decision unless all practicable steps to help him to do so have been taken without success.
3. A person is not to be treated as unable to make a decision merely because he makes an unwise decision.
4. An act done, or decision made, under this Act for or on behalf of a person who lacks capacity must be done, or made, in his best interests.
5. Before the act is done, or the decision is made, regard must be had to whether the purpose for which it is needed can be as effectively achieved in a way that is less restrictive of the person's rights and freedom of action.

1. Presumption of capacity

This has already been considered in Chapter 6. If there is a reasonable doubt about the mental capacity of a person over 16 years to make a specific decision, then the presumption of capacity can be displaced using a standard of proof of a balance of probabilities.

2. Using practical steps to assist in decision making

It is the duty of the carer, health professional or person assisting someone making decisions, to use all practical steps to help that person do so. The Code of Practice gives guidance on the kinds of help which may be required such as speech therapy or technological help. It should be noted that the word 'reasonable' is not included in this duty, which means that the cost, the time and other factors are not relevant. If a particular aid would assist the person to be able to make the decision and this aid is practicable, then it should be used.

3. Making unwise decisions

In Chapter 6, the fact that a person wishes to make unwise decisions does not necessarily mean that they lack the requisite mental capacity was discussed. The right of self-determination implies that an individual is able to make decisions which may not accord with common sense, or what others might consider to be that person's best interests.

4. Best interests

Once it is established that a person lacks the mental capacity to make a specific decision, then others have a duty to act in that person's best interests. The stages which must be followed in determining best interests are considered on pages 59–62 below.

5. Less restrictive action

The fifth and final principle requires consideration of whether the purpose for which action is needed could be effectively achieved in a way that is less restrictive of the person's rights and freedom of action. An example could be the installation of temperature controls in a shower used by a person with severe learning disabilities, so that he could shower on his own rather than be showered by someone else, but be safe. This principle requires considerable thought to be given to the options available when considering what is in the best interests of a person lacking the requisite mental capacity.

Best interests

Once an assessment leads to the conclusion that a person lacks the requisite mental capacity to make a specific decision, then in the absence of an advance decision (see Chapter 16) or a lasting power of attorney (see Chapter 11), decisions must be made in that person's best interests.

Section 4 of the MCA sets out the stages which must be followed in determining 'best interests'.

(a) No superficial judgments

Just as in the determination of mental capacity, there must be no assumptions based on superficial factors:

> the person making the determination must not make it merely on the basis of–
> (a) the person's age or appearance, or
> (b) a condition of his, or an aspect of his behaviour, which might lead others to make unjustified assumptions about what might be in his best interests.

Paragraphs 15.6 and 15.7 of the Code of Practice explain this requirement in the following way:

> 5.16 Section 4(1) states that anyone working out someone's best interests must not make unjustified assumptions about what their best interests might be simply on the basis of the person's age, appearance, condition or any aspect of their behaviour. In this way, the Act ensures that people who lack capacity to make decisions for themselves are not subject to discrimination or treated any less favourably than anyone else.

> 5.17 'Appearance' is a broad term and refers to all aspects of physical appearance, including skin colour, mode of dress and any visible medical problems, disfiguring scars or other disabilities. A person's 'condition' also covers a range of factors including physical disabilities, learning difficulties or disabilities, age-related illness or temporary conditions (such as drunkenness or unconsciousness). 'Behaviour' refers to behaviour that might seem unusual to others, such as talking too loudly or laughing inappropriately.

The Code of Practice gives the example of Martina, an elderly lady with dementia who has started to neglect herself. The Code emphasises that it cannot be assumed *simply on the basis of her age, condition, appearance or behaviour* either that Martina lacks capacity to make such a decision (of moving to a care home) or that such a move would be in her best interests.

(b) Take all relevant circumstances into consideration

The person making the determination must consider all the relevant circumstances. These are defined (S.4(11)) as

(a) of which the person making the determination is aware, and
(b) which it would be reasonable to regard as relevant.

This requirement involves a wide-ranging review of all the factors which could influence a decision on what is in a person's best interests. The MCA specifically identifies certain steps which must be taken

(i) whether it is likely that the person will at some time have capacity in relation to the matter in question, and
(ii) if it appears likely that he will, when that is likely to be.

Clearly if the person's lack of capacity is only temporary, then some significant decisions may be able to wait until the recovery of capacity. For example, if surgery is recommended for a person but a decision on whether it should go ahead could await a recovery of capacity, then that would probably be in that person's best interests. To delay the decision making enables that person's self-determination to be protected and is a less restrictive option. This may not always be practicable or realistic: it depends on the nature of the medical condition.

(c) Involve the person in the decision making

Another step required in deciding what are a person's best interests is that the decision maker must, so far as reasonably practicable, permit and encourage the person to participate, or to improve his ability to participate, as fully as possible in any act done for him and any decision affecting him. The Code of Practice gives an example, in paragraph 5.24, of Amy who has learning disabilities and whose parents are divorcing. With the help of an advocate, she is able to decide with which parent she would like to live.

(d) Life-sustaining treatment

Where the determination relates to life-sustaining treatment the decision maker must not, in considering whether the treatment is in the best interests of the person concerned, be motivated by a desire to bring about his death. (S.4(5)) Paragraph 5.31 of the Code of Practice explains this as follows:

All reasonable steps which are in the person's best interests should be taken to prolong their life. There will be a limited number of cases where treatment is futile, overly burdensome to the patient or where there is no prospect of recovery. In circumstances such as these, it may be that an assessment of best interests leads to the conclusion that it would be in the best interests of the patient to withdraw or withhold life-sustaining treatment, even if this may result in the person's death. The decision-maker must make a decision based on the best interests of the person who lacks capacity. They must not be motivated by a desire to bring about the person's death for whatever reason, even if this is from a sense of compassion. Healthcare and social care staff should also refer to relevant professional guidance when making decisions regarding life-sustaining treatment.

Life-sustaining treatment is defined in the MCA as

treatment which in the view of a person providing health care for the person concerned is necessary to sustain life.

(e) Factors to be considered

The MCA requires the decision maker to consider, so far as is reasonably ascertainable, the following factors in determining what is in a person's best interests:

(a) the person's past and present wishes and feelings (and, in particular, any relevant written statement made by him when he had capacity),
(b) the beliefs and values that would be likely to influence his decision if he had capacity, and
(c) the other factors that he would be likely to consider if he were able to do so.

Guidance on these factors is given in Paragraphs 5.38–5.48 of the Code of Practice. The effect of this requirement is that a person's earlier history, when they did have the capacity to make their own choices becomes relevant to deciding what is in their best interests at a time when that mental capacity is lacking. Even if a person has not made an advance decision or living will (see Chapter 11), their personal views on treatment they would not have accepted become relevant to the decision as to what is in their best interests. Thus a declaration refusing life-sustaining treatment which does not meet the statutory requirements for an advance decision may still be relevant in determining what is in a person's best interests.

(f) Consultation

The MCA also requires the decision maker to consult with the specified persons. He must take into account, if it is practicable and appropriate to consult them, the views of:

(a) anyone named by the person as someone to be consulted on the matter in question or on matters of that kind,
(b) anyone engaged in caring for the person or interested in his welfare,
(c) any donee of a lasting power of attorney granted by the person, and
(d) any deputy appointed for the person by the court

as to what would be in the person's best interests and, in particular, as to the matters mentioned in subsection (6) (see '(e) Factors to be considered' above).

Standard of compliance

Section 4 (9) states that:

> In the case of an act done, or a decision made, by a person other than the court, there is sufficient compliance with this section if (having complied with the requirements of subsections (1) to (7)) he reasonably believes that what he does or decides is in the best interests of the person concerned.

Paragraph 5.59 of the Code of Practice explains that the decision maker must be able to show that all the steps set out in Section 4 were followed and that it was reasonable to think that the person lacked capacity and that they were acting in the person's best interests at the time they made their decision or took action. This should then provide a defence against any legal action brought against them.

Acts in connection with care or treatment

A person is protected in making a decision in relation to care or treatment if

(a) before doing the act, D takes reasonable steps to establish whether P lacks capacity in relation to the matter in question, and

(b) when doing the act, D reasonably believes
    (i)   that P lacks capacity in relation to the matter, and
    (ii) that it will be in P's best interests for the act to be done.

The MCA makes it clear that the person making the decision does not incur any liability in relation to the act that he would not have incurred if P

(a) had had capacity to consent in relation to the matter, and
(b) had consented to D's doing the act.

Thus where the steps laid down in the Act are followed, the person making the decision or carrying out the activity is protected from any action for trespass to the person (see Chapter 2).

However, the Act does not provide protection in a situation where a person has been negligent in carrying out the act and may therefore have civil liability for loss or damage, or his criminal liability as a result of that negligence.

Use of restraint

There are specific statutory provisions relating to the use of restraint. D restrains P if he

(a) uses, or threatens to use, force to secure the doing of an act which P resists, or
(b) restricts P's liberty of movement, whether or not P resists.

D does not get the protection under Section 5 unless any restraint used satisfies two conditions. The first condition is that D reasonably believes that it is necessary to do the act in order to prevent harm to P and the second condition is that the act is a proportionate response to

(a) the likelihood of P's suffering harm, and
(b) the seriousness of that harm.

Subsequently to the passing of the Mental Capacity Act, amendments were made as a consequence of the decision of the European Court of Human Rights in the Bournewood case. This case and the Bournewood safeguards or Deprivation of Liberty safeguards introduced by the Mental Health Act 2007 by amendments to the MCA are considered in Chapter 25.

Decisions by relatives

Unfortunately, the situation in the Case scenario (Box 7.1) is a frequent occurrence in hospitals, and the Mental Capacity Act 2005 now applies to the situation. The first step to take is to carry out an assessment of Bob's mental capacity. If Bob has the mental capacity to make his own decisions, then he should be allowed to do so. However, if Bob lacks the capacity to make his own decisions, then in the absence of an advance decision (see Chapter 16) or a person appointed under a lasting power of attorney (see Chapter 11), decisions must be made on behalf of Bob in his best interests. Since it is a clinical decision, whether or not surgery should take place, then the health professionals involved in the decision making will be required to follow the steps set out above. June will be consulted on what she believes to be her father's past and present wishes and feelings, his views, and the beliefs and values that would be likely to influence his decision had he now had capacity.

An operation for an ulcerated hiatus hernia would be considered to be serious medical treatment, and in this circumstance the Act requires an independent mental capacity advocate to be appointed in the absence of someone who could be consulted about what were the patient's best interests. (This is considered in Chapter 17.) In this scenario, however, June is available to be consulted, but those consulting her must make it clear that it is not her views of Bob's best interests which are required, but her views on what Bob would have wished.

In the Department of Health guidance (DoH, 2001) on consent to examination and treatment, form 4 covers the situation where an adult is incapable of giving a valid consent because of mental disorder. Form 4 is not properly a 'consent form', since it records an absence of consent. The health practitioner recommending that treatment is in the best interests of a mentally incapable adult must record the fact of and the reason for the mental incapacity, enable the relatives to record their knowledge of the situation and the fact that the proposed treatment is in the patient's best interests. (Note that the relatives do not give consent.) A second health practitioner can also sign the form if the treatment is to be performed by another person. Where nurses become aware that relatives are being asked to give consent for a mentally incapacitated adult they should draw the attention of the health practitioner concerned to this form and the DoH forms and guidance and ensure that all the steps to determine the best interests of the patient are taken in accordance with the Act.

Bone marrow transplant

In Box 7.3 is an example of a case heard before the implementation of the Mental Capacity Act 2005.

Box 7.3 Case scenario

The claimant, aged 36 years, sought a declaration from the court that two preliminary blood tests and a conventional bone marrow harvesting operation under general anaesthetic could be lawfully taken from and performed upon her sister Y. The facts were that the applicant was suffering from a pre-leukaemic bone marrow disorder. She had undergone extensive chemotherapy and a blood stem cell transplant. She had started to deteriorate and was likely to progress to acute myeloid leukaemia over the next three months. Her only realistic prospect of recovery was a bone marrow transplant operation from a healthy compatible donor. Preliminary investigations suggested that Y her sister would be a suitable donor. Y was 25 years and severely mentally and physically handicapped. She had lived in a community home for 8 years. She was incapable of giving consent to the donation of bone marrow. The court had to decide whether it was in the best interests of Y for a declaration to be made for the blood tests and the bone marrow harvesting to take place (*Re Y (adult patient) (transplant: bone marrow)* [1997]).

The judge made it clear that it was the best interests of Y which were in dispute. The best interests of the sister were not relevant save in so far as they served the best interests of Y.

The judge argued as follows: if the sister did not have the bone marrow transplant she would die. This would be a devastating blow to her mother, who suffered from ill health. They were a very close family. The mother would find it more difficult to visit Y in the community home, especially as after the death of Y's sister she would then have to look after her only grandchild. Y would suffer as a result of the lack of contact with her mother. The risk of harm to Y from the blood tests was negligible. Although a general anaesthetic posed some risk, it was a low risk. She had already had a general anaesthetic for a hysterectomy without any apparent adverse ill effects. The bone marrow would regenerate. It was to Y's emotional, psychological and social benefit for her to be a donor. It would, therefore, be in the best interests of Y for her to have the blood tests and be a donor for her sister. From October 2007 the Mental Capacity Act 2005 and the Human Tissue Act 2004 would apply to such a situation.

The Code of Practice on the Mental Capacity Act confirmed that best interests could include the donation of bone marrow to another person and quoted the *Re Y* case. The donation of organs and tissue from live donors is considered in Chapter 14. There are considerable dangers that the case of Y could start a slippery slope. If bone marrow is justified, why not a kidney? It would be morally unacceptable for our community homes for those with learning disabilities to be seen as the source of spare parts and organ donations. Yet, in an American case, decided before *Re Y*, it was held that a mentally handicapped patient could be a live kidney donor for his brother (*Strunk* v. *Strunk*, 1996). Statutory provision for making decisions on behalf of mentally incapacitated adults, together with the statutory definition of best interests should ensure that the human rights of mentally incapacitated adults are protected.

Conclusions

The implementation of the Mental Capacity Act 2005 has amended the situation relating to decision making on behalf of those who are incapable of making their own decisions. There is now a statutory definition of mental incapacity, guidance on how decisions can be made in the best interests of a person lacking the requisite mental capacity and other tools which can protect the interests of those lacking capacity, which are considered throughout this book. The Mental Capacity Act applies in general to those over 16 years (with some exceptions) and it is the law relating to those of 16 and 17 years which we consider in the next chapter.

References

Bolam v. *Friern Hospital Management Committee* [1957] 1 WLR 582.
Department of Health (2000) *White Paper: Reforming the Mental Health Act.* Cm 5016-1. Stationery Office, London.
Department of Health (2001a) *Good Practice in Consent Implementation Guide.* DoH, London.
Department of Health (2002) Draft Mental Health Bill (issued for consultation).
Re Eve (1986) 31 DLR (4th) 1 (Can SC).
Re F (mental patient: sterilisation) [1990] 2 AC 1.
Law Commission (1995) *Mental Incapacity.* Report No 231. HMSO, London.

Lord Chancellor's Department Consultation Paper (2002) *Making Decisions: Helping People Who Have Difficulty Deciding for Themselves*; http://www.lcd.gov.uk/consult/family/decision.htm.

Lord Chancellor's Office (1997) *Who Decides? Decision Making on Behalf of the Mentally Incapacitated Adult*. Stationery Office, London.

Lord Chancellor's Office (1999) *Making Decisions: The Government's Proposals for Decision Making on Behalf of the Mentally Incapacitated Adult*. Stationery Office, London.

Strunk v. *Strunk* (1996) 445 SW 2d 145 (Ky CA).

Re Y (adult patient) (transplant: bone marrow) [1997] 2 WLR 556.

CHAPTER 8

Young persons of 16 and 17 years

Box 8.1 Case scenario

A 16-year-old girl under local authority care was suffering from anorexia nervosa. At one point she was fed by nasogastric tube and had her
arms encased in plaster. Her condition became critical and she refused
to move to a specialist hospital. The local authority applied to the High
Court for the girl to be transferred to a treatment unit without her consent, and for leave to give her medical treatment without her consent.
Leave was given by the High Court judge. By 30 June, although 5 feet
7 inches (1.70 m) tall, she weighed only 5 stone 7 pounds (35 kg). The
Court of Appeal made an emergency order enabling her to be taken to
and treated at a specialist hospital in London, notwithstanding her lack
of consent (*Re W (a minor) (medical treatment)* [1992]).

Introduction

It is only recently that the rights of children and young persons have been given
weight; some would argue that they are still treated with excessive paternalism. The
British Medical Association (BMA) has advocated that greater information should
be given to the child and young person and they should have greater involvement
in their own care, treatment and decision making (BMA, 2001). This chapter looks
at the law relating to young persons of 16 and 17 years.

Statutory right to give consent

A young person of 16 or 17 years has a statutory right to give consent under
Section 8(1) of the Family Law Reform Act 1969:

> The consent of a minor who has attained the age of 16 years, to any surgical, medical or dental treatment, which in the absence of consent, would constitute a trespass to the person, shall be as effective as it would be if he were of full age; and where a minor has by virtue of this section given an effective consent to any treatment it shall not be necessary to obtain any consent for it from his parent or guardian.

Section 8(1) makes it clear that the consent of the young person is effective in its own right; consent does not also have to be obtained from the parent or guardian. There is in law (now enacted in the MCA) a presumption that a person over 16 years has the necessary capacity, but this can be rebutted if there is evidence to the contrary, as, for example, in the case of a 16 year old with learning difficulties. The presumption can be rebutted on a balance of probabilities (see Chapter 6).

Consent to what?

Section 8(2) explains:

> In this section 'surgical, medical or dental treatment' includes any procedure undertaken for the purposes of diagnosis and this section applies to any procedures (including, in particular, the administration of an anaesthetic) which is ancillary to any treatment as it applies to that treatment.

This is a comprehensive definition and covers most care and treatment provided in hospital and the community provided by all health professionals. It does not specifically refer to complementary or alternative therapies, but if these are provided under the aegis of a registered health professional there is no reason why the young person could not give a valid consent for them. It does not cover consent to research, which would be in a different category, unless the research was part of the young person's treatment (see Chapter 21).

Parental consent and the young person

Section 8(3) makes it clear that the fact that a young person of 16 and 17 years now has a statutory right to give consent does not invalidate any other consent which would have been valid before 1969.

Nothing in the section shall be construed as making ineffective any consent which would have been effective if this section had not been enacted.

In other words, before 1969, a parent or guardian could give consent on behalf of a child and young person until he or she became an adult (i.e. 21 years before the 1969 Act, 18 years after the 1969 Act). This power of the parent or guardian to give consent, therefore, still continues and a health professional can rely on the consent of either the young person or his or her parent as a defence against an action for trespass to the person. For example, if a young man of 17 was brought unconscious into hospital following a road accident, the parents could give consent to any necessary treatment on his behalf. The health professionals could also act in the best interests of the unconscious person (see Chapters 7 and 11).

Overruling a child's consent to treatment

In a situation such as a termination of a pregnancy, the young person of 16 or 17 years may give consent for the termination, but there have been cases where the parents have attempted to prevent the termination taking place on the grounds that they would look after the child. In such a situation, the health professionals could act on the valid basis of the young person's statutory right to give consent and the parents' attempt to prevent the termination going ahead would fail. Such a dispute arose in the case of a girl of 15 years who had had a previous pregnancy and the judge refused to prevent the termination going ahead on the grounds that it was in her best interests (*Re P (a minor)* (1981)).

There may, however, be other circumstances where the treatment required by the young person was not in his or her best interests. For example, the young person might seek to be sterilised. In such circumstances the parents could seek to make the child a ward of court or invoke the court's inherent jurisdiction for the matter to be brought before the courts. The older the child, the less likely the court is to interfere with the child's wishes. In addition, the older the child, the more important it is that such disputes should go before the courts.

Refusal to consent by young person

In the case of *Re W* (see Box 8.1) the Court of Appeal held that the Family Law Reform Act 1969 section 8 did not prevent consent being given by parents or the court. While the girl had a right to give consent under the Act, she could not refuse treatment which was necessary to save her life. Her refusal was therefore overruled.

The courts would not lightly overrule the refusal of a young person. There would have to be strong evidence that it was a life-saving matter. There is a clear difference between a parent acting on behalf of a mentally incapacitated young person in his or her best interests and a parent wishing to overrule the explicit wishes of a youngster. In the latter case, referral to the courts under the Children Act 1989 or under its inherent jurisdiction to consider cases involving children would be necessary. If parents disagree over the action which should be taken in relation to a young person of 16 or 17 years, the case can be brought to court under the Children Act 1989. Where possible the court would wish to give effect to the wishes of a mentally capacitated child.

As a result of the decision in *Re W* and other cases and the view that in a life-saving situation the refusal of a young person could be overruled by the court, it is clear that young persons of 16 and 17 years are not treated as adults and do not have the same rights that a mentally competent adult would have to refuse life-saving treatment. Thus the Mental Capacity Act 2005 requires a person to be 18 years or over to be able to draw up an advance decision or living will (see Chapter 16) or to set up a lasting power of attorney (see Chapter 11). It has been suggested that competence is defined more strictly in the case of young people than in the case of adults to protect them from the worst effects of their decision (BMA, 2001). In other words, a certain paternalism lawfully exists in relation to decision making by and on behalf of young people. As yet there has not been a case where a young person has challenged such an attitude under the Human Rights Act 1998, arguing that article 3 (the right not to be subjected to inhuman or degrading treatment or punishment) is infringed when a young person's wishes are overruled. For example, if instead of suffering from anorexia nervosa the girl in the Box 8.1 was suffering from leukaemia and required a blood transfusion as a life-saving necessity, but was refusing a blood transfusion because she was a Jehovah's Witness, would the courts take the same view as it did in *Re W* and overrule her refusal? At 18 years a refusal by a mentally competent adult in such circumstances would not be overruled, but the situation for the 16- and 17-year-old still has to be clarified by the courts. The present situation could be seen as contrary to the young person's rights under Article 3 (not to be subjected to inhuman or degrading treatment or punishment) Article 9 (freedom of religious expression) and Article 14 (not to be discriminated against in the implementation of the articles).

Consent to research

While the Family Law Reform Act 1969 does not give a statutory right to the young person to give consent to research which is not part of a treatment plan, it is thought that there would be a right at common law (judge made or case law) for a young person who had the mental capacity to give a valid consent. This would be a consequence of the House of Lords ruling in the Gillick case (*Gillick* v. *W Norfolk and Wisbech Area Health Authority* [1986]), which is considered in the next chapter. Those young people over 16 years who lacked the requisite mental capacity to give consent to research would come under the provisions of the Mental Capacity Act 2005 (see Chapter 21).

Conclusion

It is likely that we shall see more cases involving children and young persons where their rights under the European Convention on Human Rights are urged. Young persons of 16 and 17 are not in law adults, but those who care for them should be able to justify (and document) decisions taken on their behalf. The next chapter considers the law relating to the child under 16 years.

References

British Medical Association (2001) *Consent, Rights and Choices in Health Care for Children and Young People*. BMJ Books, London

Gillick v. *W Norfolk and Wisbech Area Health Authority* [1986] 1 AC 112.

Re P (a minor) (1981) 80 LGR 301.

Re W (a minor) (medical treatment) [1992] 4 All ER 627.

CHAPTER 9

Children under the age of 16 years

> **Box 9.1 Case scenario**
>
> Mrs Gillick questioned the lawfulness of the Department of Health and Social Security (DHSS) circular HN[80]46 which was a revised version of part of a comprehensive memorandum of guidance on family planning services issued to health authorities in May 1974 under cover of circular HSC(IS)32. The circular stated that in certain circumstances a doctor could lawfully prescribe contraception for a girl under 16 without the consent of the parents. Mrs Gillick wrote to the acting administrator formally forbidding any medical staff employed by the Norfolk Area Health Authority (AHA) to give
>
> > 'any contraceptive or abortion advice or treatment whatever to my...daughters whilst they are under 16 years without my consent'.
>
> The administrator replied that the treatment prescribed by a doctor is a matter for the doctor's clinical judgment, taking into account all the factors of the case.
>
> Mrs Gillick, who had five daughters, brought an action against the AHA and the DHSS seeking a declaration that the notice gave advice which was unlawful and wrong and which did or might adversely affect the welfare of her children, her right as a parent and her ability to discharge properly her duties as a parent. She sought a declaration that no doctor or other professional person employed by the health authority might give any contraceptive or abortion advice or treatment to any of her children below the age of 16 without her previous knowledge and consent.
>
> Source: *Gillick v. West Norfolk and Wisbech AHA and the DHSS* [1985]

Introduction

In the last chapter it was explained that there was a statutory right for a young person of 16 or 17 years to give consent to treatment. There is no such right for those under 16 and the law there has been laid down by the courts (common law or judge made law). The leading case is that of Mrs Gillick, the facts of which are set out in Box 9.1.

Mrs Gillick had, it seemed, a very strong case. Under the Family Law Reform Act 1969, section 8(1), a young person of 16 or 17 had a statutory right to give consent, so it could be concluded that a child under 16 lacked the power in law to give consent to treatment.

Although Mrs Gillick lost the case in the High Court, her appeal to the Court of Appeal succeeded, where all three judges unanimously agreed with her and also held that a doctor who gave contraceptive advice to an underage girl would be aiding and abetting in a criminal offence, since it was unlawful for a man to have intercourse with a girl under 16 years.

The Department of Health (DoH) appealed to the House of Lords, where there was a majority decision in upholding its appeal and reversing the decision of the Court of Appeal.

Narrow interpretation of the House of Lords decision

On the narrow view, the House of Lords held that in exceptional circumstances a girl under 16 could give consent to contraceptive advice and treatment without parental consent. The exceptional circumstances listed by Lord Fraser were that:

- The girl would, although under 16, understand the doctor's advice.
- The doctor could not persuade her to inform her parents or allow her to inform the parents that she was seeking contraceptive advice.
- She was very likely to have sexual intercourse with or without contraceptive treatment.
- Unless she received contraceptive advice or treatment her physical and/or mental health were likely to suffer.
- Her best interests required him to give her contraceptive advice, treatment, or both, without parental consent.

Wider interpretation of the House of Lords decision

On a wider interpretation, the House of Lords held that a Gillick-competent (see below) boy or girl could give a valid consent to treatment which was in his or her best interests without the involvement of parents.

The Gillick-competent child

The expression 'the Gillick-competent child' has now come into regular use, but is being replaced by the phrase 'competent according to Lord Fraser's guidelines'. The phrase refers to a child of any age who has achieved sufficient understanding and intelligence to enable him or her to understand fully what is proposed. The level of understanding must, of course, relate to the nature of the decision to be made (Box 9.2).

> ## Box 9.2 Fictional case: child in need of simple treatment
>
> John, a boy of 10 years, came into the accident and emergency department accompanied by his friend of the same age. They had been playing on a refuse dump and John had fallen against some broken glass and suffered a long cut to his leg. It was bleeding profusely. John said his parents were at work and it appeared that the boys were playing truant from school. The nurse explained to John that he would have to have stitches in his leg. He understood what she was saying and appeared to give a valid consent. What is the law?

In the fictional situation in Box 9.2, it is possible that John is competent according to Lord Fraser's guidelines, that he is capable of understanding what is involved in the treatment and could therefore give a valid consent. Contact should be attempted with his parents, but in the meantime treatment could proceed on the basis of the consent given by John.

In addition, if it were felt that John was not competent, emergency treatment could be given to him under the common law power to act in the best interests of the child out of necessity.

In this situation, the health professionals also have power, under the Children Act 1989, to act in the interests of the child, as section 3(5) shows:

A person who (a) does not have parental responsibility for a particular child, but (b) has care of the child, may (subject to the provision of this Act) do what is reasonable in all the circumstances of the case for the purpose of safeguarding or promoting the child's welfare.

This would appear to include giving consent to necessary emergency treatment in the absence of the parents, as in the above situation.

If, in contrast to some stitches in his leg, John needed brain surgery or some other dangerous and risky procedure, he would probably not be seen as having the requisite level of competence and therefore health professionals would not act on the basis of his consent alone. They would still, however, have a duty to ensure that any emergency action was taken to save the child's life if parental consent could not be obtained in time.

Health professionals often find that children who suffer from chronic conditions and who receive regular hospitalisation often develop a maturity above their physical years and an understanding of the proposed treatment. They should be given as much information as is reasonable to develop their understanding, as the situation in Box 9.3 illustrates.

Box 9.3 Refusal of treatment

Jayne suffered from cystic fibrosis and her condition had deteriorated over recent years. She was now on oxygen for most of the day and night and took additional feeding through a gastrostomy tube. She was 14 years old and had been placed on a waiting list for a lung transplant. Her condition progressively deteriorated and she started rejecting the regular physiotherapy. It was explained that physiotherapy was vital to keep her as well as possible for such time as a lung transplant was available. However, she said that she did not believe that a transplant was the answer and she wanted to be allowed to die. Her parents, however, wanted all efforts to be made for her to be kept alive because of the possibility of donor organs becoming available. What is the law?

Crucial to the answer to the tragic circumstances in Box 9.3 is the mental capacity of Jayne. She probably has a very good understanding of her condition, and realises that many people on the waiting list for a transplant die before they have the operation. She may have formed a realistic view of her situation and therefore her wish to die may be a wish formed by a competent person, in which case it could be respected in law.

In contrast, her parents want active treatment to proceed. In this dilemma, much will depend on the realities of the clinical situation. If doctors assess

Jayne's chances as slim, and active intervention as not only very uncomfortable but also futile, they may support Jayne's decision as being reasonable under the circumstances. It may be that, realistically, Jayne would be too ill to have a transplant. The situation in Box 9.3 contrasts with the case shown in Box 9.5, where a 13-year-old girl's refusal to have a heart transplant was eventually respected. The situation in Box 9.3 also differs from the facts of the case shown in Box 9.4.

Box 9.4 Refusing a transplant (*Re M (medical treatment: consent)* [1999])

A girl of 15 years refused to consent to a transplant which was needed to save her life. She stated that she did not wish to have anyone else's heart and she did not wish to take medication for the rest of her life. The hospital, which had obtained her mother's consent to the transplant, sought leave from the court to carry out the transplant.

The court held that the hospital could give treatment according to the doctor's clinical judgment, including a heart transplant. The girl was an intelligent person whose wishes carried considerable weight, but she had been overwhelmed by her circumstances and the decision she was being asked to make. Her severe condition had developed only recently and she had had only a few days to consider her situation. While recognising the risk that for the rest of her life she would carry resentment about what had been done to her, the court weighed that risk against the certainty of death if the order were not made.

The difference between the situations in Boxes 9.3 and 9.4 is clear. In Jayne's case she had lived with cystic fibrosis all her life and was aware of her own situation and the fact that she might not survive for a transplant. In the case shown in Box 9.4, the girl was afflicted very suddenly with a heart condition and could not adjust easily to her new situation. In Box 9.5 a heart transplant was seen as only temporary respite, not as a long-term life saving measure as it was in Box 9.4.

Refusal by a child of 13 years

In Box 9.5 a situation where a child of 13 refused a heart transplant is described.

Box 9.5 Refusal of a heart transplant by a child of 13 years (Simon de Bruxelles, 2008)

Hannah Jones, a 13-year-old girl, who had been treated for leukaemia since the age of 5, was advised that she required a heart transplant since the chemotherapy had left her with a hole in the heart, and as her body had grown her heart had been unable to keep pace. A pacemaker had been fitted at Birmingham Children's Hospital and the heart transplant would have been carried out at Great Ormond Street. Hannah spoke to doctors at both hospitals and told her parents that she did not want the transplant since it would provide only temporary respite and drugs to prevent rejection could prompt a recurrence of the leukaemia. Her parents (the mother an intensive care nurse and the father an auditor) accepted her decision. However, a locum doctor at the Herefordshire Primary Care Trust suggested that the PCT should apply for an order to remove her from the family home, on the grounds that her parents were preventing her treatment. The doctor wanted to give her a drug to facilitate her transfer to Great Ormond Street for the transplant to take place. The parents complained to the PCT. Following an interview by a child protection officer with Hannah, the PCT decided not to apply for a court order.

Crucial to the determination of the best interests of Hannah in the case in Box 9.5 is the fact that Hannah was terminally ill, the transplant would have provided only temporary respite and Hannah, who appears, even at 13 years, to be Gillick competent, preferred to die at home than face further interventions in hospital.

In the next chapter, we will consider the case where both the patient, a boy of 15, and his parents, were Jehovah's Witnesses and both the parents' and the boy's refusal to consent to a blood transfusion were overruled.

Parental rights

In addition to the right of the child who is competent according to Lord Fraser's guidelines to give consent to necessary treatment, the parents also have the right to give consent. However, their rights must be exercised in the best interests of the child. There are examples where the parents' refusal to arrange for the necessary treatment has been overruled, and there are examples where treatment arranged by the parents has been stopped as not being in the child's best interests. In every case, the paramount consideration is the welfare of the child. This will be considered further in the next chapter. All the principles about information giving which are discussed in Chapters 4 and 5 apply to ensuring that parents have the necessary information about the care and treatment of their children. The Kennedy Report (2001) recommended that:

> Parents of those too young to take decisions for themselves should receive a copy of any letter written by one healthcare professional to another about their child's treatment or care (Recommendation 15)

Evidence that consent has been given

The Forms set out in the Department of Health's (2001) *Good Practice in Consent Implementation Guide* can be used for evidencing that consent has been given by the parent or child (where competent) or both. Form 2 is used by a child and parent of a child where it is anticipated that the child will lose consciousness and Form 3 for treatment where the patient will remain conscious. In practice some trusts are finding that Form 2 is suitable for all procedures to be carried out on children.

Conclusion

Acting in the best interests of the child and enabling the child to have as much input into critical decisions can be seen as a considerable challenge to health professionals, who are not helped by disputes between separated or divorced parents.

It is important to ensure that even in the case of very young children the child is involved in the decisions relating to his or her care, given as much information as is reasonable for his or her level of understanding and his or her autonomy promoted as fully as possible.

In the next chapter we will consider the law relating to disputes between parents and between parents and professionals.

References

Department of Health (2001) *Good Practice in Consent Implementation Guide*. DoH, London.

Dimond, B. (2002) *The Legal Aspects of Pain Management*. Quay Books, London.

Gillick v. *West Norfolk and Wisbech AHA and the DHSS* [1985] 3 All ER 402.

Re F (mental patient: sterilisation) [1990] 2 AC 1.

Kennedy (2001) *Bristol Royal Infirmary Inquiry Learning from Bristol: the Report of the Public Inquiry Into Children's Heart Surgery at the Bristol Royal Infirmary 1984–1995*. Command paper CM 5207. Stationery Office, London.

Re M (medical treatment: consent) [1999] 2FLR 1097.

de Bruxelles, Simon (2008) Girl wins fight to turn down transplant. *The Times*, 11 November, p. 3.

CHAPTER 10

Disputes with parents

> ## Box 10.1 Case scenario
>
> David has been separated from his wife Julie for several years. Their 6-year-old son, Jonathan, is in hospital and doctors have advised that he needs a tonsillectomy. David has said that he is not prepared to give consent to such an operation because he had a similar operation when he was 8 years old and believed that it was carried out simply because tonsillectomies were fashionable at the time. Julie wants the operation to proceed and is prepared to sign the consent form. What is the law?

Introduction

The last chapter considered the law relating to consent by a child under 16 years, noting that a parent could give consent on behalf of the child, but in certain circumstances, the child, if competent according to Lord Fraser's guidelines, could give consent on his or her own behalf. This chapter considers the situation where there are disputes with parents over what is in the child's best interests.

Parental rights: parental refusal overruled

In the case in Box 10.2 the parents had pleaded that the boy's refusal should be upheld because he would have been 16 years in only a few months' time. However, as discussed in Chapter 8, the case of *Re W (a minor) (medical treatment)* [1992] shows it is not until a person with the requisite mental capacity is 18 years that his or her refusal to have life-saving treatment is protected.

Box 10.2 Case of *Re E (a minor) (wardship: medical treatment)* [1993]

A youth of 15 years 9 months suffering from leukaemia required a blood transfusion as part of his treatment. Both he and his parents were devout Jehovah's Witnesses and refused to give consent. The health authority applied for him to be made a ward of court and for a declaration that the treatment could proceed. The judge held that the lad was intelligent enough to take decisions about his own well-being, but that he did not have a full understanding of what the blood transfusions would involve. The welfare of the child was the first and paramount consideration. Although the court should be very slow to interfere in a decision the child had taken, the welfare of the child led to only one conclusion: that the hospital should be at liberty to treat him with blood transfusions. The judge therefore gave leave to the hospital authority to give treatment, including blood transfusion, and the consent of the patient and his parents was dispensed with.

A case similar to that in Box 10.2 was that of *Re S (a minor) (consent to medical treatment)* [1994]. A girl of 15 years suffered from thalassaemia and had been kept alive by monthly blood transfusions and injections. She and her mother became Jehovah's Witnesses and subsequently refused to accept blood transfusions. The judge decided that the treatment could be authorised on the grounds that it was in her best interests and the court had the power to overrule a competent child's refusal of treatment. He did, however, find that the girl was not Gillick-competent because she lacked emotional maturity.

In the case of *Re S (a minor) (medical treatment)* [1993] the child was 4½ years and suffering from T-cell leukaemia. It appeared that the only clinical option for her survival was a blood transfusion as part of the treatment, but her parents, who were Jehovah's Witnesses, refused to give consent to this aspect of her care. The local authority sought leave of the court to invoke the inherent jurisdiction of the court under Section 100 of the Children Act 1989 and for a declaration that a blood transfusion could be given. The judge agreed to the declaration and considered that fears that in the future the child would believe her life to have been perpetuated by an ungodly act to have little foundation in reality. The judge stated that 'the reality seems to me to be that family reaction which recognises that the responsibility for consent was taken from them and, as a judicial act, absolved their conscience of responsibility'.

Failure by parents to arrange for the necessary treatment to be provided for their children can, in certain circumstances (i.e. where the child dies) constitute the crime of murder or manslaughter. Thus a father was imprisoned and the mother was given a suspended sentence when they treated their diabetic daughter with a herbal remedy, rather than arrange for her to have insulin (*The Times*, 1993).

Refusal of screening

In the case of Re C (HIV test) [1999] a mother was HIV positive but the parents refused to have her 4 month old baby tested for HIV. The local authority applied for a specific issue order that the baby be tested. The Court of Appeal upheld the judge's order that it was in the best interests of the child to be tested for HIV. There was no order that breast feeding of the baby should be discontinued in the event of the child being found negative. The trial judge believed that such an order (which had not been sought) would be unenforceable. The Human Rights Act 1998 had not been brought into force at the time the case was decided and it could be argued that to compel the baby to be tested was a breach of Article 8 and the right to respect for privacy and family life. However, if the test was considered to be in the best interests of the baby, then this could come under one of the exceptions to Article 8 (see Appendix 1 of this book).

The general principle is that if the parents are refusing to give consent to life-saving treatment which doctors consider is necessary in the best interests of the child, then the court can intervene and declare that it is lawful to proceed without the consent of the parents. In an emergency situation, where there is insufficient time to obtain a declaration from the courts (and there is an on-call system, so a decision can be obtained speedily), doctors would be justified in law in acting in the best interests of the child and in carrying out life-saving treatment.

In such a situation they could obtain a retrospective declaration from the courts that they acted in the child's best interests. In other words, a child should not be allowed to die because parental consent to treatment which is considered by the clinicians to be in the best interests of the child is lacking. There is also a power under the Children Act 1989 section 3(5) (see Chapter 9) which enables the carer of the child 'to do what is reasonable in all the circumstances of the case for the purpose of safeguarding or promoting the child's welfare'.

Case where parents' refusal upheld

In general it is unusual for the courts not to uphold the medical view of what is in the best interests of the child, but in the case shown in Box 10.4 the Court

Box 10.3 *Re D (a minor) (wardship: sterilisation)* [1976]

A girl of 11 years suffered from Sotos syndrome, the symptoms of which include accelerated growth during infancy, epilepsy, general clumsiness, an unusual facial appearance and behaviour problems, including emotional instability, certain aggressive tendencies and some impairment of mental function. The mother, taking the advice of the consultant paediatrician that her daughter would remain substantially handicapped and that she would always be unable to care for herself or look after any children, discussed with the obstetrician the possibility of her daughter being sterilised. An operation was arranged. However, before it was performed the educational psychologist applied for the girl to be made a ward of court. Mrs Justice Heilbron, who heard the case, was not convinced that the operation was in the best interests of the girl and so ordered that the operation should not proceed.

Box 10.4 *Re T (a minor) (Wardship: Medical Treatment* [1996]

The child was in need of a liver transplant, but parents refused to give permission for the operation to take place. Medical opinion was that the child would have a reasonable chance of success from such an operation. However, the parents were living abroad and would have to bring the child to the UK for the operation to take place. The High Court held that leave should be given for the health professions to perform the operation despite parental opposition. The Court of Appeal overruled this ruling and placed emphasis on the views of the parents and the fact that they were both health professions. It decided that it was not in the child's best interests for it to order the child to return to the UK for the transplant operation to take place.

of Appeal supported the parents' refusal to allow their child to have a liver transplant. This was an unusual decision, and specific to the atypical facts of the case.

When treatment wanted by parents is stopped

Following the case described in Box 10.3, the judge recommended that such cases of non-therapeutic sterilisations should be brought before the courts for a declaration to be made that they were in the child's best interests. Such cases are unusual, since normally treatment agreed between parents and doctors for a child would be considered to be in the child's best interests. However, the case is a precedent for any person who is concerned at the treatment which is proposed for the child. An application can be made to make the child a ward of court or, under the Children Act 1989, for a declaration to be made as to what is in the child's best interests.

Severely disabled babies and children

Disputes have arisen between clinicians and parents over the treatment plans for very severely disabled neonates and young children. Parents may be anxious for all possible measures to be taken to keep the child alive, whilst the clinicians might consider that it is in the best interests of the child to be allowed to die, i.e. for nature to take its course. The court battles between clinicians and the parents of Charlotte Wyatt illustrate the pain and suffering of such disputes. (Wyatt, 2004). See also Chapter 18 and disputes about not for resuscitation instructions.

Disputes between parents over the child's treatment

Even when parents are divorced or separated, under the Children Act 1989 section 2(1) both parents retain parental responsibility for their children. Under section 2(7) where more than one person has parental responsibility for a child each of them may act alone and without the other (or others) in meeting that responsibility. Even where one parent has a residence order in his or her favour, the other still retains parental responsibilities and can exercise these to the full. It also follows that one parent does not have the right of veto over the other's actions.

If, however, there has been a specific order by the court relating to a decision affecting the care or treatment of the child, then a single parent cannot change this or take any action which is incompatible with this order unless the approval of the court is obtained. It therefore follows that if there is a dispute between parents over treatment decisions in respect of the child, either can go to court for a specific issue or prohibited steps order to be made.

Prohibited steps order

Where one parent wishes to prevent the other taking action which he or she does not consider is in the interests of the child, that parent may seek a prohibited steps order. This can be ordered under section 8 of the Children Act 1989, which means that no step which could be taken by a parent in meeting his or her parental responsibility for a child and which is of a kind specified in the order shall be taken without the consent of the court. Thus, if one parent feared that the other was likely to agree to a mentally impaired daughter being sterilised, then that parent could obtain a prohibited steps order preventing the operation proceeding on the basis of consent by the other parent unless the court were to so direct.

If the child is considered to be competent but disagrees with actions which the parents are intending, he or she could seek the leave of the court to obtain a prohibited steps order. The child would have to apply to the High Court (*Re D (a minor) (wardship: sterilisation)* [1976]). The court must be satisfied that the child has sufficient understanding to make the proposed application (section 10(8) of the Children Act 1989).

Unmarried parents

Where parents are unmarried, the mother has the sole rights to make decisions in respect of the child unless the father has acted with the mother to have his name recorded in the child's birth registration, or completed the necessary forms to indicate that he accepts parental responsibilities. Further information can be obtained from the web site of the General Register Office (http://www.gro.gov.uk/). Even if they marry after the birth of the child, the appropriate forms still have to be completed. Even where the unmarried father has not assumed parental responsibilities, he can be called upon by the Child Support Agency to contribute to the costs of the child's upbringing. Further information is available from the Child Support Agency web site (http://www.csa.gov.uk/). Because health professionals may not always be aware of the marital status of the parents, they may have to assume that only the mother has parental responsibilities unless there is clear evidence to the contrary.

Case scenario

With regard to Box 10.1, the father is entitled to apply under the Children Act 1989 for the case to be heard on whether the operation is in the child's best interests, and whether a prohibited steps order should be made. Evidence would be brought before the court of expert views of Jonathan's clinical condition and whether reasonable practice (*Bolam* v. *Friern HMC* QBD [1957]) would justify the operation. In the light of this evidence the judge would make his order.

A dispute over whether children should be given the MMR vaccine came to the court when two sets of parents disagreed. In each case the mother was against the triple vaccine and the father wanted it given. The High Court ruled that it was in the best interest of the children to have the MMR. The Court of Appeal dismissed the appeal on the grounds that the judge had decided the applications by reference to the paramount consideration of the welfare of the two children, in accordance with section 1 of the Children Act 1989 (*Re C (A Child: immunisation: parental rights) and Others* [2003]).

Conclusion

As more marriages and relationships break down and new partnerships are formed, health practitioners on children's wards will find that they become involved in conflicts between the parties, where the child's treatment is used as an object of conflict. Health professionals should be familiar with the process for resolving any such major dilemma over what action should be taken in the best interests of the child. Where a major conflict is anticipated, it is preferable to seek the declaration of the court, earlier rather than later, since this enables all parties, including the child, to be represented. In addition disputes are likely to arise between health professionals and parents where the latter wish heroic measures to be taken where babies have severe disabilities and the clinicians consider that it is in the best interests of the baby or child to be allowed to die. Health practitioners must as always ensure that their documentation, which is likely to be produced in court, is of the highest standard.

References

Bolam v *Friern HMC QBD* [1957] 2 All ER 118.
Re C (A Child: immunisation: parental rights) and Others) [2003] 3 FCR 156 CA.

Re C (HIV test) [1999] 2 FLR 1004.

Re D (a minor) (wardship: sterilisation) [1976] 1 All ER 327.

Re E (a minor) (wardship: medical treatment) [1993] 1 FLR 386.

Re S (a minor)(medical treatment) [1993] 1 FLR 376.

Re S (a minor) (consent to medical treatment) [1994] 2 FLR 1065.

Re T (a minor) (Wardship: Medical Treatment [1996] *The Times,* 28 October 1996; [1997] 1 WLR 242.

Re W (a minor) (medical treatment) [1992] 4 All ER 627.

The Times (1993) News report. *The Times,* 29 October.

Wyatt v Portsmouth Hospital NHS Trust [2004] EWHC Civ 2247; *Wyatt v Portsmouth Hospital NHS Trust* [2005] EWHC 117 [2005] EWHC 693; *Wyatt v Portsmouth Hospital NHS Trust* [2005] EWCA Civ 1181; *Wyatt v Portsmouth NHS Trust* [2005] EWHC 2293.

CHAPTER 11

Lasting power of attorney, the Court of Protection and the Office of the Public Guardian

> ## Box 11.1 Case scenario
>
> Harry was 90 years and felt that his mental powers were declining and wished to appoint his grandson, Fred, aged 21, to make all decisions on his behalf should there come a time when he lacked the mental capacity to make his own decisions. He consulted a solicitor and all the necessary forms were signed. It was confirmed that Fred was over 18 years and both he and Harry had the requisite mental capacity. Two years later Harry is admitted to hospital following a cardiac arrest and is unable to make any decisions. What is the legal situation?

Introduction

The Mental Capacity Act 2005 (MCA) introduced several new organisations and instruments to assist in decision making on behalf of and in the protection of mentally incapacitated adults. This chapter looks at these innovations. Reference should be made to the Code of Practice on the MCA available from the Ministry of Justice website (http://www.justice.gov.uk/). There is also simple guidance in Dimond (2008).

Lasting power of attorney (LPA)

From October 2007 it has been possible for a person (known as the donor) to give authority to another person to make decisions for the donor covering personal welfare as well as property and affairs, by means of a lasting power of attorney (LPA). This authority is known as power of attorney. The enduring power of attorney (EPA), which cannot be created after October 2007 (but existing EPAs continue to be valid) can only cover decisions relating to property and affairs. LPAs which apply to personal welfare decisions only come into effect when the person setting them up (the donor) lacks the mental capacity to make his or her own decisions. In contrast, LPAs which apply to property and affairs can be used when the donor still has the requisite mental capacity. The following are the requirements for an LPA to be valid:

1. The person (the donor) creating the LPA must be aged 18 or over.
2. The donor must have the requisite mental capacity to grant a power of attorney.
3. The LPA must be a written document set out in the statutory form prescribed by regulations (the forms are available from the Office of the Public Guardian's website: http://www.publicguardian.gov.uk/).
4. The LPA must include prescribed information about the nature and effect of the LPA (as set out in the regulations).
5. The donor must sign a statement saying that they have read the prescribed information (or somebody has read it to them) and that they want the LPA to apply when they no longer have capacity.
6. The document must name people (not any of the attorneys) who should be told about an application to register the LPA, or it should say that there is no-one they wish to be told.
7. The attorneys must sign a statement saying that they have read the prescribed information and that they understand their duties – in particular the duty to act in the donor's best interests.
8. The document must include a certificate completed by an independent third party confirming that:
    (i)   in their opinion, the donor understands the LPA's purpose
    (ii) nobody used fraud or undue pressure to trick or force the donor into making the LPA and
    (iii) there is nothing to stop the LPA being created.

The attorneys

To be given the authority to make decisions on behalf of another person (i.e. to be appointed as an attorney), a person must be over 18 years and have the requisite mental capacity. More than one person can be appointed as attorney. Where they are appointed to act jointly, then they must act together; they must agree decisions and sign any relevant documents. Where they are appointed severally, then they can act independently of each other. In some situations the LPA may be a joint appointment for certain purposes, and a several appointment for others. If the donor does not specify whether it is a joint or several appointment, the MCA states that it should be regarded as a joint appointment. For LPAs covering property and affairs, the attorney could be a trust corporation such as a bank or other financial institution.

Registration

The LPA must be registered with the Office of the Public Guardian before it can be used. The application to register may be made by the donor (provided he or she still has the requisite mental capacity) or it may be made by the attorneys.

Duties of the attorney

Attorneys are required to follow the five principles set out in the Mental Capacity Act 2005, which are discussed in Chapter 7. They must also act in the best interests of the donor, following the stages discussed in Chapter 7. They also have a duty to act in accordance with the instructions set out in the LPA document. Before they act, they must ensure that the LPA has been registered, and if not they must register it themselves. In the case of personal welfare LPAs, they must ensure that the donor no longer has the requisite mental capacity to make his or her own decisions. If the donor is detained under the Mental Health Act 1983 (as amended by the 2007 Act) then the attorneys cannot take any decisions which come under the mental health legislation. If the donor has set up an advance decision refusing treatment at a future time, when he or she lacks the requisite mental capacity to make decisions, then the attorneys cannot act contrary to that advance decision. However, if the LPA was set up after the advance decision and gives the attorneys the right to give consent to the treatment identified in the advance decision, then the LPA would take precedence over the advance decision. Attorneys cannot refuse life-sustaining treatment, unless such a power is specifically given in the LPA. Attorneys are also required to act in accordance with the Code of Practice.

Guidance has been issued on LPAs by the Office of the Public Guardian, which is responsible for keeping a register of LPAs.

Application of the law to the case scenario (Box 11.1)

In this case, it is assumed that Harry has registered the LPA with the Office of the Public Guardian. If not, Fred, the grandson, can do so as attorney. An attorney cannot make decisions on behalf of the donor in respect of personal welfare until it is clear that the donor no longer has the requisite mental capacity to make his own decisions. If this is the case with Harry, then Fred can notify the Office of the Public Guardian that he is now acting as attorney on Harry's behalf. Fred should notify the ward staff of his position. They should ensure that he is given all relevant information about Harry's care and treatment and he should be invited to take part in the clinical discussions over future treatment. He would not be able on Harry's behalf to refuse life-sustaining treatment, unless that was clearly set out in the document setting up the LPA. Fred should be prepared to show the ward staff the LPA document relating to personal welfare. Fred is obliged by law to act in accordance with the five principles set out in the Mental Capacity Act and to take the necessary steps set out in section 4 to act in Harry's best interests. Fred should keep records of the actions which he takes on Harry's behalf. If anyone is concerned about Fred's actions and considers that he is not acting in the best interests of Harry, they can raise their concerns with the Office of the Public Guardian.

Office of the Public Guardian (OPG)

This organisation, established on 1 October 2007 under the MCA, is responsible for keeping a register of LPAs, a register of deputies appointed by the Court of Protection (see below) and monitoring the actions of attorneys and deputies. If anyone has concerns about an attorney, then they can be raised with the OPG, which works closely with organisations such as local authorities and NHS Trusts to carry out investigations.

It can also send Court of Protection Visitors to visit people who may lack capacity to make particular decisions and those who have formal powers to act on their behalf. A Public Guardian Board has been appointed to oversee and review how the Public Guardian carries out its duties. Since the OPG came into existence it has issued considerable guidance in the form of booklets and other information and also provides forms for Lasting Powers of Attorney. It also provides copies of the MCA UPDATE service booklets. Its website is http://www.publicguardian.gov.uk/.

Office of Public Guardian annual report

This was published in August 2008 and showed widespread use of the MCA. Nearly three times more people have applied to register their LPA than in previous years; the number of applications to the Court of Protection for a finance or health and welfare decision have exceeded expectations: nearly three times more investigations into the actions of deputies and attorneys compared to last year and more than 50 applications have been made to the Court of Protection by the Public Guardian when there are concerns about a deputy or attorney.

Annual general meeting of the Public Guardian Board

The AGM took place on 7 October 2008 and was open to members of the public. The OPG website will provide dates of future AGMs.

Court of Protection

The new Court of Protection established in October 2007 has a wider jurisdiction than its predecessor. It is now able to determine issues relating to the personal welfare of those adults lacking the mental capacity to make their own decisions as well as issues relating to property and finance. It has the power to decide on the following:

1. decide whether a person has capacity to make a particular decision for him or herself
2. make declarations, decisions or orders on financial or welfare matters affecting people who lack capacity to make such decisions
3. appoint deputies to make decisions for people lacking capacity to make those decisions
4. decide whether an LPA or EPA is valid, and
5. remove deputies or attorneys who fail to carry out their duties.

Details of how applications can be made to the Court of Protection, the fees payable and the forms to be completed are available from the website of the Office of the Public Guardian.

Deputies

The Court of Protection can appoint a deputy to make decisions on behalf of a person who lacks the capacity to make them him- or herself. The deputy has a duty to act within the instructions given by the Court of Protection, to act in the best interests of the person who lacks mental capacity and to act in accordance with the principles set out in the MCA (see Chapter 7).

A deputy appointed by the court must be either an individual who has reached 18, or when decisions relate to property and affairs, an individual who has reached 18 or a trust corporation. The Court of Protection may appoint an individual by appointing the holder for the time being of a specified office or position. A person may not be appointed as a deputy without his consent. The court may appoint two or more deputies to act and they may be appointed to act jointly or jointly and severally or jointly in respect of some matters and jointly and severally in respect of others. When appointing a deputy or deputies, the court may at the same time appoint one or more other persons to succeed the existing deputy or those deputies identifying the circumstances, or the events or a specified time which would lead to another person replacing the deputy. The deputy is entitled to be reimbursed out of P's property for his reasonable expenses in discharging his functions, and if the court so directs when appointing him, to remuneration out of P's property for discharging them. The court may confer on a deputy powers to:

(a) take possession or control of all or any specified part of P's property;
(b) exercise all or any specified powers in respect of it, including such powers of investment as the court may determine.
The court may require a deputy:
(a) to give to the Public Guardian such security as the court thinks fit for the due discharge of his functions, and
(b) to submit to the Public Guardian such reports at such times or at such intervals as the court may direct.

The Code of Practice (Paragraph 8.41) recommends that:

> Paid care workers (for example, care home managers) should not agree to act as a deputy because of the possible conflict of interest – unless there are exceptional circumstances (for example, if the care worker is the only close relative of the person who lacks capacity). But the court can appoint someone who is an office-holder or in a specified position (for example, the Director of Adult Services of the relevant local authority). In this situation, the court will need to be satisfied that there is no conflict of interest before making such an appointment (see paragraphs 8.58–8.60 of the Code of Practice).

The Deputy as agent of the person lacking the requisite mental capacity

Section 19(6) states that the deputy is to be seen as the agent of the person who lacks the requisite mental capacity. This places upon the deputy all those duties which an agent owes towards the principal. These are identified in the Code of Practice and include:

- A duty to act with care and skill
- A fiduciary duty not to take advantage of their situation
- A duty to indemnify the person against liability to third parties caused by the deputy's negligence
- A duty not to delegate duties unless authorised to do so
- A duty to act in good faith
- A duty to respect the person's confidentiality, and
- A duty to comply with the directions of the Court of Protection.

Those deputies who are appointed in relation to property and affairs also have a duty to:

- keep accounts, and
- keep the person's money and property separate from own finances.
  The Code of Practice provides detailed guidance on these duties.

Exceptions to the power of a deputy

Under section 20 there are limitations on the power of a deputy, who *cannot*:

1. make a decision on behalf of P in relation to a matter if he knows or has reasonable grounds for believing that P has capacity in relation to the matter
2. prohibit a named person from having contact with P
3. direct a person responsible for P's health care to allow a different person to take over that responsibility
4. have powers in relation to the settlement of any of P's property, whether for P's benefit or for the benefit of others
5. have powers in relation to the execution for P of a will, or
6. have the exercise of any power (including a power to consent) vested in P whether beneficially or as trustee or otherwise
7. make a decision on behalf of P which is inconsistent with a decision made, within the scope of his authority and in accordance with this Act, by the donee of a lasting power of attorney granted by P (or, if there is more than one donee, by any of them)

8. refuse consent to the carrying out or continuation of life-sustaining treatment in relation to P
9. act contrary to the principles set out in Section 1 or contrary to the best interests of the person
10. do an act that is intended to restrain P unless four conditions are satisfied.
    (i) the deputy is acting within the scope of an authority expressly conferred on him by the court
    (ii) P lacks, or the deputy reasonably believes that P lacks, capacity in relation to the matter in question
    (iii) the deputy reasonably believes that it is necessary to do the act in order to prevent harm to P
    (iv) the act is a proportionate response to
        (a) the likelihood of P's suffering harm, or
        (b) the seriousness of that harm.

Section 20(12) states that a deputy restrains P if he

(a) uses, or threatens to use, force to secure the doing of an act which P resists, or
(b) restricts P's liberty of movement, whether or not P resists, or if he authorises another person to do any of those things.

Concerns about deputies

Any person who is concerned about the conduct of a deputy can contact the OPG, which has a monitoring role of the actions of a deputy and could send a Court of Protection Visitor to investigate. Where criminal action is suspected the police and/or social services should be notified. Ultimately the Court of Protection has the power to remove a deputy who is failing in his or her duties or not acting in the best interests of the person lacking mental capacity.

Conclusions

These new tools which now cover personal welfare decisions should ensure that decision making on behalf of those who lack the requisite mental capacity is greatly facilitated and at the same time those lacking mental capacity receive greater protection. The annual reports of the OPG and the ability of members of the public to attend its AGMs should ensure openness of its activities. In time, with greater public understanding, LPAs are likely to grow in popularity and many will benefit from the fact that personal welfare decisions can be delegated to an attorney at a time when the donor lacks the requisite mental capacity. Health service professionals are likely to encounter the use of LPAs and deputies appointed by the Court of Protection more frequently in the future.

References

Dimond, B. C. (2008) *Legal Aspects of Mental Capacity*. Blackwell Publishing, Oxford.
Court of Protection and Office of Public Guardian http://www.guardian.gov.uk/.

CHAPTER 12

Compulsory Caesarean sections

Box 12.1 Case scenario

Miss MB required a Caesarean section in order to save her foetus. However, while she gave consent to the operation, she suffered from a needle phobia which caused her to panic and refuse the preliminary anaesthetic. The trust applied for a declaration that the Caesarean section could take place on the grounds that the needle phobia rendered her mentally incapacitated and therefore the operation should proceed in her best interests (*Re MB (an adult: medical treatment)* [1997]).

Introduction

It is the inalienable right of mentally competent adults to make their own decisions on treatment. Even if they refuse life-saving treatment, their refusal must be respected. This principle was upheld by the Court of Appeal in the case of *Re T (adult: refusal of medical treatment)* (1992) and underpins the provisions of the Mental Capacity Act 2005 (MCA). Where, however, a person is considered on reasonable grounds to lack the necessary mental capacity then action can be taken out of necessity in their best interests as set out in the Mental Capacity Act 2005. In the case of *Re T*, which preceded the MCA, the Court of Appeal ruled that health professionals should check, where life-saving treatment was being refused, that the patient had the necessary mental capacity to refuse. In this chapter we look at how these principles now enshrined in the Mental Capacity Act 2005 apply in the case of pregnant women and what rights, if any, the foetus has in the decision-making process.

The case of *Re S*

Mrs S, aged 30, was expecting her third child (*Re S (adult: refusal of medical treatment)*, 1992). She was admitted with ruptured membranes and in spontaneous labour. She refused a Caesarean section on religious grounds (she was described as a 'born again Christian') and was supported by her husband in her refusal. The foetus was in a transverse lie and the obstetrician formed the view that a Caesarean section was a life-saving necessity both for Mrs S and the child. The foetus could not be born alive without the Caesarean section. The health authority made an *ex parte* application (i.e. the woman was not represented) to the Family Court. The application was made at 1.30 p.m. and the case heard at 2.00 p.m. The judge, Sir Stephen Brown, who was President of the Family Division of the High Court, decided at 2.18 p.m. that the declaration could be made, authorising the surgeons and staff of a hospital to carry out an emergency Caesarean section operation upon Mrs S. The main grounds for the declaration were that the operation was in the vital interests of the woman and of her unborn child. The outcome was that the woman survived but the baby was stillborn.

Criticism of Re S

This decision came under a lot of criticism since it appeared to place the pregnant woman in a different category than any other mentally competent adult. If a Caesarean section could be forced upon a mentally competent woman in the interests of the foetus, then compulsory control over a pregnant woman's smoking, drinking, drug taking and general lifestyle – all in the interests of the foetus – could be justified. A pregnant woman would have a totally different legal status than any other mentally competent adult. Mrs S herself did not appeal against the judge's decision to the Court of Appeal. Since this case the Mental Capacity Act 2005 has been enacted and brought into force, and the crucial issue now is the ability of the woman to consent to treatment. If Mrs S had the requisite mental capacity to make a decision about a Caesarean section, then her refusal could not be overruled.

Other compulsory Caesarean cases

Re S was followed by several other cases where compulsory Caesarean section operations were carried out without the consent of the woman. In one case, the patient, who suffered from paranoid schizophrenia, was detained in a psychiatric hospital under section 3 of the Mental Health Act 1983 and was refusing to have a Caesarean section operation (*Tameside and Glossop Acute Services Trust* v. *CH*, 1996). The consultant psychiatrist gave evidence that a stillbirth would lead to a profound deterioration of the patient's mental health and once the pregnancy was over, the woman could have the antipsychotic medication which had been discontinued during the pregnancy because of dangers to the foetus. The judge declared that the operation could proceed under section 63 of the Mental Health Act 1983 as being treatment for mental disorder.

This decision could be criticised on the grounds that treatment for mental disorder was given too wide a definition: if a Caesarean section is considered to be treatment for mental disorder, it would be difficult to find any treatment which, by reason of some benefits to the mental state, would not come within the definition of treatment for mental disorder.

In a second case, a pregnant woman had a history of psychiatric treatment and had had three previous children who were delivered by Caesarean section (*Norfolk and Norwich Healthcare (NHS) Trust* v *W* [1996]). A consultant psychiatrist examined her and declared that she was not suffering from mental disorder at the time, but she was unable to balance the information given to her. The application was made to the court for a forceps delivery to take place, and if necessary a Caesarean section. The judge decided that in light of the evidence she lacked the mental competence to make a decision about treatment. A declaration was made on the lines sought.

After these decisions, which received much adverse publicity in the press, there was a need for clarification by the Court of Appeal, and this came in the case of Re *MB*.

Case of Re MB

In the case of MB (see Box 12.1) the judge held that the woman was mentally incapacitated as a result of the phobia and the operation could therefore proceed in her best interests. The same day the Court of Appeal upheld that decision. In a reserved judgment it set out how capacity was to be determined (Table 12.1) and the general principles which apply to the refusal of treatment (Table 12.2).

The Court of Appeal emphasised that every person is presumed to have the capacity to consent to or to refuse medical treatment unless and until that presumption is rebutted. A competent woman who has the capacity to decide may, for religious reasons, other reasons, rational or irrational reasons or no reason at all, choose not to have medical intervention, even though the consequence may be the death or serious handicap of the child she bears, or her own death. In that event the courts do not have the jurisdiction to declare medical intervention lawful and the question of her own best interests, objectively considered, does not arise.

Table 12.1 Determining capacity: *Re MB* (source: *Re MB (an adult: medical treatment)* [1997]).

A person lacks the capacity if some impairment or disturbance of mental functioning renders the person unable to make a decision whether to consent to or to refuse treatment. That inability to make a decision will occur when:

(a) The patient is unable to comprehend and retain the information which is material to the decision, especially as to the likely consequences of having or not having the treatment in question

(b) The patient is unable to use the information and weigh it in the balance as part of the process of arriving at the decision

Case of St George's Healthcare NHS Trust v S

The case of *St George's Healthcare NHS Trust* v *S, R v Collins ex parte S* (1998) reaffirmed the principles set out by the Court of Appeal in the case of *Re MB*. The facts were that a woman who was about 36 weeks pregnant was diagnosed as suffering from severe pre-eclampsia, severe oedema and proteinuria. She was advised to have early induction of labour as a life-saving necessity. She refused on the grounds that she would prefer to let nature take its course. She was then examined by an approved social worker and two doctors and was detained in hospital under section 2 of the Mental Health Act 1983. From there she was transferred to St George's Hospital for obstetric treatment. She was advised by a solicitor that she had the right to refuse treatment. The hospital applied in an *ex parte* application to the High Court judge stating that it was a life and death situation and the patient had gone into labour. This latter information was incorrect, and the judge was not informed that the patient had instructed solicitors. The judge made the declaration that S's consent could be dispensed with. S was then given a Caesarean section. She was transferred back to the psychiatric hospital where a doctor decided that she was not suffering from mental disorder and took her off section 2 following which she took her own discharge.

The case eventually came before the Court of Appeal which emphasised the pregnant woman's right of self-determination, that the Mental Health Act should not have been used when a person was refusing treatment for hypertension, and stated that an unborn child is not a separate person from its mother.

Lord Justice Judge held that a pregnant woman is entitled not to be forced to submit to an invasion of her body against her will, whether her own life or that of her unborn child depends on it. Her right is not reduced or diminished merely because her decision to exercise it may appear morally repugnant. The

Table 12.2 Principles laid down in *Re MB* and incorporated in guidance issued by the Department of Health(source: Department of Health (1997)).

1. The court is unlikely to entertain an application for a declaration unless the capacity of the patient to consent to or refuse the medical treatment is in issue.

2. For the time being, at least, the doctors ought to seek a ruling from the High Court on the issue of competence.

3. Those in charge should identify a potential problem as early as possible so that both the hospital and the patient can obtain legal advice.

4. It is highly desirable that, in any case where it is not an emergency, steps are taken to bring it before the court, before it becomes an emergency, to remove the extra pressure from the parties and the court and to enable proper instructions to be taken, particularly from the patient and where possible give the opportunity for the court to hear oral evidence, if appropriate.

5. The hearing should be inter parties.

6. The mother should be represented in all cases, unless, exceptionally, she does not wish to be. If she is unconscious she should have a guardian *ad litem*.

7. The official solicitor should be notified of all applications to the High Court.

8. There should in general be some evidence, preferably but not necessarily from a psychiatrist, as to the competence of the patient, if competence is in issue.

9. Where time permits, the person identified to give the evidence as to capacity to consent to or refuse treatment should be made aware of the observations made by the Court of Appeal in this judgment.

10. In order to be in a position to assess a patient's best interests the judge should be provided, where possible and if time allows, with information about the circumstances of a relevant background material about the patient.

declaration in this case involved the removal of the baby from within the body of her mother under physical compulsion. Unless lawfully justified, this constituted an infringement of the mother's autonomy. Of themselves, the perceived needs of the foetus did not provide the necessary justification.

The principles set out by the Court of Appeal in Re MB were quoted in the case of *Re B* (2002) (where a tetraplegic woman asked for her ventilator to be switched off) and can be found on pages 52–53 of Chapter 6.

The rights of the foetus

The unborn child is not recognised in law as having a legal personality. Therefore it is not until birth that the interests of the child can be taken into account. It can be seen therefore from the above cases of *Re MB* and the *St George's Healthcare Trust* that the interests of the unborn child cannot be raised against the wishes of a mentally competent mother. The mentally competent mother is entitled to make her autonomous decision, whatever the outcome for her unborn child. If the mother makes a decision which harms the unborn child, so that the child is born with a disability or injury, the child has no legal right to sue the mother for breach of her duty of care to the child. Under the Congenital Disabilities (Civil Liability) Act 1976, if an unborn child has been injured so that it is born disabled, it can only sue the mother if the injuries were caused whilst the pregnant woman was driving a car. (In this case of course, the mother would have third party insurance cover from which the injured child could benefit.) Any action against the mother (apart from one arising from these circumstances) brought by the child who was harmed whilst *in utero* is prevented by this Act. A child could not therefore sue a mother who through drinking, taking drugs or smoking, caused harm to him or her whilst a foetus.

Mental Capacity Act 2005

The common law principles set out in the cases of *Re MB* and *St George's Healthcare Trust* discussed above have now been put on a statutory footing. Since 1 October 2007, if a dispute arises over whether a Caesarean section should be carried out, the following questions should be asked and actions taken:

- Does the mother have the mental capacity, as defined in sections 2 and 3 of the MCA (see Chapter 6) to make her own decisions?
- If the answer to that question is 'Yes', then the mother's decision is binding on the health professionals.
- If the answer to that question is 'No', then health professionals must act in the best interests of the mother.
- In the absence of any specified person who can be consulted about her best interests, an independent mental capacity advocate should be appointed to report to the NHS trust on what is the woman's best interests, according to the stages set out in section 4 of the MCA (see Chapter 7).

■ If it is considered that a Caesarean is in her best interests, then an application must be made to the Court of Protection for a declaration that the mother lacks the requisite mental capacity and that a Caesarean section should be carried out in her best interests.

Conclusion

The cases of *Re MB* and the *St George's Healthcare Trust* have clarified the law which is now set out in the Mental Capacity Act 2005. The pregnant woman has the full right of autonomy, as with any other mentally competent adult. Some may find the disregard of the interests of the foetus to be morally unacceptable. However, the principles now enshrined in the MCA ensure that a pregnant woman is not simply treated as the carrier of a baby, but that her right of self-determination is protected in the same way as the right of self-determination of any other competent adult.

References

Department of Health (1997) *Circular EL (97)32*. Department of Health, London.

Re B (Consent to treatment: capacity) The Times Law Report 26 March 2002.

Re MB (an adult: medical treatment) [1997] 2 FLR 426

Re S (adult: refusal of medical treatment) (1992) 9 BMLR 69 [1993] Fam 123.

Re T (adult: refusal of medical treatment) (1992) 9 BLMR 46 [1993] Fam 95.

Norfolk and Norwich Healthcare (NHS) Trust v *W* [1996] 2 FLR 613.

St George's Healthcare NHS Trust v *S, R* v *Collins ex parte S* (1998) 44 BMLR 160 CA; [1998]3 All ER 673.

Tameside and Glossop Acute Services Trust v *CH* [1996] 1 F.L.R. 762 (1996) 31 BMLR 93.

CHAPTER 13

Organ donation after death

Box 13.1 Case scenario

Tony has been severely injured in a road accident. He is 23 years old. His parents are told that he has serious brain damage and is unlikely to survive. They are asked if they would agree to the donation of his organs. What is the law?

Introduction

The law relating to the donation of organs after death and donation from a living donor is covered by the Human Tissue Act 2004. which replaces the Human Tissue Act 1961 and the Human Organ Transplants Act 1989. The law relating to donations from a living donor and commercial transactions involving organs will be considered in the next chapter. This chapter considers the use of organs from a dead donor and the laws relating to consent.

Human Tissue Act 2004

Two distinct situations involving organ donation from a dead person arise: the first where the person has indicated his or her wishes over organ donation; and the second where there is no indication of a wish to be a donor and consent has to be obtained in another way.

Wishes expressed by the donor

> ### Box 13.2 Section 1(1) of the Human Tissue Act 2004
>
> (c) the removal from the body of a deceased person, for use for a purpose specified in Schedule 1, of any relevant material of which the body consists or which it contains
> (d) the storage for use for a purpose specified in Part 1 of Schedule 1 of any relevant material which has come from a human body
> (f) the use for a purpose specified in Part 1 of Schedule 1 of any relevant material which has come from a human body
>
> is lawful if it has the appropriate consent.
>   Transplantation is the seventh purpose specified in part 1 of Schedule 1.

The appropriate consent for the purposes of the Human Tissue Act would include the situation where a deceased person was carrying a donor card or was registered as an organ donor with the NHS organ donor register (see http://www.uktransplant.org.uk/).

The role of the relatives where the deceased has expressed his or her wishes

Clearly, the relatives must be informed of the dead person's request, be asked if they know if the deceased had withdrawn his or her wish to be a donor but they have no right to overrule the deceased person's request. In practice, relatives, despite the deceased carrying a valid donor card, may still object to organ donation. However, as a consequence of the Human Tissue Act 2004 relatives should not be permitted to overrule the clear wishes of the deceased. The Code of Practice issued by the Human Tissue Authority gives guidance on the involvement of relatives where organ donation arises. (Human Tissue Authority, 2006).

Paragraph 27 of the Code of Practice states:

If the family or those close to the deceased person object to the donation, for whatever purpose, when the deceased person (or their nominated representative – see below) has explicitly consented, clinicians should seek to discuss the matter sensitively with them. They should be encouraged to accept the deceased person's wishes and it should be made clear that they do not have the legal right to veto or overrule those wishes. There may nevertheless be cases in which donation is inappropriate and each case should be considered individually.

Where no wishes have been expressed by the donor

If the deceased person's wishes are not known and the deceased has nominated a person to deal with the use of their body after death, then consent can be given by that nominated representative or if there is no such person, by a person who was in a qualifying relationship with the deceased.

Nominated representative

The nomination and its terms and conditions can be made orally or in writing. An oral nomination must be made in the presence of at least two witnesses. A written nomination must be signed by the person making it, or signed at the direction of that person, in the presence of at least one witness who attests the signature. Where more than one nomination is made, the nominees may act jointly or individually unless the conditions of the nomination state otherwise. Nominations can be revoked by the potential donor or renounced by the nominated person at any time.

Qualifying relationship

If there is no nominated representative then consent can be given by a person who was in a 'qualifying relationship' immediately before the death of the deceased person. The qualifying relationship is shown in Box 13.3.

Box 13.3 Section 27(4) Human Tissue Act 2004 and the order of priority of a qualifying relationship

27(4) (a) spouse or partner (including civil or same sex partner)
(b) parent or child
(c) brother or sister
(d) grandparent or grandchild
(e) niece or nephew
(f) stepfather or stepmother
(g) half-brother or half-sister and
(h) friend of long standing.

27(5) Relationships in the same paragraph of subsection (4) should be accorded equal ranking.

27(6) Consent should be obtained from the person whose relationship to the person concerned is accorded the highest ranking in accordance with subsections (4) and (5).

27(7) If the relationship of each of two or more persons to the person concerned is accorded equal highest ranking in accordance with subsections (4) and (5), it is sufficient to obtain the consent of any of them.

Death of the patient

Organs can only be taken after death has been certified and this should be by different doctors than those who wish to remove the organs. Guidelines from the Department of Health (1998) cover the diagnosis of brain death and the interpretation of the Human Tissue Act 1961. Further discussion on legal issues relating to death can be found in Dimond (2008).

Ventilation of a body prior to organs being taken

Since there is a much higher success in transplants where the organs are fresh, the body may be kept ventilated until such time as the organs can be harvested.

There was concern about the legality of this prior to the Human Tissue Act 2004. Where the patient is in intensive care and on a ventilator and carries a donor card, it was argued that he or she has expressly agreed to being ventilated until the organs are removed, even though this may be several hours after brainstem death has been diagnosed. However, the converse argument was that ventilation was only justified if it was in the best interests of the dead person. The law has now been clarified in Section 47 of the Human Tissue Act 2004. Section 47 of the Human Tissue Act 2004 is set out in Box 13.4.

Box 13.4 Section 47 Human Tissue Act 2004

Where part of a body (i.e. of a deceased person) lying in a hospital, nursing home or other institution is or may be suitable for use for transplantation, it shall be lawful for the person having the control and management of the institution

(a) to take steps for the purpose of preserving the part for use for transplantation, and
(b) to retain the body for that purpose.

The authority given under section 47 only extends to the taking of the minimum steps necessary for the purpose mentioned in that provision, and to the use of the least invasive procedure.

Once it has been established that consent, which would make the removal of the part for transplantation lawful, has not been, and will not be, given, then the authority under this section ceases to apply.

Application of the law to Box 13.1

Turning back to the situation in the case scenario, Tony has made no express wish known, either in writing or by word of mouth. Nor does it appear that he has appointed a nominated representative to give consent on his behalf. Consent must therefore be obtained from the person who ranks highest in the list of qualifying relationships, as set out in Box 13.3. In addition, since he was injured in a road accident, his death would have to be reported to the coroner. The coroner would be informed if the person who was ranked as the highest in the list of qualifying relationships was prepared to give consent on behalf of the Tony and could then permit the organ removal to take place.

Proposals for change

In spite of the Human Tissue Act 2004 it is clear that the supply of organs is not meeting the needs of those awaiting organ transplants, and many patients are dying on the waiting lists. In November 2008, over 7,600 persons were awaiting an organ transplant and many would die before one became available. One suggestion is that there should be an opting-out system, rather than an opting-in system, i.e. carrying a card if you do not want your body to be used for transplant purposes, the absence of a card implying an agreement to the organs being transplanted. However, this suggestion has not met with wide acceptance. An alternative suggestion is that there should be a legal duty for the professionals to request an organ transplant from the relatives of the deceased or prospective deceased. This is described as the required request system. It has the advantage of removing some of the embarrassment that professionals feel when they have to broach the matter with relatives. It is thought that such a statutory request would lead to more organs being forthcoming, without the necessity for a change in the Human Tissue Act itself. The relatives would still have the freedom to refuse, but they would also have the opportunity to agree.

A private member's bill was put before Parliament in April 2000 recommending that there should be an opting-out system, i.e. there is a presumption that the deceased would consent to being a donor. This presumption could, however, be rebutted by evidence that the deceased would not wish to donate his or her organs. The bill was given its first reading, but did not proceed and it was never printed. An initiative supported by actors and actresses in the television soap drama *Coronation Street* was designed to increase the number of organ donors. Information for potential donors is given on a DoH website (http://www.nhs.uk/livewell/donation/pages/organdonation.aspx). It was followed by a scheme whereby credit card companies will ask customers applying for a card to sign up on the organ donor register (DoH, 2000).

The availability of organs declined after the publication of the report into the removal, retention and storage of organs at Alder Hey Children's Hospital (DoH, 2001). For example, the Royal Brompton Hospital, London, and the Queen Elizabeth Hospital, Birmingham, reported that in the 12 days ending on 5 February 2001 they had not carried out a single transplant, when normally they would carry out about three a week.

Calls for an opt-out system or presumed consent to increase the supply of organs for transplant were not accepted by Parliament and therefore not incorporated into the Human Tissue Act 2004. However, in 2007 the Medical Officer of Health recommended an opt-out system. A task force was set up to consider the issue and reported in January 2008. Following its report a sub-committee of the task force was established to look at the issue of presumed consent and reported in November 2008. The Organ Donation Taskforce 2008) reported that:

> The Taskforce reached a clear consensus in recommending that an opt out system should not be introduced in the UK at the present time. The Taskforce concluded that such a system has the potential to undermine the concept of donation as a gift, to erode trust in NHS professionals and the government, and negatively impact on organ donation numbers. It would distract attention away from essential improvements to systems and infrastructure and from the urgent need to improve public awareness and understanding of organ donation. Furthermore, it would be challenging and costly to implement successfully. Most compelling of all, we found no convincing evidence that it would deliver significant increases in the number of donated organs.

Changes in the law are necessary if more transplants are to take place, but the numbers of donors are unlikely to increase until public confidence in the system of organ removal, retention and use is restored. In the next chapter we consider donation by living donors.

References

Dimond, B. C. (2008) *Legal Aspects of Death*. Quay Books, London.

Department of Health (1998) *Code of Practice for the Diagnosis of Brain Death*. DoH, London.

Department of Health (2000) *Credit Cards to Promote Organ Donation*. DoH, London.

Department of Health (2001) *The Royal Liverpool's Children's Inquiry Report*. DoH, London

Human Tissue Authority (2006) *Code of Practice: Donation of Organs, Tissue and Cells for Transplantation, Code 2*. Stationery Office, London.

Organ Donation Taskforce (2008) *An Independent Report on the Potential Impact of an Opt Out System for Organ Donation in the UK*. Stationery Office, London.

CHAPTER 14

Organ donation from live donors

Box 14.1 Case scenario

Alice is now 12 years old and has been receiving dialysis for over three years. Her long-term chance of survival depends upon a kidney transplant and she has been on a waiting list for several years. Her condition is deteriorating and Bob, a close friend of her family, has offered to donate her a kidney. What is the law?

Introduction

The Human Tissue Act (HTA) 2004 incorporated provisions relating to transplantation from living donors and repealed the Human Organ Transplants Act 1989. Section 33 of the HTA created a criminal offence if a person

(a) ... removes any transplantable material from the body of a living person intending that the material be used for the purpose of transplantation, and
(b) when he removes the material, he knows, or might reasonably be expected to know, that the person from whose body he removes the material is alive.

However, the criminal offence does not arise in such circumstances where the Human Tissue Authority is satisfied that no reward has been given in contravention of section 33 and that the removal is in accordance with the regulations relating to the transplant of organs from living donors.

Transplant Regulations (Human Tissue Act 2004)

Regulations relating to transplants that have been or are proposed to be carried out using transplantable material removed from a human body were drawn up under the powers granted in the Human Tissue Act.

Meaning of transplantable material for the purposes of section 33 of the Act

Under Regulation 10(1) for the purposes of section 33 of the Act (restriction on transplants involving a live donor), 'transplantable material' means:

(a) an organ, or part of an organ if it is to be used for the same purpose as the entire organ in the human body,
(b) bone marrow, and
(c) peripheral blood stem cells,

where that material is removed from the body of a living person with the intention that it be transplanted into another person.

However this is subject to regulation 10(2) and (3):

10(2) The material referred to in paragraph (1)(a) is not transplantable material for the purposes of section 33 of the Act in a case where the primary purpose of removal of the material is the medical treatment of the person from whose body the material is removed.

10(3) The material referred to in paragraph (1)(b) and (c) is transplantable material for the purposes of section 33 of the Act only in a case where the person from whose body the material is removed is –

(a) an adult who lacks the capacity, or
(b) a child who is not competent,

to consent to removal of the transplantable material.

In other words, where an adult has the mental capacity to give consent to the donation of his bone marrow or peripheral blood stem cells, the Regulations do not apply and the Human Tissue Authority would not be involved.

Information to the Human Tissue Authority

Under Section 34 regulations can be drawn up covering the information which must be given to the Authority in relation to transplantable material. Transplantable material for the purposes of Section 34 means:

(a) the whole or part of any of the following organs if it is to be used for the same purpose as the entire organ in the human body–
   (i) kidney,
   (ii) heart,
   (iii) lung or a lung lobe,
   (iv) pancreas,
   (v) liver,
   (vi) bowel,
   (vii) larynx;
(b) face, or
(c) limb.

Situations where transplants involving a live donor are not criminal offences

Under regulation 11 a criminal offence relating to transplants involving a live donor does not apply if the requirements set out in the paragraphs 2 to 6 below are met.

2. A registered medical practitioner who has clinical responsibility for the donor must have caused the matter to be referred to the Authority.
3. The Authority must be satisfied that –
   (a) no reward has been or is to be given in contravention of section 32 of the Act (prohibition of commercial dealings in human material for transplantation), and
   (b) when the transplantable material is removed –
      (i) consent for its removal for the purpose of transplantation has been given, or
      (ii) its removal for that purpose is otherwise lawful.
4. The Authority must take the report referred to in paragraph (6) into account in making its decision under paragraph (3).

5. The Authority shall give notice of its decision under paragraph (3) to –

    (a) the donor of the transplantable material or any person acting on his behalf,

    (b) the person to whom it is proposed to transplant the transplantable material ('the recipient') or any person acting on his behalf, and

    (c) the registered medical practitioner who caused the matter to be referred to the Authority under paragraph (2)

6. Subject to paragraph (7), one or more qualified persons must have conducted separate interviews with each of the following—

    (a) the donor,

    (b) if different from the donor, the person giving consent, and

    (c) the recipient,

and reported to the Authority on the matters specified in paragraphs (8) and (9).

7. Paragraph (6) does not apply in any case where the removal of the transplantable material for the purpose of transplantation is authorised by an order made in any legal proceedings before a court.

8. The matters that must be covered in the report of each interview under paragraph (6) are –

    (a) any evidence of duress or coercion affecting the decision to give consent,

    (b) any evidence of an offer of a reward, and

    (c) any difficulties of communication with the person interviewed and an explanation of how those difficulties were overcome.

9. The following matters must be covered in the report of the interview with the donor and, where relevant, the other person giving consent –

    (a) the information given to the person interviewed as to the nature of the medical procedure for, and the risk involved in, the removal of the transplantable material,

    (b) the full name of the person who gave that information and his qualification to give it, and

    (c) the capacity of the person interviewed to understand –

        (i)   the nature of the medical procedure and the risk involved, and

        (ii) that the consent may be withdrawn at any time before the removal of the transplantable material.

10. A person shall be taken to be qualified to conduct an interview under paragraph (6) if –

    (a) he appears to the Authority to be suitably qualified to conduct the interview,

(b) he does not have any connection with any of the persons to be interviewed, or with a person who stands in a qualifying relationship to any of those persons, which the Authority considers to be of a kind that might raise doubts about his ability to act impartially, and

(c) in the case of an interview with the donor or other person giving consent, he is not the person who gave the information referred to in paragraph (9)(a).

Removal for medical treatment

Under Regulation 10(2), the material referred to in paragraph (1)(a) (i.e. an organ, or part of an organ if it is to be used for the same purpose as the entire organ in the human body) is not transplantable material for the purposes of section 33 of the Act in a case where the primary purpose of removal of the material is the medical treatment of the person from whose body the material is removed. An example of a situation where the organ may be removed for the medical treatment of the donor is shown in Box 14.2.

> ### Box 14.2 Case scenario: organ donation for medical purposes
>
> Glen suffered from cystic fibrosis and had been on the waiting list for a lung transplant for over two years. At the hospital, surgeons transplanted either lungs or both heart and lungs. A decision was not made definitely on the type of transplant until organs became available. When the patient was opened up, the surgeons would then decide whether to transplant both heart and lungs or merely the lungs. In the event of both heart and lungs being transplanted, it might be that the heart, provided that it was not diseased, could be available for transplant for another person. Glen was asked if he would agree to his heart being available for transplant in the event of his receiving both heart and lungs. This is known as a domino transplant.

The Code of Practice of the HTA on transplantation states that when an organ is removed as part of a patient's treatment, it may be suitable for transplant into another person (e.g. a heart originally removed from the recipient of a heart/lung transplant). Although it is a living donation, approval by an Independent Assessor will not be needed (paragraph 88).

The HTA states that:

Approval of domino transplant requires the following:

- the prospective donor is identified, informed and gives agreement for the organ to be used
- an application form is completed by the donor's clinician and signed by the donor
- the application form is sent to the HTA
- if all requirements are met, the HTA gives approval for the transplant to proceed
- after the transplant, the recipient's clinician completes all the relevant documentation
- if the organ is not used for transplantation, the HTA should be informed.

In applying the law to the situation in Box 14.2, provided the provisions set out above were followed and the Human Tissue Authority is given the appropriate information from the clinicians concerned, no offence would arise under Section 33 of the HTA.

Alice's gift from Bob

Turning now to the situation shown in Box 14.1, this transplant would be governed by the regulations passed under the Human Tissue Act 2004. The clinicians would have to follow the steps listed above and ensure that the appropriate consent was obtained and the appropriate interviews have taken place and a report made to the Authority.

Procedure of the Human Tissue Authority

Under Regulation 12 certain decisions of the authority must be made by a panel of no fewer than three members. These decisions are:

1. (a) the donor of the transplantable material is a child, and
   (b) the material is an organ or part of an organ if it is to be used for the same purpose as an entire organ in the human body.

2. (a) the donor of the transplantable material is an adult who lacks capacity to consent to removal of the material, and
   (b) the material is an organ or part of an organ if it is to be used for the same purpose as an entire organ in the human body.
3. (a) the donor of the transplantable material is an adult who has capacity to consent to removal of the material, and
   (b) the case involves–
      (i) paired donations,
      (ii) pooled donations, or
      (iii) a non-directed altruistic donation.

Interpretations

'Non-directed altruistic donation' means the removal (in circumstances not amounting to a paired or pooled donation) of transplantable material from a donor for transplant to a person who is not genetically related to the donor or known to him;

'Paired donations' means an arrangement under which–

(a) transplantable material is removed from a donor ('D') for transplant to a person who is not genetically related or known to D, and
(b) transplantable material is removed from another person for transplant to a person who is genetically related or known to D; and

'Pooled donations' means a series of paired donations of transplantable material, each of which is linked to another in the same series (for example, transplantable material from D is transplanted to the wife of another person ('E'), transplantable material from E is transplanted to the partner of a third person ('F') and transplantable material from F is transplanted to D's son).

Reconsideration of decision by the Authority

The Authority may reconsider any decision made by it under regulation 11(3) if it is satisfied that (a) any information given for the purpose of the decision was in any material respect false or misleading, or (b) there has been any material change of circumstances since the decision was made.

In addition:

(a) the donor of the transplantable material or any person acting on his behalf,
(b) the recipient of the material or any person acting on his behalf, and
(c) the registered medical practitioner who caused the matter to be referred to the Authority under regulation 11(2)

may in any case require the Authority to reconsider any decision made by it under regulation 11(3). The procedure to be followed by the Authority in reconsidering its decision is set out in regulation 14.

Transplants from living donors who lack the capacity to give consent

In Chapter 11 the case of *Re Y* (1996) was discussed where the court was asked to make a declaration that blood tests and bone marrow harvesting were in the best interests of the mentally incapacitated sister. Such a situation would now come under the provisions of the Human Tissue Act 2004 and the Regulations made under it. In its Code of Practice relating to transplants the Human Tissue Authority notes that:

> Donation of whole or part organs by adults or children who lack capacity is exceedingly rare. Should such a case arise, the HTA's advice on how to proceed should be sought. (Paragraph 67)

Independent Assessors

An Independent Assessor (who should be an NHS medical consultant or someone of equivalent registered professional status, who is not otherwise party to the transplantation process) is a trained professional who is usually, but not exclusively, based in a hospital with a transplant unit. He or she will act both as a representative of the HTA and as an advocate for the donor. Independent Assessors are trained to consider for approval all living organ donations for transplantation that fall into the following categories:

- directed:
  - genetically related
  - emotionally related
  - paired/pooled (the decision in these cases should be made by the HTA until practice is established as routine)

- non-directed:
  - altruistic (the decision in these cases should be made by the HTA until practice is established as routine).

The role of the Independent Assessor is to act on the HTA's behalf in an independent capacity in order to satisfy the requirements of the HT Act. The Assessor's responsibility is to interview the donor and recipient separately and, where appropriate, together, and to draw up a report on the proposed procedure. The Code of Practice states that there are two circumstances where the Assessor may not see the donor and recipient separately and together:

- When the recipient is a child, it is expected that the child and their parent(s) would be seen together by the Assessor, even when one parent is the potential donor and
- In non-directed altruistic donation, the Assessor would only see the donor (paragraph 85)

A panel of no fewer than three members of the Human Tissue Authority would have to decide if the donation could go ahead.

Conclusion

The Human Tissue Act 2004 has clarified the law relating to donations from live and dead donors and the Codes of Practice issued by the Human Tissue Authority should be of considerable assistance to those involved in this sensitive area. It is likely that in the absence of any change of law providing presumed consent for donations after death or a required request scheme being introduced, and the growing waiting list for those requiring transplants, more requests for transplants from live donors will arise. It is important that the strict provisions to establishing consent and capacity set out in the Regulations are followed.

In the next chapter we look at the question of organ removal, retention and storage.

References

The Human Tissue Act 2004 (Persons who Lack Capacity to Consent and Transplants) Regulations Statutory Instrument 2006 No. 1659.

The Human Tissue Authority (2006) *Code of Practice No 2 Donation of Organs, Tissue and Cells for Transplantation*. Stationery Office, London.

Re Y (1996) (Adult Patient) (Transplant: Bone Marrow) 35 BMLR 111; 4 Med LR 204.

CHAPTER 15

Organ removal, retention and storage

Box 15.1 Case scenario

Sarah was born with a congenital heart condition. Unfortunately, the subsequent operation proved unsuccessful and Sarah died. Sarah's parents were asked if they would agree to a post mortem being performed to assist in research so that in future such conditions could be successfully operated upon. The parents agreed and subsequently they were notified that the body was available for disposal. They decided upon a cremation. Several years later, following an inquiry into the pathology services of the hospital, they were notified by the Chief Executive's department that Sarah's heart, lungs, liver and other organs had been retained. The parents were shocked. What is the law?

Introduction

Unfortunately, the situation in Box 15.1 once confronted many parents across the country, as evidenced in the reports of the Bristol Royal Infirmary (Department of Health (DoH), 2000, 2001a) inquiry and the Royal Liverpool Children's (Alder Hey) inquiry (DoH, 2001b) on the retention of organs and body parts. During the Bristol Royal Infirmary inquiry into allegations of professional misconduct in carrying out paediatric heart surgery, it was learnt that human organs from children who had died had been retained. The publication of the Alder Hey report coincided with publication of a report of a census of organs and tissues retained by pathology services in England (DoH, 2001c).

Census of organs and tissues retained by pathology services

The conclusion from the census of retained organs and tissue was that a total of approximately 54,300 organs, body parts, stillbirths or foetuses were held by pathology services at the end of 1999. They had been retained from post mortems over the period 1970–1999. (This does not include the numbers held following a post mortem ordered by a coroner.) The census concluded that retention of organs, tissue and body parts after post mortem was common-place throughout the country and in the majority of cases was based on a consent form signed under the Human Tissue Act 1961. The census report listed the different pathology departments across England and the numbers of parts which they held. From the census carried out by the Chief Medical Officer it was learnt that 97 per cent of trusts during 1999 used forms to obtain a signed agreement from relatives for post mortems and 86 per cent used the same form for retention of organs or tissues after hospital post mortem. Six per cent used a separate form to record agreement to retention of organs or tissues. However, in the 1970s, 1980s and early 1990s, parents were not given full information in relation to which organs were to be removed and retained and therefore explicit consent was not obtained.

Retained Organs Commission

The Government set up a Retained Organs Commission under the Chairman-ship of Professor Margaret Brazier. It was a special health authority with spe-cific functions (Table 15.1). In addition, it was to advise ministers and provide guidance to the NHS and universities and monitor trusts to ensure that they

Table 15.1 Functions of the Retained Organs Commission.

- Oversee the return of tissues and organs from collections around the country
- Ensure that collections are accurately catalogued
- Provide information on collections throughout the country
- Ensure that suitable counselling is available
- Act as an advocate for parents if problems arise
- Advise on good practice in this area
- Handle inquiries from families and the public

dealt properly with organ returns. It also provided a national help line via NHS Direct for parents and relatives. At the end of April 2001, the Chair of the Retained Organs Commission announced that trusts were to begin to release information to people who have made inquiries about whether organs from relatives have been retained following post mortems (DoH, 2001f).

In September 2002 the first annual report of the Retained Organs Commission was published and it was announced that the Commission's existence would be extended to 31 March 2004 in order that it could complete its work. It was subsequently wound up.

Legal action by parents

Legal action by parents who had suffered as a result of the removal and retention of organs from their dead children in a group litigation action was initiated and the court agreed that the legal costs would be capped at £506,500 (*AB and Others* v. *Leeds Teaching Hospitals NHS Trust and in the Matter of the Nationwide Organ Group Litigation* 2003). On 26 March 2004 the High Court ruled, in respect of three test cases, that where hospitals had illegally removed the organs in post mortem examinations without the parents' consent, parents could claim damages if they had suffered psychological injury (*AB and Others* v. *Leeds Teaching Hospitals NHS Trust and another*, *The Times Law Report*, 12 April 2004). Damages of £2,750 were awarded in one of the test cases; the other two lost.

Human Bodies, Human Choices

A consultation paper, 'Human Bodies, Human Choices', was published in July 2002, (DoH, 2002) which invited feedback on the principles to apply to the removal, retention and storage and use of organs. It was followed by proposals for new legislation on human organs and tissue, which were published in September 2003 (DoH, 2003). These were to include:

■ Explicit consent to be the fundamental principle underpinning the lawful removal, storage and use of bodies, body parts, organs and tissue.
■ The principle that the human body and its parts should not, as such, give rise to financial gain.

- A regulatory framework within an overarching authority, the Human Tissue Authority, would be responsible for licensing and inspecting regulated activities, including public display.
- Penalties for undertaking certain activities (including DNA testing) without consent or without a licence.
- Statutory codes of practice issued in relation to matters such as the conduct of post mortems and anatomical examinations; the import and export of human body parts; communication with families about post mortem examinations; definitions of death; and disposal of human tissue.
- Human organ transplantation to continue to operate broadly under current arrangements, but within the new legislative framework.

Human Tissue Act 2004

The Human Tissue Act 2004 gave legal effect to these proposals and to the Tissue Directive of the EC (EC, 2004). It regulates the removal, storage and use of human organs and other tissues for specified purposes, specifies the appropriate consent for children and adults; creates a criminal offence in relation to the removal without appropriate consent; establishes a Human Tissue Authority and a licensing regime, arranges for the publication of codes of practice and sets up inspectorates for anatomy and pathology and of organ and tissue for human use. In addition, it makes provision for the use of DNA and creates an offence relating to non-consensual analysis of DNA, with specified exceptions. The government did not support any legal change to allow a person's organs to be donated automatically on their death unless they or their family had specifically asked otherwise, i.e. presumed consent for organ donation was not included in the Act. However the Chief Medical Officer of the DoH called in July 2007 for the introduction of an 'opt out' system (see Chapter 13). Further information is available from the web site of the Human Tissue Authority, on which the codes of practice can be found (http://www.hta.gov.uk/).

The law on removal storage and disposal

In Chapters 13 and 14 we considered the provisions of the Human Tissue Act in relation to organ donation from dead and live donors respectively. In this chapter we look at its provisions in relation to organ removal, storage and disposal. The Human Tissue Act 2004 repealed the Anatomy Act 1984 and the Human Tissue Act 1961 and set clear procedures for the removal, storage and use of organs, emphasising the importance of the appropriate consent being obtained. It published its 5th Code of Practice on the removal, storage and disposal of human organs and tissue in 2006 (Human Tissue Authority, 2006).

The HTA applies to 'relevant material', which is defined as:

material other than gametes, which consists of or includes human cells. In the HT Act, references to relevant material from a human body do not include:

(a) embryos outside the human body, or
(b) hair and nail from the body of a living person.

Removal of relevant material from living persons

The existing laws of consent apply to the removal of organs and tissue from living persons. Where the removal is part of a research project, then approval must also have been obtained from the appropriate research ethics committee and the provisions of the Medicines for Human Use (Clinical Trials) Regulations 2004 complied with.

Where the removal is from children or young persons, parental or guardian consent or the child's consent (where the child or young person has the maturity and understanding to give a valid consent – see Chapter 9) must have been obtained.

Removal of organs from deceased persons

The Human Tissue Act applies to this situation and it creates an offence where relevant material is removed from a dead body for any scheduled purposes without obtaining consent. This does not apply where material is taken under the coroner's authority or under proper authority for criminal justice purposes. The scheduled purposes are shown in Table 15.2 (Schedule 1 part 1) and Table 15.3 (Schedule 1 Part 2).

Table 15.2 Schedule 1 Part 1: Purposes requiring consent: general.

1. Anatomical examination
2. Determining the cause of death
3. Establishing after a person's death the efficacy of any drug or other treatment administered to him
4. Obtaining scientific of medical information about a living or deceased person which may be relevant to any other person (including a future person)
5. Public display
6. Research in connection with disorders, or the functioning of the human body
7. Transplantation

Table 15.3 Schedule 1 Part 2: Purposes requiring consent: deceased persons.

1. Clinical audit
2. Education or training relating to human health
3. Performance assessment
4. Public health monitoring
5. Quality assurance

Requests by the coroner for post mortems and for removal of relevant material

No consent is required where the body has become part of the coroner's jurisdiction and the coroner considers that it is necessary for a post mortem to be carried out. However, once the material is no longer required for the coroner's purposes consent must be obtained for the storage and use of material taken during the post mortem. The coroner must tell the pathologist carrying out the post mortem what material to store under their authority, and for how long. The coroner is also required to tell relatives about any material which may be stored. The 3rd Code of Practice published by the Human Tissue Authority gives guidance on the topic of post mortem examinations.

Storage of relevant materials: living persons

Under Section 1(10) of the Human Tissue Act 2004 it is lawful:

(a) to store for use for a purpose specified in Part 2 of Schedule 1 (see Table 15.3) any relevant material which has come from the body of a living person; and

(b) to use for such a purpose any relevant material which has come from the body of a living person

No consent is required for such storage and use.
However, consent is required to store tissue from the living for:

- obtaining scientific or medical information about a person which may be relevant to any other person (now or in the future)
- research into disorders, or the functioning, of the human body
- transplantation

Storage of relevant material: deceased persons

It is an offence under the HT Act to store relevant material taken after death without consent for any scheduled purposes, apart from material stored for coroners' or for criminal justice purposes. Consent can be given in advance by the deceased, by a person nominated on the deceased's behalf or by the person who is the highest in the hierarchy of qualifying relationships (see Chapter 13).

Clinical waste

Paragraphs 63 and 64 of the Code of Practice (No. 5) state that the HT Act makes it lawful to treat as 'clinical waste' any material which has come from a person who was:

- in the course of receiving medical treatment
- undergoing diagnostic testing or
- participating in research.

Material no longer used, or stored for use, for any scheduled purpose can be dealt with as waste.

Application of the law to Box 15.1

It is clear from the evidence that has emerged from the inquiries and census that many hospitals were not giving full information to relatives when the latter gave consent for a post mortem to be undertaken. Like Sarah's parents, relatives signed consent for a post mortem, but were not given the information about which organs were removed and retained. The Human Tissue Act 2004 now applies to the removal, retention, storage and use of materials from dead persons. Sarah's parents have given consent to the post mortem and their consent is also required for the removal, use and storage of any organs or tissue removed during the post mortem. When the body was released to them for the cremation, none of the organs should have been retained without their consent. The guidance issued in the Codes of Practice by the Human Tissue Authority should have been followed. Failure to follow the law and the guidance could lead to a complaint by Sarah's parents or litigation or even criminal proceedings. They may also have a claim under the Human Rights Act 1998 that they have been subjected to inhuman and degrading treatment under Article 3 of the European Convention on Human Rights.

A criminal offence may take place when the requirements of the Human Tissue Act are not complied with.

Conclusions

Paternalistic medicine, where information is kept from patients and parents supposedly for their own good, and where research interests take precedence over the interests and concerns of relatives, is no longer acceptable. As a consequence of the Human Tissue Act 2004, the emphasis now is on communication, real informed consent and bereavement support, with obligations clearly set out in the law. One of the great tragedies in the unlawful removal and retention of organs scandal was the loss of public confidence in doctors and health professionals. As a consequence of the scandal, donor cards were torn up, many more people on waiting lists for transplants died because organs were not available, and essential medical research was inhibited. There is still a major challenge for all health professionals, health trusts and the DoH to rebuild public confidence so that *bona fide* research and organ donation for transplants can take place. It is hoped that the changes brought about by the Human Tissue Act will support this rebuilding of confidence.

References

AB and Others v. *Leeds Teaching Hospitals NHS Trust and in the Matter of the Nation-wide Organ Group Litigation* (2003) Lloyd's Rep Med 7 [2003] 355.

AB and Others v. *Leeds Teaching Hospitals NHS Trust and another* (2004), *The Times Law Report*, 12 April 2004.

British Medical Association (2000) *Consent to Organ Retention*. BMA, London.

Coroners' Rules (1984) SI 1984, No 552, Rule 9. Stationery Office, London.

DHSS (1977) *Post Mortem Declaration Forms*. HC(77)28. DHSS, London.

Department of Health (2000) *The Inquiry into the Management of Care of Children Receiving Complex Heart Surgery at the Bristol Royal Infirmary. Interim Report: Removal and Retention of Human Material*. DoH, London.

Department of Health (2001a) *The Report of the Public Inquiry into Children's Heart Surgery at the Bristol Royal Infirmary 1984–1995: Learning from Bristol*. Stationery Office, London.

Department of Health (2001b) *The Royal Liverpool's Children's Inquiry: Summary and Recommendations*. Chaired by Michael Redfern QC. Stationery Office, London.

Department of Health (2001c) *Chief Medical Officer: A Report of a Census of Organs and Tissues Retained by Pathology Services in England*. DoH, London.

Department of Health (2001d) *Consent to Organ and Tissue Retention at Post Mortem Examination and Disposal of Human Materials*. DoH, London.

Department of Health (2001e) *The Removal, Retention and use of Human Organs and Tissue from Post Mortem Examination Advice from the Chief Medical Officer*. DoH, London.

Department of Health (2001f) *NHS Trusts Ready to Respond on Retained Organs*. Press release, 27 April. DoH, London.

Department of Health (2002) *Human Bodies, Human Choices: The Law on Human Organs and Tissue in England and Wales*. A consultation report. Department of Health and Wales National Assembly.

Department of Health (2003) *Proposals for New Legislation on Human Organs and Tissue*, September 2003; http://www.dh.gov.uk/tissue/.

EC (2004) Tissue Directive 2004/23/EC.

Human Tissue Authority (2006) *Code of Practice on the Removal, Storage and Disposal of Human Organs and Tissue* No 5. Stationery Office, London.

Kennedy, I. and Grubb, A. (2000) *Medical Law*, 3rd edn. Butterworths, London.

Royal College of Pathologists (2000) *Guidelines for the Retention of Tissues and Organs at Post-mortem Examination*. RCP, London.

Royal College of Pathologists and Institute of Bio-Medical Science (1999) *Consensus Statement of Recommended Policies for Uses of Human Tissue in Research, Edu-*

cation and Quality Control. (With notes reflecting UK law and practices). Working Party of the RCP and the Institute of Bio-Medical Science, London.

The Times (2000) Parents sue hospital over organs. *The Times*, 10 November.

CHAPTER 16

Living wills

> ## Box 16.1 Case scenario
>
> Since watching a programme on dementia on the television, Sam had always been terrified of losing his mental faculties. He therefore told his daughter that if he ever suffered from a disease which led to mental incapacity he would not wish to have any treatment. Some years later, early signs of motor neurone disease appeared and his condition worsened rapidly. He became incapable of swallowing and his mind deteriorated, so he was no longer able to express his views. His daughter told the healthcare staff at the hospital about his previous wishes and said that he would not wish to be fed artificially. Would staff be justified in giving him artificial feeding, contrary to the daughter's views?

Introduction

It is a basic principle of the law on consent that an adult mentally competent person can refuse treatment for a good reason, a bad reason or for no reason at all (*Re MB (adult medical treatment)* [1997]). It is also an accepted principle, now enshrined in the Mental Capacity Act 2005, that where a person has, when mentally competent, declared his or her wishes for a time when he or she may lack the mental capacity, then those previously declared views are binding upon health professionals caring for him or her during that time of incapacity. These earlier expressed views are variously known as a 'living will', an 'advance decision', an 'advanced directive' or an 'advance refusal of treatment'. The Mental Capacity Act 2005 uses the term 'advance decision'.

The previous law on advance decisions: common law

In 1993, the House of Lords discussed the situation relating to the discontinu-ation of artificial feeding for Tony Bland, victim of the Hillsborough stadium disaster who was in a persistent vegetative state (*Airedale NHS Trust* v. *Bland* [1993]). It decided that the artificial feeding could be discontinued in his best interests. It also stated that had he made an advanced directive setting out his wishes if he were to become mentally incapacitated then that directive would have been binding upon the health professionals caring for him.

A typical example of an advanced directive is the card carried by Jehovah's Witnesses. This makes it clear what treatment the person is refusing and it is signed by both the person refusing the treatment in anticipation and by another person as a witness.

In the Canadian case of *Malette* v. *Shulman* (1990), an unconscious woman who was given a life-saving blood transfusion in spite of the fact that she was carrying a card, won C$20,000 against the doctor. The reason was that the doctor was guilty of trespass to the person (i.e. battery) in treating her against her express instructions, even though she was then mentally incompetent.

The House of Lords in the Tony Bland case gave approval to the decision in this Canadian case, saying that if the same facts were to occur in this coun-try, such treatment contrary to the advanced directive of the patient would be actionable in law. In the Tony Bland case, Lord Goff stated that:

> [Respect must be given to the patient's wishes] where the patient's refusal to give his consent has been expressed at an earlier date, before he became unconscious or otherwise incapable of communicating it; though in such circumstances special care may be necessary to ensure that the prior refusal of consent is still properly to be regarded as appli-cable in the circumstances which have subsequently occurred.

Health professionals, therefore, had a duty recognised by the common law (i.e. judge made or case law) to respect the living will or advance refusal of treatment if it applies to the present situation of a mentally incapacitated adult and was made at a time when the person did have the necessary mental capac-ity.

At common law there were no specific requirements as to the drawing up of a living will. The important points were that there should be clear evidence as to:

- The fact that the person is mentally capable at the time he or she expresses an advance refusal
- What his or her refusal consists of

- That this is intended to be binding at a later time when he or she lacks the capacity
- That there is a witness to this directive

Guidance which was contained in the British Medical Association's (BMA's) code of practice on advance statements (BMA, 1995) was specifically commended by the Law Commission (Law Commission, 1995) and by the Government (Lord Chancellor's Office, 1999). This code of practice suggests the minimum information which should be contained in a living will and the value of the name of a person who could speak on behalf of the person who made the living will. It suggests that, as a minimum, the following information is included:

- Full name
- Address
- Name and address of GP
- Whether advice was sought from health professionals
- Signature
- Date drafted and reviewed
- Witness signature
- A clear statement of the person's wishes, either general or specific
- The name, address and telephone number of the nominated person, if there is one.

The case of Re T

In the case of *Re T* (which is considered in Box 16.2), Lord Donaldson warned against reliance upon the wishes of relatives when a patient lacks the requisite mental capacity:

> There seems to be a view in the medical profession that in... emergency circumstances the next of kin should be asked to consent on behalf of the patient and that, if possible, treatment should be postponed until that consent has been obtained. This is a misconception because the next of kin has no legal right either to consent or to refuse consent (*Re T (adult: refusal of medical treatment)* [1992]).

> ## Box 16.2 Case of *Re T (adult: refusal of medical treatment)* [1992]
>
> T, 34 weeks pregnant, was injured in a road accident. She had been brought up by her mother, who was a Jehovah's Witness, although she was not herself a member of that religion. After being alone with her mother, she told the staff nurse that she would not want to have a blood transfusion. At that time, it was unlikely that it would become necessary. Shortly afterwards she went into labour and it was agreed that she would have a Caesarean section. Again, after being alone with her mother, she told the medical staff that she did not want a blood transfusion. She signed a form of refusal of consent to a blood transfusion. It was not explained to her that it might be necessary to give her a blood transfusion to save her life. Following the Caesarean section, the doctors, in compliance with her wishes, did not give her blood and she was placed on a ventilator and paralysing drugs were administered. Her father (who was not a Jehovah's Witness) and her boyfriend applied to the court for a declaration that it was lawful to give her a blood transfusion. The High Court judge held at the first hearing that it was lawful for a blood transfusion to be given and at the second hearing that T had neither consented to, nor refused, a blood transfusion in the emergency which had arisen and it was therefore lawful for the doctors to treat her in whatever way they considered, in the exercise of their professional judgment, to be in her best interests.

Developments towards statutory provision for advance decisions

Whilst advance decisions were accepted by judge made law or the common law, this was not entirely satisfactory, since there were many unanswered questions: should they be in any particular format? What could be refused? Who could draw one up? Proposals to place such advance declarations on a statutory basis were therefore included in the Law Commission's report in 1995. (Law Commission, 1995). The Law Commission (an independent body which reviews our laws) published its final proposals on establishing a framework for decision making on behalf of mentally incompetent adults and its recommendations contained draft legislation in the form of a Mental Incapacity Bill. This Bill contained a clause covering the legal changes relating to advance refusal of treatment. This clause covered: the definition of an advance refusal of treatment; the contents of an advance refusal; exclusions from living wills; referral to court if doubt about validity; and legal position of health professional. The Mental Incapacity Bill was not placed before Parliament, but in 1997 the Lord Chancellor issued a consultation document (Lord Chancellor, 1997). The consultation period ended on 31 March 1998 and in October 1999 the Government published its proposals (Lord Chancellor, 1999).

In relation to advance statements it considered that in the light of the wide range of views on this complex and sensitive subject and given the flexibility inherent in developing case law, the Government believes that it would not be appropriate to legislate at the present time and thus fix the statutory position once and for all. In rejecting the need for a statute covering living wills, the Government stated for the clarity of lawyers, doctors and patients what it perceives to be the present position in law:

> The current law and medical practice is as follows. It is a principle of law and medical practice that all adults have the right to consent to or refuse medical treatment. Advance statements are a means for patients to exercise that right by anticipating a time when they may lose the capacity to make or communicate a decision (Lord Chancellor, 1999, paragraph 16).

Paragraphs 17–20 expanded on this statement by making it clear that if the advance statement requests specific treatments this did not legally bind a health professional to act contrary to his/her professional judgment. Advance statements did not permit euthanasia 'which is and will remain illegal'.

While the Government applauded the flexibility of the common law in dealing with advance statements, there were several disadvantages which arose as a result of the absence of a statute. The difficulties included:

- What, if anything, should be excluded from a living will?
- What presumptions, if any, arise from a living will?
- How can health professionals be protected?
- For how long is an advanced refusal valid?
- How should a living will be drawn up? and
- What rights, if any, should relatives have in relation to a living will?

These were discussed more fully by the author (Dimond, 2000).

Subsequently, provision was made for advance decisions in the Mental Incapacity Bill which was subjected to the scrutiny of a joint committee of both Houses of Parliament and eventually contained in the Mental Capacity Act 2005.

Mental Capacity Act 2005 and advance decisions

Sections 24–26 set out the provisions relating to advance decisions and are shown in Box 16.3.

Box 16.3 Mental Capacity Act: advance decisions to refuse treatment Sections 24–26

24 Advance decisions to refuse treatment: general

(1) 'Advance decision' means a decision made by a person ('P'), after he has reached 18 and when he has capacity to do so, that if–

   (a) at a later time and in such circumstances as he may specify, a specified treatment is proposed to be carried out or continued by a person providing health care for him, and

   (b) at that time he lacks capacity to consent to the carrying out or continuation of the treatment,

the specified treatment is not to be carried out or continued.

(2) For the purposes of subsection (1)(a), a decision may be regarded as specifying a treatment or circumstances even though expressed in layman's terms.

(3) P may withdraw or alter an advance decision at any time when he has capacity to do so.

(4) A withdrawal (including a partial withdrawal) need not be in writing.

(5) An alteration of an advance decision need not be in writing (unless section 25(5) applies in relation to the decision resulting from the alteration).

25 Validity and applicability of advance decisions

(1) An advance decision does not affect the liability which a person may incur for carrying out or continuing a treatment in relation to P unless the decision is at the material time–

   (a) valid, and

   (b) applicable to the treatment.

(2) An advance decision is not valid if P–

   (a) has withdrawn the decision at a time when he had capacity to do so,

   (b) has, under a lasting power of attorney created after the advance decision was made, conferred authority on the donee (or, if more than one, any of them) to give or refuse consent to the treatment to which the advance decision relates, or

    (c) has done anything else clearly inconsistent with the advance decision remaining his fixed decision.

(3) An advance decision is not applicable to the treatment in question if at the material time P has capacity to give or refuse consent to it.

(4) An advance decision is not applicable to the treatment in question if—

    (a) that treatment is not the treatment specified in the advance decision,

    (b) any circumstances specified in the advance decision are absent, or

    (c) there are reasonable grounds for believing that circumstances exist which P did not anticipate at the time of the advance decision and which would have affected his decision had he anticipated them.

(5) An advance decision is not applicable to life-sustaining treatment unless—

    (a) the decision is verified by a statement by P to the effect that it is to apply to that treatment even if life is at risk, and

    (b) the decision and statement comply with subsection (6).

(6) A decision or statement complies with this subsection only if—

    (a) it is in writing,

    (b) it is signed by P or by another person in P's presence and by P's direction,

    (c) the signature is made or acknowledged by P in the presence of a witness, and

    (d) the witness signs it, or acknowledges his signature, in P's presence.

(7) The existence of any lasting power of attorney other than one of a description mentioned in subsection (2)(b) does not prevent the advance decision from being regarded as valid and applicable.

26 Effect of advance decisions

(1) If P has made an advance decision which is—

    (a) valid, and

    (b) applicable to a treatment,

the decision has effect as if he had made it, and had had capacity to make it, at the time when the question arises whether the treatment should be carried out or continued.

(2) A person does not incur liability for carrying out or continuing the treatment unless, at the time, he is satisfied that an advance decision exists which is valid and applicable to the treatment.

(3) A person does not incur liability for the consequences of withholding or withdrawing a treatment from P if, at the time, he reasonably believes that an advance decision exists which is valid and applicable to the treatment.

(4) The court may make a declaration as to whether an advance decision—

    (a) exists;

    (b) is valid;

    (c) is applicable to a treatment.

(5) Nothing in an apparent advance decision stops a person—

    (a) providing life-sustaining treatment, or

    (b) doing any act he reasonably believes to be necessary to prevent a serious deterioration in P's condition

while a decision as respects any relevant issue is sought from the court.

Statutory definition of advance decision

An advance decision applies to a future situation where specific treatment is to be carried out or is being carried out and at a time when the maker no longer has the mental capacity to be able to make his or her own decisions. By the means of this statement, the maker can refuse the specified treatment. As can be seen from Box 16.3, the MCA sets down two requisites for a valid advance decision. The maker must be at least 18 years and must have the requisite mental capacity to be able to make the relevant decision. However, the advance decision will only apply when the maker lacks the requisite mental capacity to make decisions. As long as the maker has the requisite mental capacity, the advance decision will not apply.

The MCA does not set out any specific formalities to be followed in drawing up the advance decision, except where the specified treatment is life-sustaining treatment (see below). In fact it specifically states that a decision may be regarded as specifying a treatment or circumstances even though expressed in layman's terms. Even though no particular formalities or language are prescribed, it is important that it is clear to which treatments the maker is referring, so that there are no doubts about what treatments are covered when the advance decision is intended to come into effect. An advance decision will only be applicable if the treatment in question is specified in the advance decision, any circumstances specified by the maker are present and there are no reasonable grounds for believing that circumstances exist which the maker had not anticipated at the time of the advance decision was drawn up and which would have affected his decision had he anticipated them. An example of the latter situation could be the development of a new treatment for a condition, which did not exist at the time the advance decision was drawn up and which could affect the maker's decision to refuse in advance.

Alteration and withdrawal of an advance decision

No formalities are required when an advance decision is withdrawn, but the maker must have the requisite capacity to do so. The withdrawal need not be in writing. Nor are any formalities required when an advance decision is altered (the maker must have the requisite capacity), unless the alteration refers to life-sustaining treatment, in which case the provisions relating to life-sustaining treatments apply (see below).

Conflicting intentions of the maker

To be valid an advance decision must clearly affect the wishes of the maker, and if the maker acts in a way which is inconsistent with the advance decision then the advance decision would not be applicable. For example if the maker has, under a lasting power of attorney (LPA; see Chapter 11) created after the advance decision was made, given authority to the donee to give or refuse consent to the treatment to which the advance decision relates, then the advance decision would not be applicable. Any other action by the maker which is clearly inconsistent with the advance decision remaining his fixed decision will invalidate the advance decision. Apart from those situations where an LPA is drawn up after the advance decision and conflicts with it, an LPA does not prevent the advance decision from being regarded as valid and applicable.

Uncertainty about the validity or applicability of an advance decision

If it is unclear whether an advance decision is valid or applicable to a specific situation, then an application can be made to the Court of Protection for a declaration as to the existence, validity and applicability of the advance decision. The MCA states that nothing in an apparent advance decision stops a person providing life-sustaining treatment, or doing any act he reasonably believes to be necessary to prevent a serious deterioration in P's condition, while a decision as respects any relevant issue is sought from the court. This may of course undermine the very purpose of the advance decision. For example, if a person refused a blood transfusion by means of an advance decision, but there was a dispute over its validity, to give blood to keep the person alive, whilst a declaration from the Court of Protection was obtained, would defeat the object of the advance decision, if subsequently the Court declared the advance decision to be valid and applicable. If possible interim measures which do not conflict with the maker's wishes should be taken, whilst a speedy decision of the Court was sought.

Effect of an advance decision

If an advance decision meets the legal requirements, and is applicable to the treatment in question and if the maker is no longer able to make his or her own decisions, then it should be followed. An advance decision which is valid, and applicable to a treatment, has the same effect as if the maker had the capacity at the time the decision had to be made.

A person who follows the advance decision and withholds or discontinues the treatment will not be liable as a consequence, if he or she reasonably believed that the advance decision was valid and applicable. In contrast a person does not incur liability for carrying out or continuing the treatment unless, at the time, he is satisfied that an advance decision exists which is valid and applicable to the treatment.

Life-sustaining treatment

The term 'life-sustaining treatment' means treatment which in the view of a person providing health care for the person concerned is necessary to sustain life (S.4(10)).

If the maker intends to refuse life-sustaining treatment by means of an advance decision, then the formalities set out in Section 25(5) and (6) must be followed (see Box 16.3).

The maker must include a statement to the effect that the statement is to apply to that treatment even if his or her life is at risk. In addition the statement must be in writing, be signed by the maker or by another person in the maker's presence and by his direction, and the witness signs it, or acknowledges his signature, in the maker's presence.

Practical issues

There are considerable advantages in staff discussing with patients who are at an early stage of a deteriorating illness, but while they still enjoy their mental capacity, their views on active intervention. Clearly, this topic would have to be broached sensitively and the correct time chosen for such communication. It would certainly be preferable to relying entirely upon the relatives telling staff what the patient would not have wished, when this can no longer be confirmed with the patient.

The problem over what constituted a valid refusal arose in the case of *Re T* (see Box 16.2). T appealed to the Court of Appeal. The Court of Appeal held that T's refusal was the result of her mother's undue influence upon her and therefore was invalid. In addition, when she signed the form of refusal (the design of which was criticised by Lord Donaldson) she did so in ignorance of the particular circumstances which later arose (i.e. that blood may be needed in a life-saving situation for herself). It is hoped that with the implementation of the MCA, then will be greater clarity as to what constitutes an advance refusal and when that is valid and applicable.

Application of law to the Case Scenario (Box 16.1)

Has Sam created an advance directive? The difficulty with Sam's expression of his wishes to his daughter is that they lack the certainty that a living will requires to be valid:

- It is not clear that they would refer to the situation which arose when he suffered from motor neurone's disease
- There is no evidence that these wishes were repeated at the time of the early stages of this illness
- There is no evidence that he wished to put these words in writing
- How do the health professionals know that Sam's daughter is telling the truth?

The requirements of the MCA relating to life-sustaining treatments have not been complied with since there does not appear to be a statement in writing, signed and witnessed covering the treatment and an acknowledgement by Sam that he wishes his refusal to apply to life-sustaining treatments. In the absence of a valid and applicable advance decision, action must be taken in Sam's best interests if Sam is unable to make his own decisions. Reference should be made to Chapter 7 on how 'best interests' are determined. It will be noted that in deciding what are in a person's best interests, account must be taken of

(a) the person's past and present wishes and feelings (and, in particular, any relevant written statement made by him when he had capacity),
(b) the beliefs and values that would be likely to influence his decision if he had capacity, and
(c) the other factors that he would be likely to consider if he were able to do so.

This means that account must be taken of the views which Sam has expressed to his relatives at a time when he had the requisite mental capacity.

Box 16.4 Case scenario 2

Mary had cared for her invalid mentally infirm mother for many years and was determined that if she ever lost her own mental capacity she would not wish to be kept alive. She drew up a document, witnessed by her sister, which stated that in the event of her suffering from any form of mental incapacity she would not wish to be fed or have any medical or nursing intervention. Some years later she began to suffer from the early signs of Alzheimer's disease. Her sister had died, but staff were aware that Mary still carried this living will on her person. She is now refusing all food. What is the law?

Application of the law to Case Scenario 2 (Box 16.4)

It would appear that the document which Mary has drawn up complies with the statutory requirements relating to advance decisions which apply to life-sustaining treatments. She has confirmed in the document that she is refusing life-sustaining treatments and it has been signed and witnessed. There appears to be no doubt that it was signed when she was mentally capacitated. It must first be established if Mary still has the requisite mental capacity to make decisions about treatment. If she does then she must be asked to make the decision, and the advance decision will not be applicable. If, on the other hand, she no longer has the requisite mental capacity, then a valid advance decision should be applied if it is relevant to the circumstances.

In this situation, there is a difficulty since Mary is refusing food. The statutory provisions for advance decisions only relate to the refusal of treatment and providing basic nutrition, hydration, pain relief and nursing care would be seen as 'care' and not treatment. The Code of Practice therefore advises that care cannot be the subject of an advance decision – only treatment. If this is correct, then food could still be given to Mary in her best interests.

Conclusion

The fact that statutory provisions now exist for the definition and effects of an advance decision should remove considerable uncertainty from this area. An advance decision must be clearly intended to be operative in the circumstances which arise when the patient becomes mentally incapacitated. Over time, case law will develop on the interpretation of the statutory provisions as applications are made to the Court of Protection on the validity and meaning of advance decisions.

References

Airedale NHS Trust v. *Bland* [1993] 1 All ER 649.

British Medical Association (1995) *Advance Statements About Medical Treatment*. BMA, London.

Dimond, B. C. (2008) *Legal Aspects of Death*. Quay Books, London.

Dimond, B. C. (2008) *Legal Aspects of Mental Capacity*. Blackwells, Oxford.

Law Commission (1995) *Mental Incapacity Report No 231*. Stationery Office, London.

Lord Chancellor's Department Consultation Paper (2002) *Making Decisions: Helping People who have Difficulty Deciding for Themselves*; http://www.dca.gov.uk/consult/family/decision.htm.

Lord Chancellor's Office (1999) *Making Decisions: The Government's Proposals for Making Decisions on Behalf of Mentally Incapacitated Adults*. Stationery Office, London.

Malette v. *Shulman* (1990) 67 DLR (4th) 321.

Re F (a mental patient: sterilisation) [1990] 2 AC 1.

Re MB (adult medical treatment) [1997] 2 FLR 426.

Re T (adult: refusal of medical treatment) [1992] 4 All ER 649 (1992) 9 BMLR 46 CA.

CHAPTER 17

Advocacy for adults lacking mental capacity or who are mentally disordered

---

Box 17.1 Case scenario

Harry has lived in a community home for several years and now wishes to move out and live with his girlfriend. His parents oppose the move, saying that he could not cope and that he is being well cared for where he is. The social services authority are arranging the move and are anxious for a decision to be made. They do not consider that Harry has the mental capacity to make his own decision about accommodation. What is the law?

Introduction

One of the important features of the Mental Capacity Act 2005 was that an independent mental capacity advocacy service should be available for those who are unable to make their own decision. Provision for this is made in sections 35–41 which are shown in Box 17.2. In addition, the Mental Health Act 2007 introduced the duty to provide independent mental health advocates for certain qualifying persons who are detained under the Mental Health Act 1983. The provisions for independent mental capacity advocates and for independent mental health advocates are considered below in two separate sections.

A. Independent mental capacity advocates

Importance of advocacy for those lacking mental capacity

The MCA states that in arranging advocacy services the appropriate authority must have regard to the principle that a person to whom a proposed act or
decision relates should, so far as practicable, be represented and supported by
a person who is independent of any person who will be responsible for the act
or decision (S.35(4)). Advocacy in general is required:

(a) where serious medical treatment is being considered
(b) where the NHS or Local Authority are making arrangements for the accom-
    modation of a person lacking the requisite mental capacity
(c) where protective measures are being taken in respect of a person lacking
    the requisite mental capacity either because he is the perpetrator or the
    subject of abuse (this situation was added by Regulations passed in 2006;
    MCA Regs., 2006b)
(d) where there are care reviews by NHS body or LA (this situation was added
    by Regulations passed in 2006; MCA Regs., 2006b)
(e) where P is subject to detention under the Bournewood safeguards (added
    by Mental Health Act 2007)

Serious medical treatment

'Serious medical treatment' means treatment which involves providing, withholding or withdrawing treatment of a kind prescribed by regulations made by
the appropriate authority. Neither the Act nor the Regulations draw up a list of
treatments defined as serious. The Regulations provide further assistance in its
definition. Regulation paragraph 4 (MCA Regs., 2006a) defines serious medical treatment as follows:

> Treatment which involves providing, withdrawing or withholding treat-
> ment in circumstances where:
>
> a. in a case where single treatment is being proposed, there is a fine
> balance between its benefits to the patient and the burdens and risks it
> is likely to entail for him,
> b. in a case where there is a choice of treatments, a decision as to which
> one to use is finely balanced, or
> c. what is proposed would be likely to involve serious consequences
> for the patient.

Clinicians need to apply these tests to the treatment in question.

The Code of Practice gives examples of the kinds of treatment which may come under the definition of serious treatment, but this list is not of course exhaustive:

- chemotherapy and surgery for cancer
- electro-convulsive therapy
- therapeutic sterilisation
- major surgery (such as open-heart surgery or brain/neuro-surgery)
- major amputations (for example, loss of an arm or leg)
- treatments which will result in permanent loss of hearing or sight
- withholding or stopping artificial nutrition and hydration, and
- termination of pregnancy.

An IMCA must be appointed when decisions about serious medical treatment are being made if:

(a) the person lacks the requisite mental capacity and
(b) there is no person, other than one engaged in providing care or treatment for P in a professional capacity or for remuneration, whom it would be appropriate to consult in determining what would be in P's best interests.
(c) the treatment does not come under the Mental Health Act 1983 as amended by the 2007 Act.

The person who could be consulted, instead of appointing an IMCA could be a family member or informal carer (i.e. unpaid).

Accommodation arrangements made by an NHS body

Where an NHS body is considering the provision of or a change in the accommodation in a hospital or care home for a person who lacks the requisite mental capacity and there is no appropriate person who could be consulted, then an IMCA must be appointed.

Accommodation arrangements or care review made by a local authority

Where a local authority is making arrangements for the provision of or a change in residential accommodation for a person who lacks the requisite mental capacity and there is no person who could be consulted about what would be in the person's best interests, family members or unpaid carers can be consulted, not professionals or paid carers. The duty to arrange for an IMCA to be appointed does not apply if the accommodation is for less than 8 weeks or if it is required as a matter of urgency, but if the accommodation exceeds 8 weeks then the duty arises.

Protective measures

Under the Regulations, when an NHS body or LA is proposing or has taken protection measures in relation to a person P who lacks capacity to agree to one or more of the measures, then the NHS or LA *may* instruct an IMCA to represent P if it is satisfied that it would be of particular benefit to P to be so represented. The Code of Practice gives guidance on when this discretionary power may be used (paragraph 10.66–68 of Code of Practice 2007). The regulations do not require the person in an adult protection situation to have no friends or family to consult.

Care reviews by an NHS body or LA

The NHS body or LA may instruct an IMCA to represent P if it is satisfied that it would be of particular benefit to P, where a care review is proposed or in place for accommodation provided for P for at least 12 weeks. This does not apply if there is an appropriate person to be consulted.

Deprivation of Liberty Safeguards (Bournewood safeguards)

New sections 39A and 39C were added to the MCA by the Mental Health Act 2007 and apply when a person has lost his liberty under the provisions of Schedule A1. They require an IMCA to be appointed. Schedule A1 sets out the role of the IMCA when appointed under these provisions (see Chapter 25 for further information on the Deprivation of Liberty Safeguards (Bournewood safeguards)).

The role of the IMCA

An IMCA has a duty to take the necessary steps for the purpose of:

(a) providing support to the person whom he has been instructed to represent ('P') so that P may participate as fully as possible in any relevant decision;

(b) obtaining and evaluating relevant information;

(c) ascertaining what P's wishes and feelings would be likely to be, and the beliefs and values that would be likely to influence P, if he had capacity;

(d) ascertaining what alternative courses of action are available in relation to P;

(e) obtaining a further medical opinion where treatment is proposed and the advocate thinks that one should be obtained.

The Regulations give further details on how the IMCA is to function.

The general duty of the IMCA, when instructed by an authorised person to represent a person 'P', is that he must determine in all the circumstances how best to represent and support P.

In particular, the IMCA must:

(a) verify that the instructions were issued by an authorised person;

(b) to the extent that it is practicable and appropriate to do so
   (i) interview P, and
   (ii) examine the records relevant to P to which the IMCA has access under Section 35(6) of the Act;

(c) to the extent that it is practicable and appropriate to do so, consult
   (i) persons engaged in providing care or treatment for P in a professional capacity or for remuneration, and
   (ii) other persons who may be in a position to comment on P's wishes, feelings, beliefs or values; and

(d) take all practicable steps to obtain such other information about P, or the act or decision that is proposed in relation to P, as the IMCA considers necessary (Paragraph 6.4 of the Regulations).

The IMCA is required to prepare a report for the authorised person who instructed him (Reg. 6(6)) and may include in the report such submissions as he considers appropriate in relation to P and the act or decision which is proposed in relation to him (Reg. 6(7)). It should be noted that the IMCA does not actually make the decision. His or her role is to support P by ascertaining what P's wishes and feelings, beliefs and values would likely have been, had P had the requisite capacity. The IMCA collates all the relevant information and passes it on to the authority responsible for making the decision. The IMCA can also obtain a second medical opinion where he or she considers it necessary. The authority who is required to ensure the appointment of an IMCA must take account of the IMCA report in making the decision on behalf of the person lacking mental capacity. The regulations also enable the IMCA to challenge any decision which has been made, according to the power granted in Section 36(3).

Commissioning of IMCA services

Seven pilot IMCA organisations were established to test out the commissioning of IMCA services. The Department of Health advertised and competitively tendered for advocacy organisations to test out the new IMCA role. Seven organisations were selected and commissioned by the Department to provide pilot IMCA services from April 2006 to March 2007. Their experience and their meetings with the Official Solicitor and the Department of Health helped inform the IMCA chapter in the MCA Code of Practice and the provision of guidance material on the IMCA service. The Department produced commissioning guidance for local authority commissioners who were working with their local PCTs to commission the service. A Local Authority Circular explained the main requirements of the Act and announced the budgets that were being made available.

The IMCA services

The Secretary of State (for England) and the National Assembly for Wales (for Wales) (i.e. the appropriate authority (S.35(7))) must make such arrangements as it considers reasonable to enable persons (independent mental capacity advocates) to be available to represent and support persons to whom acts or decisions proposed under sections 37, 38 and 39 and those specified in the regulations relate.

The DoH decided that monitoring arrangements should be managed via local contracts/commissioning, but it would also produce an annual report on the IMCA service for the first three years.

In the first annual report published by the Department of Health on the Independent Mental Capacity Advocacy Service (DoH 2008) it stated that:

- Five thousand, one hundred and seventy five (5,175) people received representation from the IMCA service in its first year.
- Three thousand and forty seven (3047) of the representations were for decisions on accommodation moves;
- 191 people were represented in care reviews;
- 671 represented in decisions about serious medical treatment and
- 675 were represented in adult protection proceedings.

The Department of Health had the following concerns:

1. Referrals should be at a higher level for all decisions – suggesting that awareness of, or compliance with, the Act is insufficient. There are also wide geographical differences which raises concern.

2. Referrals for Serious Medical Treatment are particularly low across the whole country, raising concerns about the extent to which the NHS is, at present, complying with the requirements of the Act.

3. Gate-keeping by IMCA organisations needs to be reviewed.

Application of the law to the case scenario (Box 17.1)

The first question to be considered is whether Harry is incapable of making his own decisions. If he can make his own decisions on moving into new accommodation, then that is his right, and every practical measure must be taken to assist him in making his decision and in providing any means to help him communicate. On the other hand, even if every support were provided Harry would be unable to make the decision, then the social services authority has a duty to determine what is in Harry's best interests and if necessary ensure that an IMCA was appointed to provide a report on what Harry's best interests are. An IMCA is not required if there is a person, who is neither professionally involved in Harry's care or treatment or a paid carer, who could be consulted about Harry's best interests. In this case Harry's parents are available to be consulted. However, they have made it clear that they are opposed to Harry's move, so it could be argued that his parents would not be the best people to ensure that Harry's best interests are properly identified. If the social services authority took that view, then it could ask for an IMCA to be appointed to represent Harry. Harry's parents may well complain about the appointment. If there is a dispute which cannot be resolved through alternative dispute resolution methods, then an application could be made to the Court of Protection for a declaration as to the appointment of an IMCA or a determination as to what was in Harry's best interests.

Conclusions on IMCA

Independent advocacy is an important means of providing additional protection for those incapable of making their own decisions and the statutory provisions should provide considerable support for those lacking the requisite mental capacity. In addition, there are many charitable organisations providing advocacy services for those who do not come within the statutory provisions. It is clear from the first annual report on the IMCA service that the statutory definition of the duty to provide IMCA services is narrow and there are many situations where independent advocacy would be of value, but it is not yet a statutory duty. It is hoped that financial restrictions will not prevent an extension of the service for those lacking the mental capacity to make their own decisions.

Box 17.2 Sections 35–41 Mental Capacity Act 2005

Independent mental capacity advocate service

35 Appointment of independent mental capacity advocates

(1) The appropriate authority must make such arrangements as it considers reasonable to enable persons ('independent mental capacity advocates') to be available to represent and support persons to whom acts or decisions proposed under sections 37, 38 and 39 relate.

(2) The appropriate authority may make regulations as to the appointment of independent mental capacity advocates.

(3) The regulations may, in particular, provide–
   (a) that a person may act as an independent mental capacity advocate only in such circumstances, or only subject to such conditions, as may be prescribed;
   (b) for the appointment of a person as an independent mental capacity advocate to be subject to approval in accordance with the regulations.

(4) In making arrangements under subsection (1), the appropriate authority must have regard to the principle that a person to whom a proposed act or decision relates should, so far as practicable, be represented and supported by a person who is independent of any person who will be responsible for the act or decision.

(5) The arrangements may include provision for payments to be made to, or in relation to, persons carrying out functions in accordance with the arrangements.

(6) For the purpose of enabling him to carry out his functions, an independent mental capacity advocate–
   (a) may interview in private the person whom he has been instructed to represent, and
   (b) may, at all reasonable times, examine and take copies of–
      (i) any health record,
      (ii) any record of, or held by, a local authority and compiled in connection with a social services function, and

---

      (iii) any record held by a person registered under Part 2 of the Care Standards Act 2000 (c. 14), which the person holding the record considers may be relevant to the independent mental capacity advocate's investigation.

(7) In this section, section 36 and section 37, 'the appropriate authority' means–

    (a) in relation to the provision of the services of independent mental capacity advocates in England, the Secretary of State, and

    (b) in relation to the provision of the services of independent mental capacity advocates in Wales, the National Assembly for Wales.

36 Functions of independent mental capacity advocate

(1) The appropriate authority may make regulations as to the functions of independent mental capacity advocates.

(2) The regulations may, in particular, make provision requiring an advocate to take such steps as may be prescribed for the purpose of–

    (a) providing support to the person whom he has been instructed to represent ('P') so that P may participate as fully as possible in any relevant decision;

    (b) obtaining and evaluating relevant information;

    (c) ascertaining what P's wishes and feelings would be likely to be, and the beliefs and values that would be likely to influence P, if he had capacity;

    (d) ascertaining what alternative courses of action are available in relation to P;

    (e) obtaining a further medical opinion where treatment is proposed and the advocate thinks that one should be obtained.

(3) The regulations may also make provision as to circumstances in which the advocate may challenge, or provide assistance for the purpose of challenging, any relevant decision.

37 Provision of serious medical treatment by NHS body

(1) This section applies if an NHS body–

    (a) is proposing to provide, or secure the provision of, serious medical treatment for a person ('P') who lacks capacity to consent to the treatment, and

    (b) is satisfied that there is no person, other than one engaged in providing care or treatment for P in a professional capacity or for remuneration, whom it would be appropriate to consult in determining what would be in P's best interests.

(2) But this section does not apply if P's treatment is regulated by Part 4 of the Mental Health Act.

(3) Before the treatment is provided, the NHS body must instruct an independent mental capacity advocate to represent P.

(4) If the treatment needs to be provided as a matter of urgency, it may be provided even though the NHS body has not been able to comply with subsection (3).

(5) The NHS body must, in providing or securing the provision of treatment for P, take into account any information given, or submissions made, by the independent mental capacity advocate.

(6) 'Serious medical treatment' means treatment which involves providing, withholding or withdrawing treatment of a kind prescribed by regulations made by the appropriate authority.

(7) 'NHS body' has such meaning as may be prescribed by regulations made for the purposes of this section by–
   (a) the Secretary of State, in relation to bodies in England, or
   (b) the National Assembly for Wales, in relation to bodies in Wales.

38 Provision of accommodation by NHS body

(1) This section applies if an NHS body proposes to make arrangements–
   (a) for the provision of accommodation in a hospital or care home for a person ('P') who lacks capacity to agree to the arrangements, or
   (b) for a change in P's accommodation to another hospital or care home, and is satisfied that there is no person, other than one engaged in providing care or treatment for P in a professional capacity or for remuneration, whom it would be appropriate for it to consult in determining what would be in P's best interests.

(2) But this section does not apply if P is accommodated as a result of an obligation imposed on him under the Mental Health Act.

(3) Before making the arrangements, the NHS body must instruct an independent mental capacity advocate to represent P unless it is satisfied that–
   (a) the accommodation is likely to be provided for a continuous period which is less than the applicable period, or
   (b) the arrangements need to be made as a matter of urgency.

(4) If the NHS body—
  (a) did not instruct an independent mental capacity advocate to represent P before making the arrangements because it was satisfied that subsection (3)(a) or (b) applied, but
  (b) subsequently has reason to believe that the accommodation is likely to be provided for a continuous period—
    (i) beginning with the day on which accommodation was first provided in accordance with the arrangements, and
    (ii) ending on or after the expiry of the applicable period, it must instruct an independent mental capacity advocate to represent P.
(5) The NHS body must, in deciding what arrangements to make for P, take into account any information given, or submissions made, by the independent mental capacity advocate.
(6) 'Care home' has the meaning given in section 3 of the Care Standards Act 2000 (c. 14).
(7) 'Hospital' means—
  (a) a health service hospital as defined by section 128 of the National Health Service Act 1977 (c. 49), or
  (b) an independent hospital as defined by section 2 of the Care Standards Act 2000.
(8) 'NHS body' has such meaning as may be prescribed by regulations made for the purposes of this section by—
  (a) the Secretary of State, in relation to bodies in England, or
  (b) the National Assembly for Wales, in relation to bodies in Wales.
(9) 'Applicable period' means—
  (a) in relation to accommodation in a hospital, 28 days, and
  (b) in relation to accommodation in a care home, 8 weeks.

39 Provision of accommodation by local authority
(1) This section applies if a local authority propose to make arrangements—
  (a) for the provision of residential accommodation for a person ('P') who lacks capacity to agree to the arrangements, or
  (b) for a change in P's residential accommodation, and are satisfied that there is no person, other than one engaged in providing care or treatment for P in a professional capacity or for remuneration, whom it would be appropriate for them to consult in determining what would be in P's best interests.
(2) But this section applies only if the accommodation is to be provided in accordance with—

    (a) section 21 or 29 of the National Assistance Act 1948 (c. 29), or

    (b) section 117 of the Mental Health Act, as the result of a decision taken by the local authority under section 47 of the National Health Service and Community Care Act 1990 (c. 19).

(3) This section does not apply if P is accommodated as a result of an obligation imposed on him under the Mental Health Act.

(4) Before making the arrangements, the local authority must instruct an independent mental capacity advocate to represent P unless they are satisfied that-

    (a) the accommodation is likely to be provided for a continuous period of less than 8 weeks, or

    (b) the arrangements need to be made as a matter of urgency.

(5) If the local authority–

    (a) did not instruct an independent mental capacity advocate to represent P before making the arrangements because they were satisfied that subsection (4)(a) or (b) applied, but

    (b) subsequently have reason to believe that the accommodation is likely to be provided for a continuous period that will end 8 weeks or more after the day on which accommodation was first provided in accordance with the arrangements, they must instruct an independent mental capacity advocate to represent P.

(6) The local authority must, in deciding what arrangements to make for P, take into account any information given, or submissions made, by the independent mental capacity advocate.

40 Exceptions

Sections 37(3), 38(3) and (4) and 39(4) and (5) do not apply if there is–

(a) a person nominated by P (in whatever manner) as a person to be consulted in matters affecting his interests,

(b) a donee of a lasting power of attorney created by P,

(c) a deputy appointed by the court for P, or

(d) a donee of an enduring power of attorney (within the meaning of Schedule 4) created by P.

41 Power to adjust role of independent mental capacity advocate

(1) The appropriate authority may make regulations–

    (a) expanding the role of independent mental capacity advocates in relation to persons who lack capacity, and

> (b) adjusting the obligation to make arrangements imposed by section 35.
>
> (2) The regulations may, in particular—
>
>   (a) prescribe circumstances (different to those set out in sections 37, 38 and 39) in which an independent mental capacity advocate must, or circumstances in which one may, be instructed by a person of a prescribed description to represent a person who lacks capacity, and
>
>   (b) include provision similar to any made by section 37, 38, 39 or 40.
>
> (3) 'Appropriate authority' has the same meaning as in section 35.

B Independent Mental Health Advocates

Box 17.3 Scenario and IMHA

Jason is detained under section 3 of the Mental Health Act 1983, which means that he could be in hospital for up to 6 months with the possibility of renewal. He refused to have any treatment and said that he would prefer to die. Is he entitled to have the assistance of an advocate?

Introduction

Under a new Section 130A to the Mental Health Act 1983 the Secretary of State and the Welsh Ministers are required to make such arrangements as they consider reasonable to enable persons ('independent mental health advocates') to be available to help qualifying patients. Both authorities are given the power to make regulations to cover the appointment of persons as independent mental health advocates and the regulations may provide:

(a) that a person may act as an independent mental health advocate only in such circumstances, or only subject to such conditions, as may be specified in the regulations;

(b) for the appointment of a person as an independent mental health advocate to be subject to approval in accordance with the regulations.

Both authorities are required to have regard to the principle that any help available to a patient under the arrangements should, so far as practicable, be provided by a person who is independent of any person who is professionally concerned with the patient's medical treatment. A person is not to be regarded as professionally concerned with a patient's medical treatment merely because he is representing him in accordance with arrangements:

(a) under section 35 of the Mental Capacity Act 2005; or
(b) of a description specified in regulations under this section.

The arrangements may include provision for payments to be made to, or in relation to, persons carrying out functions in accordance with the arrangements.

IMHAs started work on 1 April 2009.

Help available for qualifying patients

A new section 130B sets out the help which is available from an independent mental health advocate. This includes help in obtaining information about and understanding:

(a) the provisions of this Act by virtue of which he is a qualifying patient;
(b) any conditions or restrictions to which he is subject by virtue of this Act;
(c) what (if any) medical treatment is given to him or is proposed or discussed in his case;
(d) why it is given, proposed or discussed;
(e) the authority under which it is, or would be, given; and
(f) the requirements of this Act which apply, or would apply, in connection with the giving of the treatment to him.

The help also includes:

(a) help in obtaining information about and understanding any rights which may be exercised under this Act by or in relation to him; and
(b) help (by way of representation or otherwise) in exercising those rights.

The powers of the independent mental health advocate are comparable to those of the independent mental capacity advocate. The advocate may:

(a) visit and interview the patient in private;
(b) visit and interview any person who is professionally concerned with his medical treatment;

(c) require the production of and inspect any records relating to his detention or treatment in any hospital or registered establishment or to any after-care services provided for him under section 117;

(d) require the production of and inspect any records of, or held by, a local social services authority which relate to him.

However, an independent mental health advocate is not entitled to the production of, or to inspect, records unless:

(a) in a case where the patient has capacity or is competent to consent (capacity is as defined by the MCA (see Chapter 6)), he does consent; or

(b) in any other case, the production or inspection would not conflict with a decision made by a donee or deputy or the Court of Protection (see chapter 11) and the person holding the records, having regard to such matters as may be prescribed in regulations under section 130A above, considers that:

(i) the records may be relevant to the help to be provided by the advocate; and

(ii) the production or inspection is appropriate.

An independent mental health advocate is required to comply with any reasonable request made to him by any of the following for him to visit and interview the patient:

(a) the person (if any) appearing to the advocate to be the patient's nearest relative;

(b) the responsible clinician for the purposes of this Act;

(c) an approved mental health professional.

Section 130B emphasises that nothing in the Act prevents the patient from declining to be provided with help under the IMHA arrangements. Guidance on access to records under S130B is provided by the DoH (2009).

A qualifying patient

A new section 130C defines a person as a qualifying patient if he is:

(a) liable to be detained under this Act (otherwise than by virtue of section 4 or 5(2) or (4) above or section 135 or 136 below);

(b) subject to guardianship under this Act; or

(c) a community patient.

A patient is also a qualifying patient if:

(a) not being a qualifying patient falling within subsection (2) above, he discusses with a registered medical practitioner or approved clinician the possibility of being given a form of treatment to which section 57 above applies; or

(b) not having attained the age of 18 years and not being a qualifying patient falling within subsection (2) above, he discusses with a registered medical practitioner or approved clinician the possibility of being given a form of treatment to which section 58A above applies.

(4) Where a patient who is a qualifying patient falling within subsection (3) above is informed that the treatment concerned is proposed in his case, he remains a qualifying patient falling within that subsection until:

(a) the proposal is withdrawn; or

(b) the treatment is completed or discontinued.

Duty to give information about independent mental health advocates

The responsible person (i.e. the managers of the hospital or registered establishment, the responsible clinician or the local social services) is required to take such steps as are practicable to ensure that the patient understands:

(a) that help is available to him from an independent mental health advocate; and

(b) how he can obtain that help.

(3) The steps to be taken under subsection (1) above shall be taken:

(a) where the responsible person falls within subsection (2)(a) above, as soon as practicable after the patient becomes liable to be detained;

(b) where the responsible person falls within subsection (2)(b) above, as soon as practicable after the conditional discharge;

(c) where the responsible person falls within subsection (2)(c) above, as soon as practicable after the patient becomes subject to guardianship;

(d) where the responsible person falls within subsection (2)(d) above, as soon as practicable after the patient becomes a community patient;

(e) where the responsible person falls within subsection (2)(e) above, while the discussion with the patient is taking place or as soon as practicable thereafter.

(4) The steps to be taken under subsection (1) above shall include giving the requisite information both orally and in writing.

(5) The responsible person in relation to a qualifying patient falling within section 130C(2) above (other than a patient liable to be detained by virtue of Part 3 of this Act) shall, except where the patient otherwise requests, take such steps as are practicable to furnish the person (if any) appearing to the

responsible person to be the patient's nearest relative with a copy of any information given to the patient in writing under subsection (1) above.

(6) The steps to be taken under subsection (5) above shall be taken when the information concerned is given to the patient or within a reasonable time thereafter.

(3) In section 134 (patients' correspondence), in subsection (3A), for paragraph (b) substitute:

(b) 'independent advocacy services' means services provided under:

  (i) arrangements under section 130A above;

  (ii) arrangements under section 248 of the National Health Service Act 2006 or section 187 of the National Health Service (Wales) Act 2006; or

  (iii) arrangements of a description prescribed as mentioned in paragraph (a) above.

Application of the law to the case scenario (Box 17.3)

Jason is a qualifying patient for the purposes of being provided with an independent mental health advocate under section 130A-D of the Mental Health Act 1983 as amended by the 2007 Act, which came into force on 1 April 2009 (MHA Regs, 2008). His agreement would be required to the appointment. If he agreed, the IMHA could get information and explain to Jason the provisions under which he is detained and about the proposed treatment. The IMHA could visit and interview the patient in private; visit and interview any person who is professionally concerned with his medical treatment; require the production of and inspect any records relating to his detention or treatment in any hospital or registered establishment or to any after-care services provided for him under section 117 and require the production of and inspect any records of, or held by, a local social services. The IMHA could also assist or represent Jason in an application to the Mental Health Review Tribunal.

Guidance for Commissioners for Independent Mental Health Advocacy was published in December 2008 (National Institute for Mental Health in England, 2008).

Conclusion

Many organisations have provided advocacy on an informal basis in a variety of situations. The provisions under the Mental Capacity Act and under the amended Mental Health legislation have established a statutory duty for independent advocacy to be provided in specified situations. This should ensure greater protection for the vulnerable and it is hoped that evidence of a need to extend statutory provision will be followed by a wider statutory remit under both the MCA and the MHA.

References

Code of Practice Mental Capacity Act 2005. Department of Constitutional Affairs, February 2007.

Dimond, B. C. (2008) *Legal Aspects of Mental Capacity*. Blackwell, Oxford.

Department of Health (2008) *First Annual Report of the Independent Mental Capacity Advocacy Service*. DoH, London.

Department of Health (2009) *Independent Mental Health Advocates – supplementary guidance on access to patient records under S130B of the Mental Health Act 1983*. DoH, London.

MCA Regs (2006a) The Mental Capacity Act 2005 (Independent Mental Capacity Advocates)(General) Regulations 2006 SI 2006 No 1832.

MCA Regs (2006b) Mental Capacity Act 2005 (Independent Mental Capacity Advocates) (Expansion of Role) Regulations 2006 SI 2006 No 2883.

MHA Regs (2008) Mental Health Act 1983 (Independent Mental Health Advocates) (England) Regulations 2008 SI 2008 No 3166.

National Institute for Mental Health in England (2008) *Independent Mental Health Advocacy Guidance for Commissioners*. DoH, London.

CHAPTER 18

Not for resuscitation instructions

> ## Box 18.1 Case scenario
>
> Ben, aged 75 years, was extremely depressed following the death of his wife. He was admitted to hospital in an emergency for an appendectomy. A young doctor told the nurse that he had spoken to Ben's son and it was agreed that in the event of a cardiac arrest Ben should not be resuscitated. This instruction was not put in writing. Unfortunately, after his return to the ward from the recovery room, Ben arrested. What should the nursing staff do?

Introduction

Life and death decisions over whether or not a person is to be resuscitated, if not considered before an emergency arises, can lead to a difficult situation for nursing staff and others. In the above case scenario (Box 18.1), a nurse who decided that Ben should be resuscitated and called out the team might be criticised by medical staff who say that the instructions were that Ben should not be resuscitated. On the other hand, if the nurse, conforming to the instructions of the junior doctor, did not call out the crash team, the consultant could subsequently criticise her on the grounds that the junior doctor had not discussed this with the medical team and there were no 'not for resuscitation' (NFR) or 'do not resuscitate' (DNR) instructions written in the notes.

Clarity of instructions based firmly on the legal principles is essential both to protect the rights of the patient and to protect the position of staff.

The patient's rights

A patient has a right to be resuscitated if the procedure is reasonably likely to be successful and if he or she has a reasonably good prognosis following resuscitation. Failure to provide necessary treatment in such circumstances could amount to murder or manslaughter (*R (on the application of Burke)* v. *GMC and Disability Rights Commission and the Official Solicitor to the Supreme Court* [2004]).

European Convention on Human Rights

Under article 2 of the European Convention on Human Rights, every person has a right to life. It could be argued that failure to resuscitate in circumstances favourable to the patient is a denial of this right.

Article 2

Article 2 states:

> Everyone's right to life shall be protected by law. No one shall be deprived of his life intentionally save in the execution of a sentence of a court following his conviction of a crime for which this penalty is provided by law.

Recent decisions of the courts show how this right is interpreted. For example, in one case (*A National Health Service Trust* v. *D*, 2000), parents lost their attempt to ensure that a severely handicapped baby born prematurely was resuscitated if necessary. The judge ruled that the hospital should provide him with palliative care to ease his suffering, but should not try to revive him as that would cause unnecessary pain.

In another case, the President of the Family Division, Dame Elizabeth Butler-Sloss, held that the withdrawal of life-sustaining medical treatment was not contrary to article 2 of the Human Rights Convention and the right to life where the patient was in a persistent vegetative state (PVS). The ruling was made on 25 October 2000 in cases involving Mrs M, a 49-year-old woman, who suffered brain damage during an operation abroad in 1997 and was diagnosed as being in a PVS in October 1998, and in the case of Mrs H, aged 36, who fell ill in America as a result of pancreatitis during Christmas 1999 (*NHS*

Trust A v. *Mrs M* and *NHS Trust B* v. *Mrs H*). In the light of these decisions, it would appear that failure to resuscitate a patient when circumstances justify the decision would not amount to a breach of article 2.

Article 3

Article 3 of the European Convention of Human Rights states that:

> No one shall be subjected to torture or to inhuman or degrading treatment or punishment.

Failure to resuscitate Ben when all the circumstances (likely success and good prognosis) are favourable may be defined as inhuman treatment.

Duty of care in the law of negligence

Ben is also owed a duty of care by the medical and nursing staff caring for him. The standard of care of this duty, as defined by the Bolam Test (*Bolam* v. *Friern Barnet Management Committee* [1957]), would require staff to follow a reasonable standard of care conforming to the acceptable approved practice of a competent body of professional opinion.

If, in a case such as Ben's, reasonable practice would have indicated resuscitation, then it could be argued that failure to resuscitate was a breach of the duty of care. If as a result of this failure Ben suffered harm (i.e. death), then his relatives could sue in his name for breach of the duty of care owed to him.

What if Ben were able to express his own wishes?

If Ben were asked before the operation what he would wish to happen in the event of a cardiac arrest and stated that he would not wish to be resuscitated, then his wishes should prevail. Care should be taken to ensure that he has the mental capacity to make such a decision. It may be, for example, that Ben is severely depressed following the bereavement and this is affecting his thinking. His request for no resuscitation may be a result of that depression and therefore not a competent decision.

There is a statutory presumption that an adult has the mental capacity to make decisions, but this presumption can be rebutted if there is evidence to the contrary. Professionals have a duty when a person refuses what could be life-saving treatment to ensure that the person is mentally competent (*Re T (adult: refusal of medical treatment)* [1992]. The facts of *Re T* are set out on page 140 in Chapter 16). If, however, it is clear that Ben has the necessary mental capacity and clearly indicates that he does not wish to be resuscitated then it is Ben's legal right to refuse treatment (*Re MB (adult medical treatment)* [1997] (see Chapters 2 and 12).

What if Ben were incompetent?

As a result of the Mental Capacity Act 2005 there is now a statutory presumption that an adult has the requisite mental capacity to make a specific decision. However this presumption can be rebutted or removed on a balance of probabilities if the evidence exists. If Ben were assessed as lacking the requisite mental capacity (as defined in the Mental Capacity Act 2005 – see Chapter 6), then staff would have to decide what was in his best interests in determining whether or not NFR instructions were appropriate. Acting in the best interests of a mentally incapacitated adult was considered in chapter 7. The Mental Capacity Act 2005 enshrined the principle which the House of Lords laid down in the case of *Re F* (*Re F (mental patient: sterilisation)* [1990]; see Chapter 7) that health professionals have a duty in law to act out of necessity in the best interests of a mentally incapacitated adult person.

What rights do the relatives have?

Where serious medical treatment is concerned such as in this situation, the decision as to what was in the best interests of the patient would normally be made by the clinicians. In ascertaining the best interests of the patient, the relatives would have to be consulted over what the patient's views and beliefs were in order to ascertain the decision that he would have made had he had the requisite mental capacity. Relatives should describe what the patient's wishes would have been. It is not the relatives' view as to the patient's best interests, which are being sought. In Ben's situation, his son has already told the medical staff that Ben should not be resuscitated. The relatives' views on what would have been Ben's wishes should be sought. In the absence of an advance decision (living will or advance refusal of resuscitation (see Chapter 17)), it is extremely uncertain what Ben wants. In this case he has to be treated as an adult who lacks the requisite mental capacity and actions must be taken in his best interests. It is, of course, important to ascertain statements which the patient made in order to determine what is in his best interests. In determining best interests the MCA states that 'where the determination relates to life-sustaining treatment he must not, in considering whether the treatment is in the best interests of the person concerned, be motivated by a desire to bring about his death' (MCA S.4(5)).

Professional guidance

Before the implementation of the Human Rights Act 1998, the Department of Health drew attention to guidance which had been drawn up by the Resuscitation Council, the Royal College of Nursing and the British Medical Association in 1999. (This guidance has since been updated: BMA/RCN/Resuscitation Council (UK), 2007). The guidance was commended to NHS trusts in September 2000 by the NHS Executive (2000) in a NHS circular.

By this circular, chief executives of NHS trusts are required to ensure that appropriate resuscitation policies which respect patients' rights are in place, understood by all relevant staff, and accessible to those who need them, and that such policies are subject to appropriate audit and monitoring arrangements. The action required to be taken by NHS trusts is shown in Table 18.1.

The Healthcare Commission) has been asked by the Secretary of State to pay particular attention to resuscitation decision-making processes as part of its rolling programme of reviews of clinical governance arrangements put in place by NHS organisations. Guidance emphasises that there must be no blanket policies, each individual patient must be assessed personally and policy cannot depend solely on the age of the patient. Since April 2009 the Care Quality Commission has taken over the work of the Healthcare Commission.

Withholding of resuscitation

According to the guidelines, cardiopulmonary resuscitation (CPR) should only be withheld in the following four situations (NHS Executive, 2000):

- The mentally competent patient has refused treatment.
- A valid advance decision (living will), which complies with the statutory provisions for refusing life-sustaining treatment and which covers such circumstances has been made by the patient.

Table 18.1 Resuscitation policies: action to be taken by NHS trusts.

Action to be taken by NHS trusts to ensure:

- Patients' rights are central to decision making on resuscitation

- The trust has an agreed resuscitation policy in place which respects patients' rights

- The policy is published and readily available to those who may wish to consult it, including patients, families and carers

- Appropriate arrangements are in place for ensuring that all staff who may be involved in resuscitation decisions understand and implement the policy

- Appropriate supervision arrangements are in place to review the resuscitation decisions

- Induction and staff development programmes cover the resuscitation policy

- Clinical practice in this area is regularly audited

- Clinical audit outcomes are reported in the trust's annual clinical governance report

- A non-executive director of the trust is given designated responsibility on behalf of the trust board to ensure that a resuscitation policy is agreed, implemented, and regularly reviewed within the clinical governance framework

- Effective CPR is unlikely to be successful.
- Where successful CPR is likely to be followed by a length and quality of life which would not be in the best interests of the patient to sustain.

Table 18.2 provides a matrix showing how the factors of mental competence and prognosis impact on each other in NFR decisions.

A situation may arise where the patient is asking for resuscitation and the medical view is that it would not succeed or the prognosis of the patient is so appalling that it would not be a justification for resources to be used. For example, imagine that in the situation of Ben he is suffering from the final stages of cancer of the pancreas. He asks to be resuscitated, but medical staff know that he has very few days left and in his very poor state of health CPR may not succeed. In such circumstances, while Ben may want the treatment, medical staff may consider that it is unjustified. A patient cannot insist upon treatment which would not be in accordance with the professional judgment of health

Table 18.2 A matrix for not for resuscitation decisions.

Is the patient competent?	No	Yes: patient asks for treatment	Yes: patient refuses treatment
Good prognosis	Resuscitate	Resuscitate	NFR
Bad prognosis	NFR	?*	NFR

*Indicates a situation where the patient is asking for resuscitation and the medical view is that it would not succeed or the prognosis of the patient is so appalling that it would not be a justification for resources to be used.

staff (*Burke* v. *GMC* 2004). This also applies to parents seeking treatment for their child. In the case discussed above (*A National Health Service Trust* v. *D*, 2000), the court held that the decision by doctors that a child should not be placed upon a ventilator was not an infringement of the child's right to life and parents could not compel the doctors to act contrary to their professional discretion.

Withholding and withdrawing life saving treatment in children

Parents of children under 18 years of age do have decision-making rights on behalf of the child, as long as such decisions are in the best interests of the child. Guidance has been issued by the Royal College of Paediatric and Child Health (RCPCH, 1997 reissued 2004). The Royal College identified five situations in which withholding or withdrawing treatment may be considered:

- The brain dead child
- The permanent vegetative state
- The 'no chance' situation
- The 'no purpose' situation
- The 'unbearable' situation

At the present time there are no clear guidelines as to when the approval of the court should be sought for withholding or withdrawing of treatment in a child, and in practice it is probably only where there is a dispute between parents and physicians or surgeons or a third party wishes to seek a court review of what is being proposed in relation to the treatment or non-treatment of a child that an application is made to court. In the case of *Re J* (1992), the baby suffered from a severe form of cerebral palsy with cortical blindness and severe epilepsy. The Court of Appeal held that the court would not exercise its inherent jurisdiction over minors by ordering a medical practitioner to treat the minor in a manner contrary to the practitioner's clinical judgement. In the practitioner's view, intensive therapeutic measures such as artificial ventilation were inappropriate. The Court of Appeal declared that it would be lawful for doctors in their professional judgment to allow a severely disabled child to die. The many court appearances in the dispute between clinicians and the parents of Charlotte Wyatt illustrate the difficulties which can arise in determining the best interests of a severely disabled child. (Wyatt, 2005) For further information on this subject see Dimond (2008, Chapter 14). See also Chapter 10.

Conclusion

The guidance from the Resuscitation Council and other bodies and from the DoH should be of considerable assistance to health professionals, who are entitled to request that any NFR instructions are in writing and that each patient is individually assessed. Such blanket policies as 'patients over 80 are not for resuscitation' are illegal. The Healthcare Commission (and from April 2009 the Care Quality Commission) has a duty to ensure that NFR policies are in place and are being implemented and this should ensure the protection of patients' rights and also the benefit of staff.

References

A National Health Service Trust v. *D* (2000) *The Times Law Report* 19 July.

BMA, Resuscitation Council, RCN (1999) *Decisions Relating to Cardiopulmonary Resuscitation*. BMA, London

BMA/RCN/Resuscitation Council (UK) (2007) *Decisions Relating to Cardiopulmonary Resuscitation. A Joint Statement from the British Medical Association, the Resuscitation Council (UK) and the Royal College of Nursing*. BMA/RCN/Resuscitation Council (UK), London.

Bolam v. *Friern Barnet Management Committee* [1957] 1 WLR 582.

Dimond, B. C. (2008) *Legal Aspects of Nursing*, 5th edn. Pearson Education, Harlow.

NHS Executive (2000) *Resuscitation Policy* HSC 2000/028 September. NHS Executive, London.

NHS Trust A v. *Mrs M* and *NHS Trust B* v. *Mrs H* Family Division *The Times* 25 October 2000; [2001] 1 All ER 801; [2001] 2 F.L.R. 367.

Re F (mental patient: sterilisation) [1990] 2 AC 1.

Re J (a minor) (wardship, medical treatment) [1992] 4 All ER 614

Re MB (adult medical treatment) [1997] 2 FLR 426.

R (on the application of Burke) v. *GMC and Disability Rights Commission and the Official Solicitor to the Supreme Court* [2004] EWHC 1879; [2004] LRM 451.

Royal College of Paediatric and Child Health (1997 reissued 2004) *Withholding or Withdrawing Life Saving Treatment in Children; a Framework for Practice.* RCPCH, London.

Re T (adult: refusal of medical treatment) [1992] 4 All ER 649, (1992) 9 BMLR 46 CA.

The Times (2000) Frances Gibb: Rights Act does not bar mercy killing. *The Times* 26 October 2000.

Wyatt v. *Portsmouth Hospital NHS Trust* [2005] EWCA Civ 1181.

CHAPTER 19

Issues relating to euthanasia

Box 19.1 Case scenario

Norah was in the terminal stages of cancer. She lived with her single daughter, Jane, and was being cared for by Macmillan nurses who came to see her daily. She was on a high level of morphine but still suffered considerable pain. A consultant in palliative care visited her to reassess her medication levels, but Norah found that the new medication still left her with considerable discomfort and pain. Norah asked her daughter to help her end her life. What is the law?

Introduction

In contrast to the Netherlands and Switzerland, the laws of this country make it a criminal offence to assist another person to die. Any person involved in the death of another could face a charge of murder or manslaughter and the Suicide Act 1961 creates a specific offence where a person assists or attempts to assist in the death of another person. This offence arises even when the victim has made the request for help with full mental capacity. The consent of that individual does not constitute a defence to any of these offences. These offences will be considered in the light of Norah's situation in Box 19.1.

Murder

The definition of murder derives from a 17th century case:

> Murder is when a man of sound memory, and of the age of discretion, unlawfully killeth within any country of the realm any reasonable

creature in rerum natura under the King's peace, with malice afore-
thought, either expressed by the party or implied by law, so as the party
wounded, or hurt, etc. die of the wound or hurt, etc...

(Sir Edward Coke, 1797, cited in Dine and Gobert, 2000)

The original definition set a time limit of a year and a day in which the
person must die of the wound or hurt. This limitation of time was removed in
1996. If, therefore, Norah's daughter Jane was to comply with Norah's wishes
and end her life deliberately she could be found guilty of murder. In this case,
at the present time, a judge has no discretion following a plea or conviction of
guilty of murder, other than to sentence the accused to life imprisonment, but
there are recommendations that the judge can make about parole dates.

Manslaughter

In certain circumstances what would have been a crime of murder may be
reduced to manslaughter. Manslaughter is divided into two categories: voluntary and involuntary. Voluntary covers the situation where there is the mental
intention to kill or complete disregard as to the possibility that death could
arise from one's actions, i.e. there is the mental requirement (*mens rea*) but
there are extenuating factors. For example:

- Provocation
- Death in pursuance of a suicide pact
- Diminished responsibility

The effect of these extenuating facts is that a murder verdict could not be
obtained, but the defendant could be guilty of voluntary manslaughter.

Involuntary manslaughter exists when the *mens rea* (i.e. the mental element) for murder is absent. Such circumstances would include:

- Gross negligence
- Killing recklessly may or may not be insufficient to be murder
- An intention to escape from lawful arrest
  Defences to a charge of murder or manslaughter include:
- Killing in carrying out the sentence of the court
- Killing in the course of preventing crime or arresting offenders
- Killing in the defence of one's own person or that of another
- Killing in defence of property

Use of excessive force will negate the defence of protecting one's own person or that of another or defending property.

Where the accused is convicted of manslaughter the judge has complete discretion over sentencing, in contrast to where there is a murder conviction.

Reforms are contained in the Coroners and Justice Bill which if enacted would change the the laws relating to manslaughter.

If Norah were to be given a lethal injection by Jane, that action would probably constitute murder, but Jane may succeed in obtaining a plea of not guilty of murder but guilty of manslaughter by reason of diminished responsibility.

In the case presented in Box 19.2 (R v. Cox, 1992) the doctor was found guilty of attempted murder. It is noticeable that in this case Dr Cox was not charged with murder. Had he been so and found guilty of that, then the judge would have had no choice other than to impose a sentence of life imprisonment. Dr Cox also faced proceedings before the professional conduct committee of the General Medical Council and before his employers, Wessex Regional Health Authority. The case came to light because a nurse, in fulfilment of her professional duty, reported to senior management the fact that potassium chloride had been administered. Management then brought in the police. As the case of Dr Cox shows, voluntary euthanasia, by which is meant the killing of a person with that person's consent, is unlawful. The fact that the patient had pleaded with the doctor for her life to be ended was not a defence against attempted murder.

Box 19.2 The case of Dr Cox (*R* v. *Cox*, 1992)

Lillian Boyes, an elderly patient, suffered from rheumatoid arthritis. She was in extreme pain and was terminally ill. She asked her consultant Dr Cox and others to kill her. Dr Cox administered a lethal dose of potassium chloride and she died almost immediately. He was prosecuted for attempted murder and convicted. The judge gave him a suspended prison sentence.

The outcome in the case of Dr Cox can be contrasted with a case where a husband killed his wife who was suffering from motor neurone disease (see below).

Assistance in a suicide bid

If the act of the person in causing a person's death amounts to assistance in a suicide bid, then it is illegal under section 2(1) of the Suicide Act 1961, which is shown in Box 19.3.

> ## Box 19.3 Suicide Act 1961, relating to assisting a person to commit suicide
>
> A person who aids, abets, counsels or procures the suicide of another or an attempt by another to commit suicide, shall be liable on conviction on indictment to imprisonment (up to 14 years).

If Norah were able to end her own life without the assistance of any other person it would not be a criminal offence. Before the Suicide Act 1961 any person who attempted to commit suicide and failed could be prosecuted for the attempt to take their own life (of course, if they succeeded, they were beyond the reach of the laws of this country). The Suicide Act 1961 made it no longer a criminal offence to attempt to commit suicide, but retained the criminal offences of aiding and abetting another person's suicide.

The situation is therefore that if Norah succeeds in taking her own life without the involvement of any other person, then no crime has been committed. Yet, if Jane helps her in any way at all – and it will be noted that the words 'aids', 'abets', 'counsels', 'procures' or 'attempts' any such action are extremely wide in meaning, then such help would constitute an offence under the Suicide Act 1961. The words used in the Act would cover Jane obtaining a publication giving advice on suicide, or leaving tablets by Norah's bed if she knew that Norah wanted to take her own life, and any other form of encouragement or assistance by Jane. The Coroners and Justice Bill currently being debated in Parliament would replace section 2(1) of the Suicide Act 1961 and add in more provisions to clarify the law relating to assisted suicide.

Letting die and killing

While assisting a person to die is illegal in this country, it may in certain circumstances be lawful to allow a person to die, i.e. to let nature take its course. This could arise where either a mentally capacitated person had refused treatment or it was considered to be in the best interests of the person to be allowed to die.

The Tony Bland case (*Airedale NHS Trust* v. *Bland* [1993]) is an example where the House of Lords held that it was in the best interests of this person, who was in a persistent vegetative state, to be allowed to die and for the artificial feeding to cease. Where the patient has the necessary mental capacity, then he or she is entitled to refuse life-saving treatment. Thus Norah could refuse any further treatment in the hope that she would die quicker. As a result of the Mental Capacity Act 2005 statutory provisions now determine how best interests are defined. The MCA provides that where the decision relates to life-sustaining treatment, then the decision maker must not, in considering whether the treatment is in the best interests of the person concerned, be motivated by a desire to bring about his death.

Treatment which reduces life expectancy

Since Norah is in extreme pain it may be necessary to increase her level of morphine to such a point that the medication will actually reduce her life expectancy. However, if the intention is to control her pain and not to bring about her death, and the level of medication is in accordance with reasonable medical practice, then giving her medication would not constitute a criminal offence of murder or manslaughter. The dose level would have to accord with the Bolam Test (*Bolam* v. *Friern Barnet HMC* [1957]) as to what is reasonable practice.

This issue arose in the trial of Dr Bodkin Adams who was charged with the murder of an elderly woman who was receiving 24 hour nursing care in Eastbourne by giving her excessive amounts of morphine (*R* v. *Adams (Bodkin)* [1957]). The trial judge made it clear to the jury that a doctor has a duty to care for a dying patient and is able to ensure that the patient is given appropriate pain relief, even if the effect of the medication is to reduce the life expectancy of the patient. If, however, the doctor administered medication with the intention of reducing the life of the patient that would be unlawful.

The Netherlands

Several countries have brought in legislation to decriminalise voluntary euthanasia, so that a mentally competent person who is dying can have assistance in ending his or her life which is recognised as lawful. In the Netherlands (Battin, 1992), for example, a doctor will not be prosecuted if he or she has assisted a dying person to die, provided that the doctor has followed specific requirements, including obtaining the written consent of a mentally capacitated patient.

Switzerland

In recent years, patients with terminal illnesses have sought end of life assistance from a hospital in Switzerland. Dignitas, the centre for assisted dying in Zurich, released figures in October 2008 that over 100 Britons had travelled to the clinic to end their lives (Gibb, 2008a). The number included a 23-year-old man, Daniel James, who had been paralysed by a rugby injury. He was not terminally ill, but he found life to be unbearable and attempted suicide several times. His parents assisted him in his journey to the Swiss clinic. At the time of writing police are investigating the circumstances (Brown, 2008).

The case of Diane Pretty (R. (On the application of Pretty) v. DPP [2001])

In a well-publicised case, Diane Pretty, a sufferer of motor neurone disease, appealed to the House of Lords that her husband should be allowed to end her life and not be prosecuted under the Suicide Act 1961. The House of Lords did not allow her appeal. It held that if there were to be any changes to the Suicide Act to legalise the killing of another person, then these changes should be made by Parliament.

As the law stood, the Suicide Act made it a criminal offence to aid and abet the suicide of another person and the husband could not be granted immunity from prosecution were he to assist his wife to die. The House of Lords held that there was no conflict between the human rights of Mrs Pretty as set out in the European Convention on Human Rights (see Chapter 1 of this book). Mrs Pretty then applied to the European Court of Human Rights in Strasbourg, but the European Court of Human Rights did not find in her favour.

It held that there was no conflict between the Suicide Act 1961 and the European Convention of Human Rights. The Council of Europe issued a press release entitled 'Chamber judgement in the case of *Pretty* v. *the United Kingdom*' published on 29 April 2002. It stated that the European Court of Human Rights had refused an application by Diane Pretty, a British national dying of motor neurone disease, for a ruling that would allow her husband to assist her to commit suicide without facing prosecution under the Suicide Act 1961 section 2(1). The applicant was paralysed from the neck downwards and had a poor life expectancy, whilst her intellect and decision-making capacity remained unimpaired. She wanted to be given the right to decide when and how she died without undergoing further suffering and indignity. The court unanimously found the application inadmissible, with no violations under the

European Convention of Human Rights under Art. 2 the right to life, Art. 3 prohibition of human or degrading treatment or punishment; Art. 8 the right to respect for private life; Art. 9 freedom of conscience and Art. 14 prohibition of discrimination.

It was subsequently reported that Diane Pretty had died.

The case of Debbie Purdy (R. (On the application of Purdy) v. DPP [2008])

The legality of the help given by relatives in accompanying these patients to the clinic in Switzerland was considered in a case brought in October 2008 by Debbie Purdy, a member of Dignitas. She was diagnosed as suffering from multiple sclerosis in 1995 and had been a wheelchair user since 2001. She sought a declaration that the Crown Prosecution Service should issue guidelines on the circumstances in which prosecutions for assisted suicide were likely. Such guidelines exist for crimes of domestic violence and driving and football-related offences. She specifically wanted a ruling on whether her husband would be immune from prosecution if he were to take her to the Swiss clinic for her life to be ended. She argued that the uncertainty of prosecution meant that she might have to go to the clinic to end her life earlier than necessary, because if she left it too late and was unable to go on her own and her husband had to help her then he could face prosecution. She failed in her application. The High Court held that it had great sympathy for Ms Purdy, her husband and others in a similar position to know in advance whether they will face prosecution for doing what many would regard as something that the law should permit, namely to help loved ones to go abroad to end their suffering when they are unable to do it on their own. However, it said that this would involve a change in the law. The offence of suicide is very widely drawn to cover all manner of different circumstances: only Parliament can change it. The court also held that the Code of Practice for Crown Prosecutors issued by the Director of Public Prosecutions, coupled with the general safeguards of administrative law, satisfied human rights convention standards and met the need for clarity and foreseeability and there was no breach of article 8 of the European Convention on Human Rights and the right to private and family life.

Ms Purdy was given leave to appeal to the Court of Appeal and the hearing took place on 19 February 2009 (*R. (on Applic. of Purdy)* v. *DPP* [2008]). The Court of Appeal held that she was not entitled to have the specific guidance she was seeking, but that there were broad circumstances in which aiding and abetting suicide would not be prosecuted. Even if there were a prosecution, the court had power to order that the offender should be discharged and might well question publicly the decision to prosecute. The Court of Appeal also said that it was for Parliament to change the law. On 2 June 2009 she appealed to the House of Lords. A decision was still awaited at the time of writing.

The House of Lords

The House of Lords in a Select Committee report (House of Lords Select Committee on Medical Ethics, 1993–1994) had strongly advocated against any relaxation of the laws which would permit voluntary euthanasia in the UK. This has also been the stance of the Government in its White Paper on decision making on behalf of mentally incapacitated adults (Lord Chancellor, 1999).

Mercy killing

Even though the law treats voluntary euthanasia as a criminal offence, the actual punishment given to offenders depends upon the attitude taken by the judge in sentencing. A conviction for murder, as was noted above, is followed by life imprisonment; the judge has no discretion. However, there have been cases where a person found guilty of manslaughter in a mercy killing situation has been given a non-custodial sentence. For example, in one case (Peek, 2002), Mr Lionel Bailey, the husband of a woman suffering from motor neurone disease, smothered his wife with a pillow to release her from pain. He pleaded guilty to manslaughter on the grounds of diminished responsibility. A plea of not guilty to murder was accepted by the prosecution. The judge sentenced him to a three-year community rehabilitation order. The judge said that

> In my view, the interests of justice do not require me to impose a custodial sentence in this case. I accept that the strain you were under watching a much-loved wife deteriorate due to the cruelty of illness must have been well-nigh unbearable. You were in your 70s, in poor health, and yet continued to do your loving best to care for her as a loyal husband should. That anguish must have been intense. You couldn't bear to see her suffering any longer. I'm sure you did what you did to end her suffering without a thought for yourself and I make that quite plain.

Some have argued that in the light of such judgements, the law should be amended to recognise voluntary euthanasia as lawful. However, it does not follow that because, in some cases, the perpetrators of mercy killing are treated leniently the law recognises such actions as justified. They are still criminal offences and an offender cannot be sure how he or she will be treated by the courts.

Proposals for reform

Since 2002 Lord Joffe has introduced into the House of Lords several Bills which would legalise assisted suicide or assisted dying. A bill for 'Assisted Dying for the Terminally Ill' was introduced by Lord Joffe into Parliament in 2004. This would have enabled a competent adult who is suffering unbearably as a result of a terminal illness to receive medical assistance to die at his own considered and persistent request. It also made provision for a person suffering from such a condition to receive pain relief medication. It was subjected to considerable criticism. A Select Committee of the House of Lords was set up to examine the provisions of the 'Assisted Dying for the Terminally Ill' bill. Its Report (House of Lords Select Committee, 2005) was published in April 2005 and is a comprehensive analysis of the arguments for and against the legalising of voluntary euthanasia. Sixty organisations gave evidence to the Select Committee and it received over 14,000 letters and emails from individuals. The Committee also visited Oregon, the Netherlands and Switzerland, where laws permitted some form of assisted dying.

In November 2005 Lord Joffe introduced an amended Bill, which was described as follows:

> A Bill to enable an adult who has capacity and who is suffering unbearably as a result of a terminal illness to receive medical assistance to die at his own considered and persistent request and for connected purposes.

The Bill covered the following topics:

- Authorisation of assisted dying
- Qualifying conditions
- Declaration
- Duties of attending physician
- Revocation of declaration
- Conscientious objection

- Protection for health care professionals and other persons
- Offences
- Insurance
- Requirements as to documentation in medical records and reporting requirements
- Monitoring commission
- Interpretation
- Power to make orders and regulations
- Amendment of Suicide Act 1961
- Short title and extent

The main provisions of this ill-fated Bill are shown below in italics.

Main provisions of the Assisted Dying for the Terminally Bill 2005

The Bill makes it lawful for a physician to assist a patient who is a qualifying patient to die–

(i) by prescribing such medication, and (ii) in the case of a patient for whom it is impossible or inappropriate orally to ingest that medication, by prescribing and providing such means of self-administration of that medication, as will enable the patient to end his own life. It also legalises a person who is a member of a health care team to work in conjunction with a physician to whom paragraph (a) of this section applies.

Qualifying conditions

There are several qualifying conditions. Two are laid down in relation to the attending physician and the consultant physician. In addition, the patient must have the mental capacity necessary to make the request for assistance to die, and must have drawn up a written declaration.

Attending physician

The first condition places obligations upon the attending physician.
The attending physician shall have–

(a) been informed by the patient in a written request signed by the patient that the patient wishes to be assisted to die;

(b) examined the patient and the patient's medical records and satisfied himself that the patient does not lack capacity;

(c) determined that the patient has a terminal illness;

(d) concluded that the patient is suffering unbearably as a result of that terminal illness ('unbearable suffering' means suffering whether by reason of pain, distress or otherwise which the patient finds so severe as to be unacceptable);

(e) informed the patient of–
    (i)   his medical diagnosis;
    (ii) his prognosis;
    (iii) the process of being assisted to die; and
    (iv) the alternatives to assisted dying, including, but not limited to, palliative care, care in a hospice and the control of pain;

(f) ensured that a specialist in palliative care, who shall be a physician or a nurse, has attended the patient to inform the patient of the benefits of the various forms of palliative care;

(g) recommended to the patient that the patient notifies his next of kin of his request for assistance to die;

(h) if the patient persists with his request to be assisted to die, satisfied himself that the request is made voluntarily and that the patient has made an informed decision; and

(i) referred the patient to a consulting physician.

Terminal illness *is defined as:*

an illness which in the opinion of both the attending and the consulting physician–

(a) is inevitably progressive,

(b) cannot be reversed by treatment (although treatment may be successful in relieving symptoms temporarily), and

(c) will be likely to result in the patient's death within six months.

Consulting physician

The second condition is that the consulting physician shall have–

(a) been informed by the patient that the patient wishes to be assisted to die;

(b) examined the patient and the patient's medical records and satisfied himself that the patient does not lack capacity;

(c) confirmed the diagnosis and prognosis made by the attending physician;

(d) concluded that the patient is suffering unbearably as a result of the terminal illness;

(e) informed the patient of the alternatives to assisted dying including, but not limited to, palliative care, care in a hospice and the control of pain;

(f) if the patient still persists with his request to be assisted to die, satisfied himself that the request is made voluntarily and that the patient has made an informed decision; and

(g) advised the patient that prior to being assisted to die the patient will be required to complete a declaration which the patient can revoke.

Definition of lack of capacity

For the purposes of the Bill, a person lacks capacity in relation to being assisted to die if at the material time he is unable to make a decision for himself in relation to that matter because of an impairment of, or a disturbance in the functioning of, the mind or brain resulting from any disability or disorder of the mind or brain.

Determination of lack of capacity

If, in the opinion of either the attending or the consulting physician, a patient who wishes to make a declaration may lack capacity, the attending physician shall refer the patient to a consultant psychiatrist, or a psychologist, who shall be independent of the attending and consulting physicians, for an opinion as to the patient's capacity.

No assistance to end the patient's life may be given unless the consultant psychiatrist or the psychologist has determined that the patient does not lack capacity.

Declaration

(1) When the qualifying conditions have been met, a patient who wishes to be assisted to die must make a declaration of his wish to die in the form prescribed by regulations made by the Secretary of State.

(2) The declaration must be witnessed by two individuals one of whom shall be either a solicitor who holds a current practising certificate or a public notary.

(3) The solicitor or public notary may only witness the declaration if–
  (a) the patient is personally known to, or has proved his identity to, him;
  (b) it appears to him that the patient is of sound mind and has made the declaration voluntarily; and
  (c) he is satisfied that the patient understands the effect of the declaration.
(4) The patient and witnesses shall sign and witness the declaration respectively at the same time and each in the presence of the others.
(5) Neither the attending or consulting physician, nor a member of the health care team, a consultant psychiatrist or a psychologist consulted under section 3, nor a relative or partner (by blood, marriage or adoption) of the patient who wishes to be assisted to die, may witness the declaration.
(6) No person who owns, operates or is employed at a health care establishment where the patient is a resident or is receiving medical treatment may witness the declaration.

Duties of assisting physician

(1) The assisting physician shall be either the attending physician or the consulting physician.
(2) The assisting physician shall not take any action to assist the patient to die until after the expiration of a period of 14 days from the date on which the patient informed the attending physician under section 2(2)(a) that the patient wished to be assisted to die.
(3) Before taking any step to assist the patient to die the existing physician shall have–
  (a) informed the patient of his right to revoke the declaration, and
  (b) asked the patient to confirm that the declaration has not been revoked, and received such confirmation.

Revocation of declaration

A patient may revoke his declaration orally or in any other manner and irrespective of his physical or mental state. In the event of a declaration being revoked, the assisting physician, or if there is no assisting physician, the attending physician, shall ensure that a note recording its revocation is made on the patient's file.

Conscientious objection

No person shall be under any duty to participate in any diagnosis, treatment or other action authorised by this Act, apart from subsection (6), to which he has a conscientious objection.

No hospice, hospital, nursing home, clinic or other health care establishment shall be under any obligation to permit an assisted death on its premises. No person shall be under any duty to raise the option of assisted dying with a patient, to refer a patient to any other source for obtaining information or advice pertaining to assistance to die, or to refer a patient to any other person for assistance to die under the provisions of this Act.

If an attending physician whose patient makes a request to be assisted to die in accordance with this Act has a conscientious objection as provided in subsection (1), the patient shall be free to consult another physician who does not have a conscientious objection and who, for the purposes of this Act, shall then be the patient's attending physician. If a consulting physician to whom a patient has been referred in accordance with section 2(2)(i) has a conscientious objection as provided in subsection (1), the patient shall be free to consult another consulting physician who does not have a conscientious objection and who, for the purposes of this Act, shall then be the patient's consulting physician. (6) Where a patient has consulted a physician under subsection (4) or (5) the physician who has a conscientious objection shall immediately, on receipt of a request to do so, transfer the patient's medical records to the new physician.

Protection for health care professionals and other persons

A physician who assists a qualifying patient to die, or attempts to do so, in accordance with the requirements of this Act, shall not, by so doing, be guilty of an offence. A member of a health care team who works in conjunction with a physician who assists a qualifying patient to die, or attempts to do so, in accordance with the requirements of this Act, or in reliance on information supplied to him that the requirements of this Act in relation to the patient had been fully complied with, shall not by so doing be guilty of an offence. A person who is present when–

(a) a qualifying patient dies, having received assistance to die, or
(b) an attempt is made to assist a qualifying patient to die,

shall not be guilty of an offence provided that he is present in reliance on information provided to him that the requirements of this Act in relation to the patient have been complied with.

(4) A physician to whom subsection (1) of this section applies or a member of a health care team to whom subsection (2) of this section applies, shall be deemed not to be in breach of any professional oath or affirmation.

(5) No physician, psychiatrist, psychologist or member of a health care team may take any part in assisting a qualifying patient to die, or in giving an opinion in respect of such a patient, nor may any person act as a witness, if he has grounds for believing that he will benefit financially or in any other way, except for his proper professional fees or salary, as a result of the death of that patient.

Offences

A person commits an offence if he wilfully falsifies or forges a declaration made or purporting to be made under section 4 with the intent or effect of causing the patient's death and shall be liable, on conviction on indictment, to imprisonment for life.

A person commits an offence if he makes a statement as a witness to a declaration made, or purporting to be made, under section 4 that he knows to be false.

A person commits an offence if he wilfully conceals or destroys a declaration.

A physician, psychiatrist, psychologist, or member of a health care team who takes any part in assisting a qualifying patient to die, or who gives an opinion in respect of such a patient, and who has grounds for believing that he will benefit financially or in any other way, except for his proper professional fees or salary, as the result of the death of that patient, contrary to section 8(5) commits an offence.

A person guilty of an offence under subsections (3) to (5) shall be liable on conviction on indictment to imprisonment for a period not exceeding five years or a fine or both.

No provision of this Act shall be taken to affect a person's liability on conviction to criminal penalties for conduct which is inconsistent with the provisions of this Act.

Insurance

No policy of insurance which has been in force for 12 months as at the date of the patient's death shall be invalidated by reason of a physician having assisted a qualifying patient to die in accordance with this Act.

Requirements as to documentation in medical records and reporting requirements

The assisting physician shall ensure that the following are documented and filed in the patient's medical records—

(a) all evidence, data and records which demonstrate that the qualifying conditions have been met;

(b) any written request by the patient for assistance to end his life;

(c) the declaration; and

(d) a note by the assisting physician stating that he was satisfied, at the date and time of his having assisted the patient to die, that all requirements under this Act had been met and indicating the steps taken to end the patient's life including the description and quantity of the medication and any means of self-administration prescribed or provided.

The assisting physician shall send a copy of each of the documents referred to in subsection (1) of this section to the monitoring commission for the region concerned within seven days of the qualifying patient having been assisted to die or of an attempt so to assist having been made.

Monitoring commission

The Secretary of State shall by order establish such number of monitoring commissions covering regions forming parts of England and Wales as he may determine, to review the operation of this Act and to hold and monitor records maintained pursuant to this Act.

A monitoring commission shall consist of three members appointed by the Secretary of State, of whom—

(a) one shall be a registered medical practitioner;

(b) one shall be a solicitor or barrister; and

(c) one shall be a lay person having first hand experience in caring for a person with a terminal illness.

If, in relation to documents sent to a monitoring commission in accordance with section 11(2), two of its members consider that the qualifying conditions have not been met, the declaration had not been validly made or had been revoked, or that the requirements of this Act had not been complied with, the monitoring commission shall refer the matter to the district coroner.

A monitoring commission to which documents have been sent in accordance with section 11(2) shall confirm to the assisting physician concerned whether all the requirements of this Act have been complied with as soon as reasonably possible after the date of receiving such notification of the patient having been assisted to die or of an attempt so to assist having been made.

The Secretary of State shall publish an annual statistical report of information collected under this section.

Power to make orders and regulations

(1) The Secretary of State may at any time by order make such supplementary, incidental, consequential or transitional provision as appears to him to be necessary or expedient for the general or particular purposes of this Act or in consequence of any of its provisions or for giving full effect to it.

(2) The Secretary of State may make regulations under this Act–

(a) determining classes of persons who may or may not witness a declaration;

(b) regulating the custody of records and the collection of information regarding the operation of this Act;

(c) making provision about appointments to and the operation of the monitoring commissions; and

(d) providing a code of practice for the guidance of physicians, members of health care teams and other persons acting in accordance with the provisions of this Act.

(3) The power to make orders and regulations under this Act is exercisable by statutory instrument and includes power to make different provision for different cases.

(4) A statutory instrument containing regulations made under section 4(1) is subject to annulment in pursuance of a resolution of either House of Parliament and no other statutory instrument may be made under this Act unless a draft of the instrument has been laid before, and approved by a resolution of, each House of Parliament.

The Suicide Act 1961 is amended *by inserting after subsection (3)–*

'(3A) Subsection (1) does not apply where a person assists another person to die, or where a person helps another person to assist a third person to die, or where a person is present when another person ends his own life or attempts to do so, in accordance with sections 1 and 8 of the Assisted Dying for the Terminally Ill Act 2005.'

In spite of the many amendments to earlier Bills and the provisions to ensure that the person has the requisite mental capacity to decide to end their life and the restriction of the protection to a terminal illness situation, the Bill was talked out by the House of Lords and failed to be enacted.

Conclusion

At present the law is clear: health professionals cannot deliberately shorten the lives of their patients or assist them in a suicide attempt. They must, however, respect the wishes of their mentally capacitated patients to refuse treatment and where patients lack the mental capacity and their prognosis is appalling or they are in a situation such as persistent vegetative state, then they can, if it is in their best interests, be allowed to die. They also have a duty of care to the patient to use the appropriate level of pain medication, even if this were incidentally to shorten the patient's life. However, there are clear advantages in seeking the views of the court in the latter circumstances, and in the case of patients in a persistent vegetative state (PVS), a Practice Direction (Practice Note [1996]) was issued by the courts requiring a court declaration to be sought before any life saving procedures can be withdrawn. Subsequently, new guidance has been issued which incorporates this 1996 guidance as well as guidance on sterilisation of mentally incapacitated adults (see Chapter 7). (Practice Note [2001]) The Mental Capacity Act 2005 applies since October 2007 and applications should be made to the Court of Protection for a determination as to the best interests of the patient. For decisions relating to the withholding or withdrawing of treatment in children see Chapter 18 of this book. As a consequence of the Purdy decision, Lord Joffe has indicated his intention to reintroduce a bill so that the family and friends who wished to help to end their loved ones' suffering knew whether or not they were committing an offence. At the present time the chances of success of further attempts by Lord Joffe and others to obtain legislation permitting assisted suicide would seem to be dubious. The Coroners and Justice Bill contains provisions to amend the law relating to manslaughter and assisted suicide, and proposals to legalise the assistance given by relatives and friends to those who wish to end their lives are being debated at the time of writing.

References

Airedale NHS Trust v. *Bland* [1993] 1 All ER 821.

Battin, M. (1992) Voluntary euthanasia and the risk of abuse: can we learn anything from the Netherlands. *Law Med Health Care*, **20**(1–2), 133–43.

Bolam v. *Friern Barnet HMC* [1957] 2 All ER 118.

Brown, D. (2008) Paralysed in a scrum, rugby player chose assisted death at age of 23. *The Times*. 18 October, p. 4.

Dine, J. and Gobert, J. (2000) *Cases and Materials on Criminal Law*, 3rd edn. Blackstone Press, London.

Gibb, F. (2008) Swiss clinic has helped 100 Britons to die. *The Times*, 2 October, p. 5.

House of Lords Select Committee on Medical Ethics (1993–1994) HL Paper 21, House of Lords Select Committee on Medical Ethics, London.

House of Lords Select Committee (2005) on the Assisted Dying for the Terminally Ill Bill HL Paper 86-1, 4 April 2005. The Stationery Office, London.

Lord Chancellor (1999) *Making Decisions: The Government's Proposals for Making Decisions on Behalf of Mentally Incapacitated Adults*. The Stationery Office, London

Peek, L. (2002) Mercy for husband who killed wife in pain. *The Times*, 7 September.

Practice Note [1996] (Official Solicitor to the Supreme Court: Vegetative State); [1996] 4 All ER 766; [1996] 2 F.L.R. 375.

Practice Note [2001] (Official Solicitor: Declaratory Proceedings: Medical and Welfare Proceedings for Adults who lack Capacity) [2001] 2 F.L.R. 158; [2001] 2 F.C.R. 94.

Pretty v. *United Kingdom ECHR*. The full judgement is available on http://www.echr. coe.int/Eng/Press/apr/Prettyjudepress.htm. (Current Law 380 June 2002).

R. (On the application of Pretty) v. *DPP* [2001] UKHL 61 [2001] 3 WLR 1598.

R. (On the application of Purdy) v. *DPP* [2008]) *The Times Law Report* 17 November 2008; [2009] EWCA Civ 92.

R v. *Cox* (1992) 12 BMLR 38. Winchester Crown Court.

R v. *Adams (Bodkin)* [1957] Crim LR 365.

CHAPTER 20

Research and the mentally competent adult

Box 20.1 Case scenario

Sylvia was admitted to hospital for a hysterectomy. Before the operation, she agreed to take part in a research project designed to test the effectiveness of different forms of operative care, and understood that some additional tissue would be removed. The day after the operation she suffered from extreme pain and felt sure that this was because of the additional procedure undertaken. She now regrets agreeing to participate in the research and is wondering what action she can take. What is the law?

Introduction

Research-based, clinically effective practice is becoming part of the reasonable standard of care, and over the next few years there will be increasing pressure to ensure that every activity, task and item of care and treatment by all health professionals is subjected to scientific analysis as to its effectiveness. Research activities will therefore become an increasingly important part of health care, and there is additional pressure for those who use complementary or alternative therapies to prove that these are effective.

Nursing staff will increasingly find that they are caring for patients who are research subjects. In addition, nurses will have to keep abreast of research findings to ensure that their professional practice accords with approved clinically effective practice. The National Institute for Health and Clinical Excellence (NICE), through its publications, promotes research-based practice.

In this chapter we consider the law which applies to research involving mentally competent adults. The next chapter examines issues relating to children and mentally incapacitated adults in the context of the law on consent.

Principles of consent to research participation

To be valid, consent to participation in research by mentally competent people must be given voluntarily, without coercion or deceit, and in the light of information about the risks of significant harm arising from the research. People should have the right to withdraw from the research when they wish (this, however, would be subject to ensuring that they did not suffer as a result of the withdrawal). They should not suffer any discrimination as a result of their wish to withdraw from, or refuse to participate in, the research. These basic principles are recognised by case law (i.e. common law, judge made law) in this country. An EC Directive (EC Directive 2001/20/EC (Medicines for Human Use)) relating to medicines research with clinical trials has been incorporated into the UK law and subjects in research projects are entitled to ensure that their human rights are respected. There are several international codes or conventions which are recognised by professional organisations in this country, but these codes have not been incorporated into the laws of this country, unlike the European Convention on Human Rights, which came into force in England, Wales and Northern Ireland on 2 October 2000, and in Scotland on devolution.

International conventions

Nuremberg Code

At the end of the Second World War, military trials were held in Nuremberg where some of the worst perpetrators of crimes against humanity in the Nazi party were prosecuted. In its judgment, the court set out 10 basic principles which should be observed in order to satisfy moral, ethical and legal concepts. These have become known as the Nuremberg Code (Kennedy and Grubb, 2000) (Table 20.1).

Declaration of Helsinki

The World Medical Association published a Declaration of Helsinki in 1964 which set out principles for the carrying out research on human subjects. Amendments were made in 2000 following a conference in Edinburgh (Euro-

Table 20.1 Research principles from the Nuremberg Code (source: http://www.ushmm.org/research/doctors/Nuremberg_Code.htm).

- The voluntary consent of the human subject is absolutely essential.

- The experiment should be such as to yield fruitful results for the good of society, unprocurable by other methods.

- The experiment should be based on results of animal experiments and a knowledge of the natural history of the disease or other problem so that the anticipated results should justify the performance of the experiment.

- The experiment should be so conducted as to avoid all unnecessary physical and mental suffering and injury.

- No experiment should be conducted where there is an *a priori* reason to believe that death or disabling injury will occur; except, perhaps, in those circumstances where the experimental physicians also serve as subjects.

- The degree of risk to be taken should never exceed that determined by the humanitarian importance of the problem to be solved by the experiment.

- Proper preparations should be made and adequate facilities provided to protect the experimental subject against even remote possibilities of injury, disability or death.

- The experiment should be conducted only by a scientifically qualified person.

- The highest degree of skill and care should be required through all stages of the experiment of those who conduct or engage in the experiment.

- During the course of the experiment the human subject should be at liberty to bring the experiment to an end if he has reached the physical or mental state where continuation of the experiment seems to him to be impossible.

- During the course of the experiment the scientist in charge must be prepared to terminate the experiment at any stage, if he has probable cause to believe, in the exercise of the good faith, superior skill and careful judgment required of him that a continuation of the experiment is likely to result in injury, disability, or death to the experimental subject.

Table 20.2 Clauses in the Declaration of Helsinki relating to research.

5. In medical research on human subjects, considerations related to the wellbeing of the human subject should take precedence over the interests of science and society.

6. The primary purpose of medical research involving human subjects is to improve prophylactic, diagnostic and therapeutic procedures and the understanding of the aetiology and pathogenesis of disease. Even the best proven prophylactic, diagnostic, and therapeutic methods must continuously be challenged through research for their effectiveness, efficiency, accessibility and quality.

7. In current medical practice and in medical research, most prophylactic, diagnostic and therapeutic procedures involve risks and burdens.

8. Medical research is subject to ethical standards that promote respect for all human beings and protect their health and rights. Some research populations are vulnerable and need special protection. The particular needs of the economically and medically disadvantaged must be recognised. Special attention is also required for those who cannot give or refuse consent for themselves, for those who may be subject to giving consent under duress, for those who will not benefit personally from the research and for those for whom the research is combined with care.

9. Research investigators should be aware of the ethical, legal and regulatory requirements for research on human subjects in their own countries as well as applicable international requirements. No national, ethical, legal or regulatory requirement should be allowed to reduce or eliminate any of the protections for human subjects set forth in this Declaration.

pean Forum for Good Clinical Practice, 1999). The principle clauses in this declaration relating to consent are shown in Table 20.2.

Convention on Human Rights and Biomedicine

A Convention for the Protection of Human Rights and Dignity of the Human Being with Regard to the Application of Biology and Medicine: Convention on Human Rights and Biomedicine (Council of Europe, 1997) also sets principles for the conduct of research.

Local research ethic committees (LRECS)

The Department of Health (DoH) requested each health authority to ensure that an LREC was set up to examine research proposals (DoH Local Research Ethics Committees, 1991). Any NHS body asked to agree a research proposal falling within its sphere of responsibility should ensure that it has been submitted to the appropriate LREC for research ethics approval. Guidance is provided on every aspect of its work, including the special procedure for multicentre research (King's College, 1997).

In certain cases, multicentre research ethics committees (MRECs), established by the DoH, oversee research which is carried on across several LREC catchment areas. Where fewer than five LRECs are involved, one LREC can act on behalf of the others. The role of the LREC is defined as being: 'To consider the ethics of proposed research projects which will involve human subjects and to advise the NHS body concerned' (DoH Local Research Ethics Committees, 1991).

The LREC comprises multidisciplinary members, including lay persons. The Royal College of Physicians published guidelines on the practice of ethics committees (Royal College of Physicians, 1996). Every research project involving patients or their records must be approved by an LREC. The LREC will look at the assessment of risks, if any, to all participants. It will also consider the consent form, the written information given to the patient about the research and ensure that there is justification for the research taking place. Any health professional who is caring for patients who are involved in a research project would be entitled to see evidence of LREC approval.

New provisions for the work and the control of LRECs were put in place in 2002 following new guidelines issued by the Department of Health (2001), which can be accessed on the DH website (http://www.dh.gov.uk/en/Publicationsandstatistics/Publications/PublicationsPolicyAndGuidance/DH_4005727).

How much information should be given to data subjects?

There is justification for believing that people who volunteer for research projects as healthy volunteers who have no immediate benefit from the research should be given more information about any potential risks that a patient who stands to benefit personally from the treatment which is the subject of the research. Such a presumption is based on a distinction between therapeutic and non-therapeutic research. This distinction was recognised in the Helsinki Declaration (i.e. research which is linked with the treatment of the patient being described as 'therapeutic', whereas research which has no immediate benefit to that particular patient is described as 'non-therapeutic').

However, in the discussions which took place between 1998 and 2000 on revisions to the Declaration of Helsinki it was agreed that the distinction should be dropped from the Declaration. In practice the distinction may be important, particularly in the care of children and mentally incapacitated adults, where therapeutic research may be justified in their best interests (see Chapter 21).

The principles set out by the House of Lords in the case of *Sidaway* v. *Bethlem Royal Hospital Governors* [1985] would apply to the giving of information to the subject in a research project, i.e. that the researcher should follow the reasonably accepted practice. However, it could be argued that where a healthy volunteer is offering his or her services, there is no room for the therapeutic privilege of withholding information from the person. The volunteer is entitled to all information about the project. It could also be argued that in the case of the healthy volunteer participating in non-therapeutic research, there would be a duty in law for the researcher to pass on every item of information available to him or her which might affect participation in the research or which might be asked for by the research subject. The General Medical Council (1998) advises its registered members to be sure that anyone asked to take part in the research is given the fullest possible information, presented in terms and in a form that they can understand.

What is meant by voluntary?

In relation to the scenario outlined in Box 20.2, while the pharmaceutical company might consider that £1000 is pin money and unlikely to be an inducement, from Brenda's perspective such wealth and the opportunity to clear her

---

Box 20.2 Inducement to participate in research

Brenda is a single mother dependent on income from social security. She has three children and finds it difficult to manage financially, being over £500 in debt. A local pharmaceutical company is advertising for volunteers for their drug testing programme and offering up to £1000 as inconvenience payments. Brenda decides to volunteer. What is the law?

debts is a significant attraction. To what extent, therefore, can it be said that Brenda has voluntarily consented to the research? According to the DoH Local Research Ethics Committees (1991) guidance:

> Payment in cash or kind to volunteers should only be for expense, time and inconvenience reasonably incurred.

Whether a person is truly a volunteer is a question of the fact of each case. On the facts it would seem that the assessment of the cost of inconvenience in Brenda's case is not related to her economic circumstances. The difficulty, however, is that Brenda may still be prepared to be a volunteer for half or even a quarter of that payment. Perhaps people in Brenda's situation should not be seen as potential volunteers. One could conclude that, in law, Brenda gave full consent to participation in the research, but that the ethical principles laid down in the international codes requiring no inducement have been broken.

Harm suffered by the research subject

The main remedies in law for failures by the researcher are:

- Trespass to the person if there is no consent or consent has been obtained by fraud or duress.
- An action for negligence if there has been a failure to fulfil the duty of care in relation to the safety of the research subject or if there has been a failure to provide reasonable information about the risks which could arise from the research.

Turning to the plight of Sylvia as outlined in Box 20.1, there is no clear evidence that the pain she is suffering from is the result of the research or pain she would have had anyway from that type of operation. At present there is no system of strict liability for those undertaking research. To obtain compensation, Sylvia would have to show, like any other patient claiming compensation for negligence, that she was owed a duty of care, that there was a failure to follow the reasonable standard of care and as a reasonably foreseeable consequence she has suffered harm.

The Royal Commission Report chaired by Lord Pearson (1978) recommended that both volunteers and patients who take part in medical research and clinical trials and who suffer severe damage as a result should receive compensation on the basis of strict liability. This recommendation has never been implemented in law, although the Association of British Pharmaceutical Industry has recommended that such persons should obtain compensation without proof of negligence if harm arose as a result of the research project.

Research ethics committees are required to establish that there has been an agreement to pay compensation before any research on medicinal products takes place. In Sylvia's case it would not appear that a pharmaceutical company is involved, so she would have to pursue a remedy through the courts, with a very dubious chance of success.

Full and informed consent

If we really wish to ensure that volunteers and participants in research projects are fully informed, then there is much to be said for requiring the same high standards of consent as are required of those prepared to donate an organ whilst alive (see Chapter 14). Here specific conditions of consent are required by law (the Human Tissue Act 2004 and regulations made under the Act). Adapting these for the purpose of consent to research we would have the conditions shown in Table 20.3.

Table 20.3 Conditions for giving consent to participation in a research project.

(a) That a registered medical practitioner has given the potential research subject an explanation of the nature of the medical procedure for, and the risk involved in, the research in question

(b) That the potential research subject understands the nature of the medical procedure and the risks, as explained by the registered medical practitioner, and consents to participation in the research in question

(c) That the potential research subject's consent to the participation in the research in question was not obtained by coercion or the offer of an inducement

(d) That the potential research subject understands that he is entitled to withdraw his consent if he wishes, but has not done so

(e) That the potential research subject and the researcher have both been interviewed by a person who appears to the authority to have been suitably qualified to conduct such interviews and who has reported to the authority on the conditions contained in subparagraphs (a)–(d) above and has included in his report an account of any difficulties of communication with the potential research subject or the researcher and an explanation of how those difficulties were overcome

Researchers may well protest that there is considerable difference between a living person donating an organ to someone and a mentally competent person participating in a research project. However, statutory conditions of consent with an external person verifying this might well be justified in the interests of research subjects.

Conclusion

LRECs have a considerable responsibility in ensuring that all research involving patients complies with the law and ethical principles. There would now seem to be justification for legislation to implement the recommendations of the Lord Pearson (1978) report that any person suffering harm during a research project should obtain compensation on the basis of strict liability. In the next chapter we consider the law as it applies to children and mentally incapacitated adults taking part in research.

References

Council of Europe (1997) Convention for the Protection of Human Rights and Dignity of the Human Being with Regard to the Application of Biology and Medicine. 4.iv. Council of Europe http://conventions.coe.int/treaty/en/treaties/html/164.htm

Department of Health (1991) *Local Research Ethics Committees* HSG(91)5. DoH, London

Department of Health (2001) *Governance, Arrangements for NHS Research Ethics Committees* (replaces HSG(91)5 (The Red Book) and HSG(97)23 on multicentre research ethics committees).

European Forum for Good Clinical Practice (1999) *Bulletin of Medical Ethics: revising the Declaration of Helsinki: a fresh start.* Bulletin of Medical Ethics, London

General Medical Council (1998) *Seeking Patients' Consent: The Ethical Considerations.* General Medical Council, London

Kennedy, I. and Grubb, A. (2000) *Medical Law*, 3rd edn. Butterworths, London.

King's College (1997) *Manual for Research Ethics Committees.* Centre for Medical Law and Ethics, King's College, London.

Lord Pearson (1978) *Royal Commission on Civil Liability and Compensation for Personal Injury.* Chaired by Lord Pearson. Cmnd 7054. HMSO, London.

Royal College of Physicians (1996) *Guidelines on the Practice of Ethics Committees in Medicines for Human Use (Clinical Trials)* SI 2004 No 1031 (Amended SI 2006 No 1928 and SI 2006 No 2984.

Medical Research Involving Human Subjects, 3rd edn. Royal College of Physicians, London.

Sidaway v. *Bethlem Royal Hospital Governors* [1985] 1 All ER 643 [1985] AC 871.

CHAPTER 21

Research using children or mentally incapable adults

Box 21.1 Case scenario

James is 10 years old and is suffering from leukaemia. He has had a bone marrow transplant which at first appeared to succeed, but has now failed. The health authority has refused, in the best interests of James, to fund further chemotherapy and a second bone marrow transplant. However, the pioneer of a new treatment for leukaemia has offered to provide treatment for James without any cost to the family. The family is tempted by the possibility of James' life being saved. What is the law?

Introduction

In the last chapter, the basic principles of law which applied to consent by mentally capable adults in research projects were considered. In this chapter we examine the law relating to children and mentally incapable adults and their participation in research projects. It was noted in the previous chapter that there is no statutory scheme for research participation and compensation, but several international codes or conventions are recognised by professional associations in this country. These also apply to research participation by children and mentally incapacitated adults. In addition, the United Nations' Convention on the Rights of the Child protects the rights of the child (United Nations, 1989).

Where patients lack the capacity to make their own decisions, it is considered that different principles arise depending on whether or not the research has therapeutic benefits for the research subject. Thus, although this distinction has been abandoned in the revisions to the Declaration of Helsinki (see Chapter 20), it is submitted that it still has a place where the care of those lacking mental capacity is considered.

Children

The United Nations' Convention on the Rights of the Child and profession guidance

The 1989 United Nations' Convention on the Rights of the Child represents clear guidance for the development of rights-based and child-centred health care. The UK ratified the Convention in 1991. Most health professional organisations have produced guidelines in respect of different aspects of research along the lines of the international conventions. Thus, the Royal College of Paediatrics and Child Health (in its previous identity of the British Paediatric Association) provided a guide to the UN Convention (British Paediatric Association, 1995). Subsequently, the Royal College of Paediatrics and Child Health has published guidelines on clinical research involving newborn babies and infants (Royal College of Paediatrics and Child Health, 1999) and children (Royal College of Paediatrics and Child Health, 2000).

Therapeutic research

Statutory right of 16- and 17-year-olds

Under section 8(1) of the Family Law Reform Act 1969, a young person of 16 or 17 can give a valid consent to medical, dental and surgical treatment (see Chapter 8). Treatment is defined in section 8(2) as including:

> ...any procedure undertaken for the purposes of diagnosis and this section applies to any procedures (including, in particular, the administration of an anaesthetic) which is ancillary to any treatment as it applies to that treatment (Family Law Reform Act 1969, section 8(1)).

There is no mention of participation in research in this definition, so it could be assumed that a young person of 16 or 17 does not have a statutory right to participate in non-therapeutic research as a healthy volunteer. This right might exist at common law (see below), but there could be circumstances where the research is such an integral part of the treatment, i.e. the treatment would proceed anyway, but the researchers want to compare this patient group with another on a different treatment. In this case it could be argued that there would be a statutory right under section 8(1). It all depends upon the ratio of treatment to research in the aims of the health professional.

Common law powers of child to give consent to participation in research

If the statutory right does not apply, then under the Gillick principles (*Gillick* v. *W Norfolk and Wisbech Area Health Authority* [1986]) a youngster of 16 and 17 years may have the mental capacity to give a valid consent to participation in the research project. So also may a child under that age, but clearly the test of competence must cover the capacity to understand any potential risks arising from the research project.

Common law powers of the parents to give consent

If the child stands to benefit from participation in the research, then it is probable that parents could give consent on the child's behalf, providing that such participation was in the child's best interests. This is only likely to apply if the research is therapeutic and therefore part of a treatment plan for that child. If, however, there are recognised existing treatments which work, then it could be argued that participation in unknown treatments carry a risk to which the parent could not give consent on the child's behalf.

Looking at the situation in Box 21.1, it could be argued that the existing treatments have failed, and therefore the parents could give consent on James' behalf to participation in this new pioneering treatment. However, there are many unanswered questions:

- Is James likely to suffer pain and discomfort in participating?
- Do the benefits of the possible success outweigh the risks of harm?
- Since the welfare of James is the paramount consideration, would any court justify participation in his best interests?
- If the health authority had decided against funding more treatment in his best interests, it could apply for James to be made a ward of court, so that the court could decide if it was in the best interests of James for him to participate in the research.

Non-therapeutic research and children

It could be argued that parents have no right to make any decision which is not in the best interests of their children. It would therefore follow that they could not give consent to the child's participation in research as a healthy volunteer whatever the level of risk. In a sense this is to deny a child the right of being altruistic. Only if a child was competent according to the guidelines set by Lord Fraser in the Gillick case and had the requisite level of competence required for participation in a research project and gave an informed and entirely voluntary consent, could a child participate as a healthy volunteer. In practice this rigid rule is not followed and provided that there is no or only minimal risk to the child, parental consent can be given.

Adults who lack the requisite mental capacity to give consent

The Mental Capacity Act 2005 now applies to adults who do not have the mental capacity to consent to participation in a research project and regulations have been made under the Act covering such participation. Where clinical trials are involved, these come outside the Mental Capacity Act and are covered by the clinical trial regulations.

Therapeutic research

There are now statutory provisions relating to the decision making on behalf of mentally incapacitated adults which replaces the common law power to act in their best interests (*Re F (mental patient: sterilisation)* [1990]). There are strict rules relating to participation which are considered below. In addition specific approval to the participation of those lacking the mental capacity to give consent must be obtained from the local research ethics committee (LREC).

Statutory provisions Section 30–36 MCA

Intrusive research (i.e. research which would be unlawful if consent were not obtained) is unlawful unless it is carried out as part of a research project which

> # Box 21.2 Improved memory: case scenario
>
> A psychologist was researching into hemisphere function of the human brain and linked up with a pharmaceutical company which was researching into preparations which appeared to reduce memory loss. The psychologist approached a psychiatrist to inquire if he would be prepared to permit, as part of their treatment plan, those patients suffering from Alzheimer's disease to participate in this research as part of a randomly controlled test. What is the law?

is for the time being approved by the appropriate body for the purposes of this Act in accordance with section 31, and in accordance with Sections 32 and 33.

Sections 31 is shown in Box 21.3 and Sections 32 and 33 are shown in Box 21.4.

> # Box 21.3 Sections 31 of the MCA
>
> (1) The appropriate body (i.e. the Secretary of State or the Welsh Assembly) may not approve a research project for the purposes of this Act unless satisfied that the following requirements will be met in relation to research carried out as part of the project on, or in relation to, a person who lacks capacity to consent to taking part in the project ('P').
> (2) The research must be connected with–
>   (a) an impairing condition affecting P, or
>   (b) its treatment.
> (3) 'Impairing condition' means a condition which is (or may be) attributable to, or which causes or contributes to (or may cause or contribute to), the impairment of, or disturbance in the functioning of, the mind or brain.
> (4)1 There must be reasonable grounds for believing that research of comparable effectiveness cannot be carried out if the project has to be confined to, or relate only to, persons who have capacity to consent to taking part in it.
> (5) The research must–
>   (a) have the potential to benefit P without imposing on P a burden that is disproportionate to the potential benefit to P, or

(b) be intended to provide knowledge of the causes or treatment of, or of the care of persons affected by, the same or a similar condition.

(6) If the research falls within paragraph (b) of subsection (5) but not within paragraph (a), there must be reasonable grounds for believing—

(a) that the risk to P from taking part in the project is likely to be negligible, and

(b) that anything done to, or in relation to, P will not—

(i) interfere with P's freedom of action or privacy in a significant way, or

(ii) be unduly invasive or restrictive.

(7) There must be reasonable arrangements in place for ensuring that the requirements of sections 32 and 33 will be met.

Box 21.4 Sections 32 and 33 of the MCA

(1) This section applies if a person ('R')—

(a) is conducting an approved research project, and

(b) wishes to carry out research, as part of the project, on or in relation to a person ('P') who lacks capacity to consent to taking part in the project.

(2) R must take reasonable steps to identify a person who—

(a) otherwise than in a professional capacity or for remuneration, is engaged in caring for P or is interested in P's welfare, and

(b) is prepared to be consulted by R under this section.

(3) If R is unable to identify such a person he must, in accordance with guidance issued by the appropriate authority, nominate a person who—

(a) is prepared to be consulted by R under this section, but

(b) has no connection with the project.

(4) R must provide the person identified under subsection (2), or nominated under subsection (3), with information about the project and ask him—

(a) for advice as to whether P should take part in the project, and

(b) what, in his opinion, P's wishes and feelings about taking part in the project would be likely to be if P had capacity in relation to the matter.

(5) If, at any time, the person consulted advises R that in his opinion P's wishes and feelings would be likely to lead him to decline to take part in the project (or to wish to withdraw from it) if he had capacity in relation to the matter, R must ensure—

    (a) if P is not already taking part in the project, that he does not take part in it;

    (b) if P is taking part in the project, that he is withdrawn from it.

(6) But subsection (5)(b) does not require treatment that P has been receiving as part of the project to be discontinued if R has reasonable grounds for believing that there would be a significant risk to P's health if it were discontinued.

(7) The fact that a person is the donee of a lasting power of attorney given by P, or is P's deputy, does not prevent him from being the person consulted under this section.

(8) Subsection (9) applies if treatment is being, or is about to be, provided for P as a matter of urgency and R considers that, having regard to the nature of the research and of the particular circumstances of the case—

    (a) it is also necessary to take action for the purposes of the research as a matter of urgency, but

    (b) it is not reasonably practicable to consult under the previous provisions of this section.

(9) R may take the action if—

    (a) he has the agreement of a registered medical practitioner who is not involved in the organisation or conduct of the research project, or

    (b) where it is not reasonably practicable in the time available to obtain that agreement, he acts in accordance with a procedure approved by the appropriate body at the time when the research project was approved under section 31.

(10) But R may not continue to act in reliance on subsection (9) if he has reasonable grounds for believing that it is no longer necessary to take the action as a matter of urgency.

33 Additional safeguards

(1) This section applies in relation to a person who is taking part in an approved research project even though he lacks capacity to consent to taking part.

(2) Nothing may be done to, or in relation to, him in the course of the research—

(a) to which he appears to object (whether by showing signs of resistance or otherwise) except where what is being done is intended to protect him from harm or to reduce or prevent pain or discomfort, or

(b) which would be contrary to—
  (i) an advance decision of his which has effect, or
  (ii) any other form of statement made by him and not subsequently withdrawn, of which R is aware.

(3) The interests of the person must be assumed to outweigh those of science and society.

(4) If he indicates (in any way) that he wishes to be withdrawn from the project he must be withdrawn without delay.

(5) P must be withdrawn from the project, without delay, if at any time the person conducting the research has reasonable grounds for believing that one or more of the requirements set out in section 31(2) to (7) is no longer met in relation to research being carried out on, or in relation to, P.

(6) But neither subsection (4) nor subsection (5) requires treatment that P has been receiving as part of the project to be discontinued if R has reasonable grounds for believing that there would be a significant risk to P's health if it were discontinued.

Loss of capacity during research project

In situations where a mentally capable adult gave consent to participation in a research project but subsequently lost capacity during the time of the research, the MCA makes specific statutory provision in section 34. This enables regulations to be made to cover the situation.

Regulations (The Mental Capacity Act 2005 (Loss of Capacity during Research Project) (England) Regulations 2007 SI No 679) covering the situation where an adult who had give consent to participation in research lost the requisite mental capacity during the research project were published and consulted upon in June 2006 and enacted in 2007. They provide that in such circumstances, despite P's loss of capacity, research for the purposes of the project may be carried out using information or material relating to him if certain specified conditions exist:

(a) the project satisfies the requirements set out in Schedule 1,

(b) all the information or material relating to P which is used in the research was obtained before P's loss of capacity, and

(c) the person conducting the project ('R') takes in relation to P such steps as are set out in Schedule 2.

Schedule 1 is shown in Box 21.5.

Box 21.5 Schedule 1 to the Regulations on loss of capacity during the research project

Requirements which the project must satisfy:

1. A protocol approved by an appropriate body and having effect in relation to the project makes provision for research to be carried out in relation to a person who has consented to take part in the project but loses capacity to consent to continue to take part in it.
2. The appropriate body must be satisfied that there are reasonable arrangements in place for ensuring that the requirements of Schedule 2 will be met. (see Box 21.6 for Schedule 2.)

Schedule 2 of the Regulations is shown in Box 21.6.

Box 21.6 Schedule 2 to the Regulations on loss of capacity during the research project

Steps which the person conducting the project must take:

1. R must take reasonable steps to identify a person who—
   (a) otherwise than in a professional capacity or for remuneration, is engaged in caring for P or is interested in P's welfare, and
   (b) is prepared to be consulted by R under this Schedule.
2. If R is unable to identify such a person he must, in accordance with guidance issued by the Secretary of State, nominate a person who—
   (a) is prepared to be consulted by R under this Schedule, but
   (b) has no connection with the project.
3. R must provide the person identified under paragraph 1, or nominated under paragraph 2, with information about the project and ask him—

(a) for advice as to whether research of the kind proposed should be carried out in relation to P, and

(b) what, in his opinion, P's wishes and feelings about such research being carried out would be likely to be if P had capacity in relation to the matter.

4. If, any time, the person consulted advises R that in his opinion P's wishes and feelings would be likely to lead him to wish to withdraw from the project if he had capacity in relation to the matter, R must ensure that P is withdrawn from it.

5. The fact that a person is the donee of a lasting power of attorney given by P, or is P's deputy, does not prevent him from being the person consulted under paragraphs 1 to 4.

6. R must ensure that nothing is done in relation to P in the course of the research which would be contrary to—
   (a) an advance decision of his which has effect, or
   (b) any other form of statement made by him and not subsequently withdrawn, of which R is aware.

7. The interests of P must be assumed to outweigh those of science and society.

8. If P indicates (in any way) that he wishes the research in relation to him to be discontinued, it must be discontinued without delay.

9. The research must be discontinued without delay if at any time R has reasonable grounds for believing that one or more of the requirement set out in Schedule 1 is no longer met or that there are no longer reasonable arrangements in place for ensuring that the requirements of this Schedule are met in relation to P.

10. R must conduct the research in accordance with the provision made in the protocol referred to in paragraph 1 of Schedule 1 for research to be carried out in relation to a person who has consented to take part in the project but loses capacity to consent to take part in it.

A possible scenario is shown in Box 21.2. In this scenario, there would have to be clear analysis of any potential risks to the patients together with potential benefits and the full facts would have to be given to the LREC. (In practice this is likely to be a multicentred research project so would be scrutinised by a multicentred research ethics committee.) It would have to be shown that it was in the best interests of each individual patient to have this treatment and the statutory provisions followed.

Where there is a dispute as to whether therapeutic research is in fact in the best interests of the patient, an application could be made to the Court of Protection for a declaration.

Non-therapeutic research

In contrast to therapeutic research, it could be argued that the participation of mentally incapable adults in research from which they will never benefit can never be in their best interests and that they should be protected from such activities. The statutory provisions apply. The MCA prevents the argument that the interests of science and society would benefit from the research being used as a justification to overrule the interests of the mentally incapable adult. Section 33 (3) states that the interests of the person must be assumed to outweigh those of science and society. (see Box 21.4).

Conclusion

Mentally incapacitated adults are now protected by the Mental Capacity Act 2005 in respect of their participation in research projects. Children are protected by the Children Act 1989 (but only if a person challenges proposed treatment or research) Scotland has since April 2002 had the benefit of the Adults with Incapacity (Scotland) Act 2000 – see chapter 7).

References

British Paediatric Association (1995) *A Paediatrician's Brief Guide to the UN Convention on the Rights of the Child*. British Paediatric Association, London.

Gillick v. *W Norfolk and Wisbech Area Health Authority* [1986] 1 AC 112.

Law Commission Mental Incapacity (1995) *Report No 231*. HMSO, London.

The Mental Capacity Act 2005 (Loss of Capacity during Research Project) (England) Regulations 2007 SI No 679.

Re F (mental patient: sterilisation) [1990] 2 AC 1.

Royal College of Paediatrics and Child Health (1999) *Safeguarding Informed Parental Involvement in Clinical Research Involving Newborn Babies and Infants*. Royal College of Paediatrics and Child Health, London.

Royal College of Paediatrics and Child Health (2000) Guidelines for the ethical conduct of medical research involving children. *Arch Dis Child*, **82**, 1777–82.

United Nations (1989) *Convention on the Rights of the Child*. United Nations, http://www.unhchr.ch/html/menu3/b/k2crc.htm.

CHAPTER 22

Amputation of healthy limbs

> ## Box 22.1 Case scenario
>
> Martina suffered from apotemnophilia, a rare psychological condition related to body dysmorphic disorder. Her GP referred her to a general surgeon, Mr Walker. She pleaded with him that he should amputate her left leg. Mr Walker saw no signs of disease, and said that there was no physical justification for surgery. Martina said that she would put her leg over the railway line or cut it off herself if he did not operate. As a consequence Mr Walker carried out the amputation but is now facing an investigation by his employers. What is the law?

Introduction

The condition of body dysmorphic disorder came to light when publicity was given to a surgeon who had removed the healthy limbs of some patients (Gillian, 2000). One patient, a social worker, stated that she had fantasised about losing both her legs from the age of 6 years. She sought out disabled people, wanting to learn about the realities of the condition. She often pretended to be disabled, and was considering having both legs amputated. A man of 75 years from Florida could not find a doctor to help him and shot his knee, leaving it so badly mutilated that the hospital had to amputate the leg.

In February 2000, Robert Smith, a consultant orthopaedic surgeon at Falkirk and District Royal Infirmary, removed one lower leg from each of two private patients, one from England and the other from Germany. He is reported as saying:

> It took me 18 months to pluck up the courage, but it was the most satisfactory operation I have ever performed. The patients were well informed about their condition, and they were the most grateful patients I have ever dealt with.

Mr Smith also explained that his two patients had had a course of antipsychotic drugs, to which they had failed to respond, had received psychological counselling and a psychiatric assessment before surgery. From Mr Smith's perspective, he clearly believed that there was clinical justification for the operations and the patients were undoubtedly satisfied. The hospital subsequently announced that it was banning any further such amputations after a report by its ethical issues subcommittee.

The condition is also known as Body Integrity Identity Disorder (BIID) or amputee identity disorder.

The law: the patient

In theory, it could be argued that a mentally competent adult could give consent to any action upon him or her, provided that it was voluntary, and that no fraud, deceit, or compulsion had been involved. However, in a criminal case where sadomasochists were prosecuted for inflicting serious bodily harm on each other, the House of Lords refused to allow a defence of consent to the acts to prevail (*R* v. *Brown* [1993]). The House of Lords stated that surgical or medical treatment is justified in law providing it is consented to or is otherwise justified in law.

Clearly, if consent is lacking then surgical or medical intervention would constitute both the criminal offence of assault and battery, or the offence of inflicting grievous bodily harm. It may also constitute the crime of maim, an old offence of causing an injury which disables a person. Treatment without consent would also constitute the civil wrong of trespass to the person.

What has not been decided by the House of Lords is whether the consent of a patient to an operation which others would see as clinically unacceptable would be sufficient to protect the surgeon from a criminal prosecution. Clearly, consent to an operation which is accepted as reasonable professional practice is very different from consent to an operation which is not supported by reasonable professional opinion.

Law Commission recommendations

The Law Commission (1995) recommended that consent in criminal law should be on a statutory basis and that there should be a clear statutory exception for medical treatment. It recommended that a person should not be guilty of an offence, notwithstanding that he or she causes injury to another of whatever degree of seriousness, if such injury is caused during the course of proper medical treatment or care administered with the consent of that other person.

It proposed that proper medical treatment should include procedures taken for the purposes of diagnosis, the prevention of disease, and the prevention of pregnancy. It lists specific procedures which should be included, i.e. sterilisations, transsexual operations, abortions, operations for cosmetic purposes and procedures for the donation of regenerative tissue or non-regenerative tissue not essential for life. However, neither the general definition of medical treatment or care nor the specific examples given could be interpreted as including the amputation of healthy limbs, unless such an operation was supported by reasonable professional opinion.

The Law Commission's recommendations have not been incorporated in statute law. Even if they were to be there is no certainty that a surgeon who performed the amputation of healthy limbs would be protected from prosecution.

Case scenario

In the case scenario presented in Box 22.1, if Mr Walker carried out a procedure which does not have the support of reasonable professional practice, then he could face certain consequences in law:

- Criminal prosecution for battery and criminal assault
- Professional conduct proceedings by the General Medical Council (GMC)
- Disciplinary proceedings by his employer.

Criminal prosecution for battery and criminal assault

The patient's consent is the main defence against an action for trespass to the person. Therefore, if the treatment is not clinically justified, in the event of the surgeon being prosecuted for criminal assault, as a result of the House of Lords' decision in the case of *R* v. *Brown* [1993] he could probably not use successfully the fact that the patient had consented as a defence to the criminal charge.

Professional conduct proceedings by the GMC

Mr Walker also faces professional conduct proceedings by the GMC. Crucial to the determination of the proceedings would be the extent of reasonable professional opinion which supported the surgeon's actions. Also vital to its decision would be the nature of the patient's consent and the extent to which the patient had received full information about the surgery and had thoroughly explored all other treatment options before agreeing to the surgery of her healthy limbs.

Disciplinary proceedings by his employer

In the case scenario it is not clear if Mr Walker carried out the operation as part of his private practice or as an employee, so both situations will be considered.

If Mr Walker undertook the operation privately he might still face disciplinary proceedings from any employer for whom he also works. An employer's disciplinary machinery is not confined to actions undertaken during the course of employment. For example, a nurse found guilty of shoplifting could face disciplinary action from his or her employer and may lose his or her job (and also face professional conduct proceedings, as a result of which he or she could be struck off the register). If there is a nexus between unacceptable actions of an employee outside of the course of employment, then the employer would be justified in holding disciplinary proceedings. Even if he worked full time in private practice and had no employer, the hospital in which he carried out his operations could make it clear that no such operations are to take place on its premises, even though they are conducted as part of private practice.

If Mr Walker conducted the operation as an employee, then he could be disciplined by the employer for carrying out unacceptable surgery.

Acceptable clinical practice

The key issue is whether the actions of the surgeon are acceptable clinical practice. Research is clearly necessary on this condition and clear statements necessary from the Royal College of Psychiatry on whether there is the research evidence which would lead it to support surgery for this mental condition.

Social revulsion

Such an operation naturally results in considerable disgust. It seems to make a mockery of those who are disabled, through no fault of their own, who have to cope with missing limbs, wheelchairs and considerable restrictions on their lifestyle. The view is also held on why more is not done for the patients on a psychological level. They are clearly suffering from a major psychiatric disorder and to treat this by such drastic physical means seems quite wrong. More should be done to help them psychologically before there is a resort to amputation.

There are other treatments and operations which are religious and cultural requirements in certain societies, but which the West finds unacceptable. For example, female circumcision is a criminal offence under the Female Genital Mutilation Act 2003, which replaced the Prohibition of Female Circumcision Act 1985. Guidance has been issued by the Royal College of Nursing (RCN) and British Medical Association (BMA) (RCN, 1998; BMA, 2001) to practitioners, but there is evidence that female circumcision is taking place in this country (Charter and Kennedy, 2001). The House of Lords overruled a Court of Appeal decision that held that a 19-year-old from Sierra Leone was not protected by the asylum laws since she did not belong to a particular social group fearing prosecution. The House of Lords held that the fear of genital mutilation if she were to return enabled her to stay in Britain (*Secretary of State* v. *Fornal* 2006). Baroness Hale stated that female genital mutilation is in breach of international human rights law and standards. The Metropolitan police have offered £20,000 to anyone giving information which leads to successful prosecution for female genital mutilation (Pidd, 2007).

Other mutilations may also take place, such as the insertion of needles and other objects in all manner of places, but there is no specific statute law outlawing such invasions of the body. The usual laws of consent would apply.

Public policy

Public policy has to find a way between the criminalisation of unacceptable social practices causing bodily injury (such as female circumcision) and the acceptance of other practices, which also cause bodily harm or disfigurement (such as male circumcision and tattoos), which are tolerated.

Martina's situation

Martina may consider herself fortunate in having found Mr Walker, who is prepared to operate on her. Nowadays it is very unlikely that any surgeon in this country would carry out this operation. Even private practice would not permit such an operation, as the surgeons would risk being struck off the GMC register and if they are also NHS employees, lose their NHS employment. It may be that surgeons overseas would be prepared to carry out the operation.

Conclusion

Clearly, what is required is more research into body dysmorphic disorder and the development of treatments to ameliorate or cure the condition. It may be that less drastic medical treatments, such as the temporary paralysis of the limb, may assist the sufferer. The danger is that unless such alternatives are found, in the absence of any law making these operations an exception to our criminal laws and acceptable according to standards of professional practice, patients such as Martina will end up on the railway line, possibly suffering much greater harm.

References

British Medical Association (2001) *Guidelines on Female Genital Mutilation.* BMA, London.

Charter, D. and Kennedy, D. (2001) Doctors put on alert for girl butchery. *The Times,* 21 August.

Gillian, H. (2000) Surgeon happy he removed healthy limbs. *The Times,* 1 February, p. 7.

Law Commission (1995) *Consent in the Criminal Law.* No 139. HMSO, London.

Pidd, H. (2007) Met's unique £20,000 reward to stop mutilation of women. 11 July.

Royal College of Nursing (1998) *Position Paper 20. Female Genital Mutilation (Female Circumcision).* RCN, London.

R v. *Brown* [1993] 2 All ER 75.

Secretary of State for the Home Department (respondent) v. *Fornah (FC) (Appellant)* [2006] UKHL 46.

CHAPTER 23

Consent and the scope of professional practice

> ## Box 23.1 Case scenario
>
> Staff nurse Fawn was asked to take on the role of getting the patients to sign the consent forms before surgery was carried out. She was concerned at the legality of her being asked to undertake this, since she would not be carrying out the operations. What is the law?

Introduction

In relation to consent, it should always be remembered that the signed consent form is not the consent, but evidence that consent has been given (see Chapter 3). To be valid, the patient must be mentally competent and understand what invasion of his or her person is intended. Consent is, therefore, part of a process in which the patient is given the necessary information relating to the decisions which have to be made and then, without duress or fraud, the patient must agree that the proposed treatment can go ahead.

In addition, information must be given to the patient about any reasonably foreseeable risks of harm which could occur even if all care were taken. Failure to provide this information according to the reasonable professional standard (i.e. the Bolam test) (*Bolam* v. *Friern Hospital Management Committee* [1957]) could, if harm were to occur to the patient, leave the trust open to an action for its vicarious liability for negligence by staff in failing to give the appropriate information to patients.

What should be taken into account in obtaining the consent?

It follows from the above that the person giving the information to the patient must understand what is proposed and must be able to explain to the patient, in words which he or she can understand, the nature of the proposed operation. Any additional procedures which may be necessary, and for which the patient's consent is required, would also have to be explained to the patient. If the person who is giving the information to the patient is not the same person who is to carry out the procedure, great care is necessary to ensure that the patient is not given any inaccurate information or any false assurances. For example, the patient may inquire if the operation is to be carried out by a consultant. If, in fact, it is a junior doctor who is to carry out the operation, it would clearly be wrong for the patient to be told that the consultant would be performing it.

Where the patient seeks additional information, the person discussing the treatment with the patient must be able to provide this information. If the questions cannot be answered, there must be a referral to the appropriate person before the form is signed so that the patient can have these questions answered fully and accurately.

The scope of professional practice

It is legally possible for nurses and other health professionals, such as physiotherapists or radiographers, to obtain consent for procedures which are to be carried out by doctors. This would be regarded as an expanded role activity. Therefore, all the principles which relate to the Scope of Professional Practice as laid down by the UKCC would apply (UKCC, 1992a). These principles are summarised in Table 23.1.

The UKCC Scope Document was revoked by the publication of a new Code of Professional Practice of the NMC in 2002 (updated in 2008). However, the principles set out in Table 23.1 are still valid. The revised Code of Professional Practice came into force in June 2002. Clause 6 required the registered practitioner to maintain her professional knowledge and competence. Clause 6.2 stated:

> To practise competently, you must possess the knowledge, skills and abilities required for lawful, safe and effective practice without direct supervision. You must acknowledge the limits of your professional

Table 23.1 Principles for adjusting the Scope of Professional Practice (UKCC, 1992a).

The registered nurse, midwife or health visitor:

1. Must be satisfied that each aspect of practice is directed to meeting the needs and serving the interests of the patient or client.

2. Must endeavour always to achieve, maintain and develop knowledge, skill and competence to respond to those needs and interests.

3. Must honestly acknowledge any limits of personal knowledge and skill and take steps to remedy any relevant deficits in order effectively and appropriately to meet the needs of patients and clients.

4. Must ensure that any enlargement or adjustment of the scope of personal professional practice must be achieved without compromising or fragmenting existing aspects of professional practice and care and that requirements of the Council's Code of Professional Conduct (UKCC, 1992b) are satisfied throughout the whole area of practice.

5. Must recognise and honour the direct or indirect personal accountability borne for all aspects of professional practice.

6. Must, in serving the interests of patients and clients and the wider interests of society, avoid any inappropriate delegation to others which compromises those interests.

competence and only undertake practice and accept responsibilities for those activities in which you are competent.

This clause could apply to all health professionals undertaking expanded role activities. The essential requirement was that the health professional must act within the scope of his or her competence. It would be wise to ensure, as in any other expanded role activity, that a procedure is drawn up specifying the level of competence required by the health professional, the actions which he or she should take in the event of certain questions being raised, and that all patients could, if they so wish, speak to a doctor.

The standard which the health professional must satisfy is the reasonable standard of care of the health professional who would usually undertake that role. It would be no defence for a physiotherapist to argue that the reason certain information was omitted, which would usually have been given to a patient, was because a physiotherapist, rather than a doctor, was carrying out that activity.

The NMC updated the code in 2004 and then in 2008 (NMC 2008).

Under the heading 'Provide a high standard of practice and care at all times', the NMC requires registrants to:

- Keep your skills and knowledge up to date
- You must have the knowledge and skills for safe and effective practice when working without direct supervision
- You must recognise and work within the limits of your competence
- You must keep your knowledge and skills up to date throughout your working life
- You must take part in appropriate learning and practice activities that maintain and develop your competence and performance

Training and competence of the health professional

Any expanded role activity requires appropriate training and supervised practice to be made available to the health professional. In the case of the expanded role of explaining procedures to the patient and communicating to the patient (so that the patient ultimately signs the consent form) the health professional should be sure that he or she has the necessary supervised practice, always admits ignorance and refers the patient to the doctor who is to carry out the procedure when necessary.

The Department of Health (DoH, 2001a) guidance on consent is given in Box 23.2.

> ### Box 23.2 The Department of Health's guidance on consent (DoH, 2001a)
>
> The clinician providing the treatment or investigation is responsible for ensuring that the patient has given valid consent before treatment begins, although the consultant responsible for the patient's care will remain ultimately responsible for the quality of the medical care provided.
>
> The General Medical Council guidance states that the task of seeking consent may be delegated to another health professional, as long as that professional is suitably trained and qualified. In particular, they must have sufficient knowledge of the proposed investigation or treatment, and understand the risks involved, in order to be able to provide any information the patient may require. Inappropriate delegation (e.g. where the clinician seeking consent has inadequate knowledge of the procedure) may mean that the 'consent' obtained is not valid. Clinicians are responsible for knowing the limits of their own competence and should seek the advice of appropriate colleagues when necessary.

More recent guidance has been given by the GMC in its consent booklet (GMC, 2008). It states that:

Responsibility for seeking a patient's consent

26 If you are the doctor undertaking an investigation or providing treatment, it is your responsibility to discuss it with the patient. If this is not practical, you can delegate the responsibility to someone else, provided you make sure that the person you delegate to:

(a) is suitably trained and qualified

(b) has sufficient knowledge of the proposed investigation or treatment, and understands the risks involved

(c) understands, and agrees to act in accordance with, the guidance in this booklet.

27 If you delegate, you are still responsible for making sure that the patient has been given enough time and information to make an informed decision, and has given their consent, before you start any investigation or treatment.

Bristol Royal Infirmary inquiry into paediatric cardiac surgery

The report of the inquiry into paediatric cardiac surgery at the Bristol Royal Infirmary (DoH, 2001b) made clear recommendations about the process of consent (Table 23.2) (see also Chapters 2, 4 and 5, where other recommenda-

Table 23.2 Recommendations in relation to consent from the report of the inquiry into paediatric cardiac surgery at Bristol Royal Infirmary (DoH, 2001b).

Recommendation 24: The process of informing the patient, and obtaining consent to a course of treatment, should be regarded as a process and not a one-off event consisting of obtaining the patient's signature on a form

Recommendation 25: The process of consent should apply not only to surgical procedures, but also to all clinical procedures and examinations which involve any form of touching. This must not mean more forms; it means more communication

Recommendation 26: As part of the process of obtaining consent, except when they have indicated otherwise, patients should be given sufficient information about what is to take place, the risks, uncertainties, possible negative consequences of the proposed treatment, any alternatives, and the likely outcome to enable them to make a choice about how to proceed

tions are discussed.) The Bristol report also recommends that patients should be referred to information relating to the performance of the trust, of the specialty and of the consultant unit (a consultant and the team of doctors who work under his or her supervision).

The health professional who takes on this expanded role of giving information to the patient and obtaining the patient's consent to the treatment proceeding would also have to understand the performance figures and be able to explain the figures and their significance accurately to the patient.

Staff nurse Fawn's situation

It is clear from what has been said that to delegate to one staff nurse, i.e. staff nurse Fawn in Box 23.1, the task of obtaining consent from patients for all the surgery which is to be undertaken is too vast a role for a nurse to take on competently and lawfully. However, it would be possible for staff nurse Fawn, after specific training, to discuss with patients who are having a specific type of surgery the details of that surgery and, the associated risks and implications, and to answer the patients' questions and thereby obtain a valid consent. However, for staff nurse Fawn to take on an undefined responsibility over areas of treatment in which she has not had specific training would mean that she would not have the competence to undertake them safely. Further clarification is required of what staff nurse Fawn should undertake and the training and knowledge necessary for her to be competent.

Conclusion

As the professional role of the different health professionals expands, it is probable that obtaining the consent of the patient to proposed treatment and diagnostic procedures will increasingly become the responsibility of health professionals other than the person carrying out the treatment. There are no legal barriers to prevent other health professionals undertaking this expanded role activity; there are no statutes which make it illegal for health professionals other than doctors to carry this activity out.

However, the common law rule that the health professional must satisfy the reasonable standard of care according to the Bolam Test does apply. It is the health professional's personal and professional responsibility to ensure that he or she is competent to undertake this activity and the onus is upon him or her to refuse to undertake it, if there are reasonable grounds for believing that he or she lacks the capacity.

References

Bolam v. *Friern Hospital Management Committee* [1957] 1 WLR 582.

Department of Health (2001a) *Reference Guide to Consent for Examination or Treatment*. DoH, London.

Department of Health (2001b) *Learning from Bristol: the Report of the Public Inquiry into Children's Heart Surgery at the Bristol Royal Infirmary 1984–1995*. Command Paper CM 5207. DoH, London; http://www.bristol-inquiry.org.uk/.

General Medical Council (2008) *Consent: Patients and Doctors Making Decisions Together*, GMC, London.

Nursing and Midwifery Council (2002) *Code of Professional Conduct*. NMC, London.

Nursing and Midwifery Council (2008) *Code of Professional Conduct: Standards of Conduct, Performance and Ethics for Nurses and Midwives*. NMC, London.

UKCC (1992a) *The Scope of Professional Practice*. UKCC, London.

UKCC (1992b) *Code of Professional Practice for the Nurse, Midwife and Health Visitor*. UKCC, London.

CHAPTER 24

Consent and fertility treatment

> **Box 24.1 Case scenario (*R* v. *Human Fertilisation and Embryology Authority ex p. Blood* [1997] 2 WLR 806)**
>
> Diane Blood was refused permission by the Human Fertilisation and Embryology Authority to use the stored sperm from her dead husband on the grounds that the husband had not given written consent for this use as required by the 1990 Act.

Introduction

As can be seen from the previous chapters in this book, much of the law on consent derives from case law: common law principles laid down by the judges which relate in particular to the law on trespass to the person (see Chapter 3) and the law of negligence (see Chapters 4 and 5). However, the area of fertilisation is one where there has been since 1990 a clear statutory framework for obtaining consent from the patient and others and covering the information which must be made available. (Another area where consent provisions have been laid down by statute is in organ donation; see Chapters 13 and 14). The Human Fertilisation and Embryology Act 1990 provided the statutory context within which fertilisation and the use of embryos could take place and has now been amended by the Human Fertilisation and Embryology Act 2008. The consent provisions relating to fertilisation and embryology were set out in Schedule 3 of the 1990 Act. There were significant amendments made by the 2008 Act and the amended Schedule is shown in Appendix 2. The Human Fertilisation and Embryology Authority is responsible for issuing licences to approved centres which undertake work on fertilisation treatments under the provisions of the 1990 Act (as amended by the 2008 Act).

Consent provisions for retrieval, storage and use of human gametes under the Human Fertilisation and Embryology Act 1990

In the case scenario shown in Box 24.1 Diane Blood brought a case seeking judicial review of the Authority's refusal to license the infertility treatment. She and her husband, who were married in 1991, decided to start a family at the end of 1994. Unfortunately before she had conceived the husband contracted meningitis and she arranged for the sperm to be taken by electro-ejaculation from her husband as he lay in a coma. He died not long after. The Human Fertilisation and Embryology Authority refused to agree to allow her to have the necessary treatment using the sperm on the grounds that the statutory consent requirements had not been complied with. In addition, they refused to allow the export of the sperm so that the treatment could be carried out abroad. The Court of Appeal (*R* v. *Human Fertilisation and Embryology Authority ex p. Blood* [1997] 2 WLR 806) held that as a result of the restrictions under Section 4(1)(b) and Schedule 3 the 1990 Act (see below) she could not be lawfully treated with the sperm in this country. However, she would be permitted to receive treatment in Belgium according to Article 59 of the EC treaty. She subsequently became pregnant and gave birth. In 2002 it was reported that she had given birth to a second child, again conceived through use of the dead husband's sperm.

The statutory provisions

Section 4(1) of the 1990 Act (as amended by the 2008 Act states that:

No person shall
(a) store any gametes, or
(b) in the course of providing treatment services for any woman, use the sperm of any man unless the services are being provided for the woman and the man together or use the eggs of any other woman
except in pursuance of a licence.

In a new Section 4A the Act also prohibits activities in connection with genetic material not of human origin:

(1) No person shall place in a woman –
       (a) a human admixed embryo,

(b) any other embryo that is not a human embryo, or

(c) any gametes other than human gametes.

In addition a licence is needed for the following activities:

(a) mix human gametes with animal gametes,

(b) bring about the creation of a human admixed embryo, or

(c) keep or use a human admixed embryo.

Under section 12 the general conditions of granting a licence require that there is compliance with the consent provisions set out in Schedule 3 (S.12(c)).

Schedule 3 of the Human Fertilisation and Embryology Act 1990 sets out the provisions relating to consent in relation to the removal, storage and use of gametes, embryos and cells for fertility treatment and research. Significant amendments were made by the 2008 Act and although these do not come into force till October 2009, the paragraphs of Schedule 3 with their amendments are shown in Appendix 2.

Consents to use or storage of gametes, embryos or human admixed embryos etc.

The general requirements for the use or storage of gametes, embryos or human admixed embryos are set out in Paragraph 1 of Schedule 3 (see Appendix 2). The consent to or the withdrawal of variation of consent to any activities under the Act must be in writing and signed by the person. If the person is unable to sign because of illness, injury or physical disability, then the requirement can be satisfied if it is signed at the direction of the person unable to sign, in the presence of the person unable to sign and in the presence of at least one witness who attests the signature. A consent to the use of any human admixed embryo must specify use for the purposes of any project of research and may specify conditions subject to which the human admixed embryo may be so used. A consent to the use of any embryo must specify one or more of the purposes listed in paragraph 2 of Schedule 3 (see Appendix 2). Under the amendments the purposes can now include use for the purpose of training persons in embryo biopsy, embryo storage or other embryological techniques. A consent to the use of any human admixed embryo must specify use for the purposes of any project of research and may specify conditions subject to which the human admixed embryo may be used.

Under the Act an effective consent is one which has not been withdrawn.

Procedure for giving consent

Paragraph 3 of Schedule 3 sets out the procedure which must be followed before a person gives consent under the Schedule. The person must be given a suitable opportunity to receive proper counselling about the implications of taking the proposed steps, and he must be provided with such relevant information as is proper. (See Appendix 3 Schedule 3ZA added to the 1990 Act by the 2008 Act, setting out the circumstances in which an offer of counselling is required as a condition of a licence for treatment.) In addition, before consent is given, he must be informed of the effect of paragraph 4 and if relevant paragraph 4A. Paragraph 4 covers the variation and withdrawal of consent and paragraph 4A introduces a new cooling off period where consent is withdrawn: 12 months must elapse before the destruction of the embryos.

The new paragraph 4A introduces a 'cooling off period' where one person in a couple seeking fertility treatment withdraws their consent to the storage of an embryo or, where donated gametes are used, where the gamete donor withdraws consent. This provision does not alter the requirement that the consent of both parties is required to store the embryos, but it is intended to provide a year-long period during which the embryos will not be destroyed unless all interested persons (see paragraph 4A(3)) consent. There is also to be a cooling off period where a single woman seeks fertility treatment and the gamete donor or donors withdraw consent.

Paragraph 5 of Schedule 3 prevents the receipt or use of a person's gametes for the treatment of others ('or non-medical fertility services' added by 2008 Act) unless there is an effective consent by that person to their being so used and they are used in accordance with the terms of the consent. (This paragraph does not apply to the use of a person's gametes for the purpose of that person, or that person and another together, receiving treatment services. The Court of Appeal considered that this exception could not cover the situation of Diane Blood since the husband was dead and so the treatment services could not be described as for the use of 'that person and another together').

Paragraph 6 requires an effective consent to be given to the use of a person's gametes for the creation of any embryo in vitro. Paragraph 6 of Schedule 3 to the 1990 Act is amended by paragraph 9 of Schedule 3 to the Act to require an effective consent from a person whose gametes or human cells are used to create an embryo *in vitro* for use in treatment services (not including implantation) or for a project of research. ('Human cells' are defined by new paragraph 22 to exclude reproductive cells.)

Consent is also required from each 'relevant person' in relation to an embryo for its use for any purpose (see paragraph 6(3)). In addition consent from each 'relevant person' must be in place before an embryo is received by any person. A 'relevant person' means:

- each person whose gametes or human cells were used to bring about the creation of the embryo (embryo A);
- each person whose gametes or human cells were used to create *in vitro* an embryo which was then used to create embryo A; and
- each person whose gametes or human cells were used to create *in vitro* a human admixed embryo, which was then used to create embryo A.

Paragraph 7 requires an effective consent to be given by a woman before an embryo is taken from her for any purpose. (This paragraph does not apply to the use of a woman's embryo for her own treatment purposes.) The 2008 Act amends this paragraph so that an embryo taken from a woman must not be used to bring about the creation of any embryo *in vitro* or any human admixed embryo *in vitro*.

Paragraph 8 relates to the storage of gametes and embryos. A person's gametes must not be kept in storage unless there is an effective consent by that person to their storage and they are stored in accordance with the consent. In addition, an embryo which was created *in vitro* must not be kept in storage unless there is an effective consent, by the relevant person in relation to the creation of an embryo, to the storage of the embryo and the embryo is stored in accordance with those consents. Effective consent can be given by a person with parental responsibility for a person under the age of 18.

Developments prior to the 2008 Act

Following the Diane Blood case, the Minister of Health appointed a committee under the Chairmanship of Professor Sheila McLean to review the consent provisions in the Human Fertilisation and Embryology Act 1990. A questionnaire was sent out for public consultation and the committee published its Report in December 1998 (Department of Health 1998). In general it recommended that there should be no change in the common law. However, it was suggested that there could be an amendment to the requirements of written consent to storage so that the HFEA had the discretion to waive the consent requirements in Schedule 3 of the 1990 Act for storage in the situation of an unconscious patient where it may be in the best interests of that person to remove and store gametes if treatment was likely to result in sterility on recovery. In August 2000 the Government published its response to the McLean Report (Department of Health Press announcement, 25 August 2000).

The Department accepted all the recommendations of the report and went further, suggesting a retrospective effect:

- The Father's name should be allowed to appear on birth certificates where his sperm has been used after his death.
- The legal position on consent and removal of gametes should remain unchanged: gametes can be taken from an incapacitated person who is likely to recover if the removal of gametes is in their best interests.
- The HFEA should have the power to permit the storage of gametes where consent has not been given, so long as the gametes have been lawfully removed. This will also benefit children who are about to undergo treatment which will affect their future fertility.
- Families will be able to make these birth certificate changes retrospectively.
- The best practice is for written consent to be obtained, since this most clearly constitutes effective consent. Where there is doubt over whether an effective consent has been obtained, this should be a matter for the courts.

The Government did not recommend that there should be any legislative change over permitting the export of gametes that have been removed lawfully, since the Court of Appeal in the Diane Blood case held that sperm stored with consent can be the subject of export. Legislative provision was contained within the Human Fertilisation and Embryology Bill 2008 following the Consultation Report *Human Bodies, Human Choices* (DoH, 2002); see below.

Centre for Reproductive Medicine v. U [2002]

Similar issues over the use of sperm posthumously arose in a case in 2002. A wife appealed against a High Court decision which permitted the destruction by the reproductive centre of her late husband's sperm, which had been surgically removed and stored. Prior to the sperm being removed, the husband had signed a consent form in which he had agreed, *inter alia*, that the sperm could be used after his death. He later withdrew this aspect of his consent at the request of a specialist nursing sister. Both the Centre and the nursing sister had ethical objections to the posthumous use of sperm. The wife contended that the husband had withdrawn his consent reluctantly and only because he believed that if he did not, the Centre would cease or postpone fertility treatment. The Court of Appeal dismissed the wife's appeal. It held that the husband's withdrawal of consent to the posthumous storage and the use of his sperm had not been actuated by undue influence. Without an effective consent from the husband, the continued storage and later use of his sperm by the Centre had been rendered unlawful by virtue of the Human Fertilisation and Embryology Act 1990.

Separated women and the right to use embryos

A further challenge to the provisions of the Human Fertilisation and Embryology Act 1990 started in September 2002 when two women sought to stop their former partners destroying their frozen fertilised embryos (Gibb, 2002).

In the case of one woman, she had cancer and before the treatment started she placed six frozen embryos into storage. During treatment her ovaries were removed. Subsequently she and her partner split up and the partner refused to give consent to the continued storage and use of the frozen embryos. The Act requires that both partners must give consent. The case was heard in 2003 (*Evans* v. *Amicus Healthcare Ltd and Others* 2003). The judge held that the court had no power to override the unconditional statutory right of either party to withdraw or vary consent to the use of embryos in connection with *in vitro* fertilisation treatment at any time before the fertilised embryo was implanted in the woman. In addition, where consent for treatment had originally been given for treatment together with a named partner, that consent remained neither effective nor valid once the parties ceased to be together. Ms Evans lost her appeal to the Court of Appeal in June 2004 (*Evans* v. *Amicus Healthcare* 2004). Her application to the ECHR (*Evans* v. *UK* 2007) for breach of articles 2, 8 and 14 failed but a dissenting judgment held that there had been a breach of article 8 and article 14 in conjunction with article 8.

Human Bodies, Human Choices (DoH, 2002)

Issues concerning gametes were included in a Consultation Report, *Human Bodies, Human Choices*, issued by the Department of Health (2002). Views were invited on such issues as to: whether the HFEA should have the power to waive the requirement for personal consent to the storage of gametes for the duration of a child's incapacity and if so should parental or court consent be required; should courts have a power to consent to continued storage of gametes once someone reaches the age of 18; should the courts have the power to remove gametes from a mentally incapable adult and also be able to specify what should happen to the gametes in the event of a person's death or permanent incapacity? Subsequently amendments to the 1990 Act were made by the Human Fertilisation and Embryology Act 2008.

Human Fertilisation and Embryology Act 2008

The Act amends the 1990 Act to take into account scientific developments which had taken place since 1990 and other changes in social attitude to assisted fertility. The Act includes:

- Ensuring that the creation and use of all human embryos outside the body (whatever the process used in their creation) are subject to regulation.
- Provisions clarifying the scope of legitimate embryo research activities, including regulation of 'inter-species embryos' (embryos combining human and animal material).
- A ban on sex selection of offspring for non-medical reasons. This puts into statute a ban on non-medical sex selection currently in place as a matter of HFEA policy. Sex selection is allowed for medical reasons – for example to avoid a serious disease that affects only boys.
- A provision to recognise same-sex couples as legal parents of children conceived through the use of donated sperm, eggs or embryos. These provisions enable, for example, the civil partner of a woman who carries a child via IVF to be recognised as the child's legal parent.
- The retention of a duty to take account of the welfare of the child in providing fertility treatment, but replacing the reference to 'the need for a father' with 'the need for supportive parenting' – hence valuing the role of all parents
- Altering the restrictions on the use of HFEA-collected data to help enable follow-up research of infertility treatment.

The timetable for these changes to be implemented is as follows:

April 2009   Part 2 of the Act, the revised definitions of parenthood, take effect.
October 2009   The amendments to the 1990 legislation take effect.
April 2010   The parental orders take effect.

Further information on the legislation can be found on the DoH website (http://www.dh.gov.uk/) which provides details of the 1990 Act as amended by the 2007 Regulations and the 2008 Act, and also from the website of the Human Fertilisation and Embryology Authority (http://www.hfea.gov.uk/). The changes to Schedule 3 and the consent provisions which have been introduced by the 2008 Act can be found in Appendix 2. They are due to come into force in October 2009.

Storage without consent

Concern had arisen about the storage of gametes from persons undergoing radiotherapy or chemotherapy. In some cases the patients, especially where the patient was a child, might not have the capacity to consent to the removal and storage of the gametes. As a consequence, new paragraphs 9 and 10 of Schedule 3 to the 1990 Act will allow the storage of gametes, without written consent, providing a medical practitioner certifies that the conditions set out in those paragraphs have been met. The gametes cannot be used for any purpose unless the gamete provider becomes competent and consents to such use.

Adults who lack capacity

Paragraphs 16 to 19 are added to Schedule 3 by the 2008 Act to provide an exception to the requirement for an effective consent for the use of cells from a person who has attained 18 years of age to bring about the creation of an embryo or human admixed embryo and for the subsequent storage and use of any resulting embryo. This exception to the requirement for an effective consent is subject to the specific conditions set out in paragraphs 17 and 18. The HFEA must be satisfied that:

(i) the adult lacks capacity and is unlikely to have capacity again;
(ii) the adult suffers from, or is likely to develop a serious disease, serious disability or other serious medical condition;
(iii) the proposed embryonic research is intended to increase knowledge about that disease/disability/condition or its treatment and care (or similar conditions);
(iv) there is no evidence that the adult would have refused to participate at any time they may have had capacity in the past;
(v) there are reasonable grounds for believing research of comparable effectiveness could not be carried out using the cells of a person who could consent themselves;
(vi) the licence holder has taken steps to identify a carer for the adult who could be consulted or has nominated someone if a carer could not be found;
(vii) the carer or nominee has been consulted as to their opinion of what the adult who lacks capacity's wishes or feelings would be about the proposed use of their cells – if they indicated they did not think that they would want them to be used then the researcher could not use their cells.

Under paragraph 19, an adult donor who acquires capacity can give notice that their cells are not to be used to create any further embryos, or that any existing embryos may not be used in research.

Deceased fathers and use of sperm

Following the Diane Blood case, the Human Fertilisation and Embryology (Deceased Fathers) Act 2003 made provision for the legal status of the man where his sperm had been used after his death. The 2008 Act replaced these provisions by a new section 39. Where a man's sperm, or an embryo created with his sperm, is used after his death, the man may be treated as the child's father, for the purposes of birth registration only, if specified conditions are met:

- The man must have consented, in writing, to the use of the sperm or embryo after his death and to being treated as the child's father for the purposes of birth registration.
- The woman must elect that he should be treated in this way within 42 days (or, in Scotland, 21 days) of the child's birth.
- This provision applies whether the embryo or gametes were transferred to the woman in the UK or elsewhere.

There is also provision in section 40 for the recognition of the status of fatherhood for a deceased man where the sperm was donated subject to specified conditions.

Conclusions

This is an interesting area and the advantages of statutory regulation over the consent provisions are clearly in the interests of all those involved in fertility treatments, although as the Diane Blood case illustrated, there were grounds for a less restrictive framework. It is too early to determine the effect of the changes introduced by the 2008 Act, many of which are still to be brought into force. This is an area of tight control over consent provisions and it may be that some of the lessons learnt from statutory provisions for consent in fertility treatments and also statutory provisions for consent in organ donation by live donors (see Chapter 14) could pave the way to statutory provisions for consent to treatment.

References

Centre for Reproductive Medicine v. *U* [2002] EWCA Civ 565, *The Independent* May 1 2002 CA.

Department of Health (1998) *Sheila McLean Review of the Common Law Provisions Relating to the Removal of Gametes and of the Consent Provisions in the Human Fertilisation and Embryology Act* 1990.

Department of Health Press announcement, 25 August 2000.

Department of Health (2002) *Human Bodies, Human Choices: The law on human organs and tissue in England and Wales. A Consultation Report.* Department of Health and Wales National Assembly.

Evans v. *Amicus Healthcare Ltd and Others* (2003); *Hadley* v. *Midland Fertility Services Ltd and Others, The Times Law Report*, 2 October 2003 [2003] EWHC 2161.

Evans v. *Amicus Healthcare* [2004] EWCA 727.

Evans v. *United Kingdom* [2007] ECHR 264 (application No 6339/05).

Gibb, F. (2002) Separated women seek right to use frozen embryos. *The Times*, 12 September.

R v. *Human Fertilisation and Embryology Authority ex p. Blood* [1997] 2 WLR 806.

CHAPTER 25

Consent and the mentally disordered

> **Box 25.1 Case scenario**
>
> There was a history of mental illness in Ashmed's family and he hated the time that his mother had been given ECT. He made it clear to his family that if he ever became mentally ill and there was any discussion as to whether he should have ECT, he would not want it. He drew up an advance decision making this refusal clear, signed it and had it witnessed. Some years later, Ashmed was detained for six months under the Mental Health Act 1983 (as amended) and clinicians discussed with the family the possibility of his being given ECT. His daughter showed the consultant psychiatrist Ashmed's advance decision. The consultant was uncertain of its validity, since Ashmed was now a detained patient under the Mental Health Act and the consultant was of the view that ECT was in his best interests.

Introduction

In Chapter 7 we considered the law relating to decision making on behalf of those adults who lacked the mental capacity to make their own decisions and noted the new provisions under the Mental Capacity Act 2005 for decisions to be made in the best interests of such persons. In the same chapter we discussed what was meant by the term 'best interests'. In this chapter we look at the statutory provisions relating to mentally disordered adults including the amendments to the 1983 Mental Health Act made by the Mental Health Act 2007. The introduction of the European Convention of Human Rights into the laws of the UK has resulted in many cases brought by the mentally disordered with significant results. In general, where patients are being treated under the provisions of the Mental Health Act 1983 (as amended by the 2007 Act), then they do not come under the provisions of the Mental Capacity Act 2005. Section 28 of the MCA states that:

(1) Nothing in this Act (i.e.MCA) authorises anyone–
    (a) to give a patient medical treatment for mental disorder, or
    (b) to consent to a patient's being given medical treatment for mental disorder,

    if, at the time when it is proposed to treat the patient, his treatment is regulated by Part 4 of the Mental Health Act.
(2) 'Medical treatment', 'mental disorder' and 'patient' have the same meaning as in that Act.

A new Section 1A was added to Section 28 by the Mental Health Act 2007:

(1A) Subsection (1) does not apply in relation to any form of treatment to which section 58A of that Act (electro-convulsive therapy, etc.) applies if the patient comes within subsection (7) of that section (informal patient under 18 who cannot give consent).

Subsection of 7 section 58A states:

(7)1 This section shall not by itself confer sufficient authority for a patient who falls within section 56(5) above to be given a form of treatment to which this section applies if he is not capable of understanding the nature, purpose and likely effects of the treatment (and cannot therefore consent to it).

(Section 56(5) applies to patients who are not under short-term detention, not a community patient; and have not attained the age of 18 years). This provides greater protection to those patients who are to have ECT and other specified treatments.

Long-term detained patients

Under the provision of Part IV of the Mental Health Act 1983 (as amended by the 2007 Act) those patients who are detained under long-term detention provisions (e.g. sections 2, 3, 37 and 41) can in certain circumstances be given compulsory treatment for mental disorder. The definition of medical treatment given in section 145 of the 1983 Act was expanded by the 2007 Act and now includes psychological intervention and specialist mental health habilitation, rehabilitation and care. In addition, a new subsection 4 to section 145 states that

> Any reference in this Act to medical treatment, in relation to mental disorder, shall be construed as a reference to medical treatment the purpose of which is to alleviate, or prevent a worsening of, the disorder or one or more of its symptoms or manifestations.

This will hopefully prevent treatment for mental disorder under the Mental Health Act being used to cover a caesarean section (see page 254 and Chapter 12).

For long-term detained patients, the Act covers treatments for mental disorder in both emergency and non-emergency situations. The provisions are set out in Box 25.2.

Box 25.2 Provisions under Part IV of the Mental Health Act 1983 on consent to treatment (Sections 57, 58, 58A and 63)

1. Treatments involving brain surgery or hormonal implants can only be given with the patient's consent, which must be certified and only after independent certification of the consent and of the fact that the treatment should proceed (Section 57).

2. Treatments involving electroconvulsive therapy, or medication where 3 months or more have elapsed since medication was first given during that period of detention can only be given either (a) with the consent of the patient and it is certified by the patient's own registered medical practitioner or another registered medical practitioner appointed specifically for that purpose that he is capable of understanding its nature, purpose and likely effects, or (b) the registered medical practitioner appointed specifically certifies that the patient has refused or is incapable of consenting but agrees that the treatment should proceed (Section 58). A new Section 58A in relation to ECT treatments has been added by the Mental Health Act 2007 and is discussed below.

3. All other treatments (i.e. those not covered by S 57, 58 and 58A) can be given without the consent of the patient provided they are for mental disorder and are given by or under the direction of the approved clinician in charge of the treatment (Section 63).

Section 58A: new provisions relating to ECT and other specified treatments

Under the amendments to Section 58 by the Mental Health Act 2007, which created a new section 58A, a patient cannot be given ECT unless he falls into one of three categories A, B or C. These provisions are subject to an urgent treatment situation (Sections 62 and 62A; see below).

A. A patient falls within this subsection if–
(a) he has attained the age of 18 years;
(b) he has consented to the treatment in question; and
(c) either the approved clinician in charge of it or a registered medical practitioner appointed as mentioned in section 58(3) above has certified in writing that the patient is capable of understanding the nature, purpose and likely effects of the treatment and has consented to it.

B. A patient falls within this subsection if–
(a) he has not attained the age of 18 years; but
(b) he has consented to the treatment in question; and
(c) a registered medical practitioner appointed as aforesaid (not being the approved clinician in charge of the treatment) has certified in writing–
   (i) that the patient is capable of understanding the nature, purpose and likely effects of the treatment and has consented to it; and
   (ii) that it is appropriate for the treatment to be given.

C. A patient falls within this subsection if a registered medical practitioner appointed as aforesaid (not being the responsible clinician (if there is one) or the approved clinician in charge of the treatment in question) has certified in writing*–
(a) that the patient is not capable of understanding the nature, purpose and likely effects of the treatment; but
(b) that it is appropriate for the treatment to be given; and
(c) that giving him the treatment would not conflict with–
   (i) an advance decision which the registered medical practitioner concerned is satisfied is valid and applicable; or
   (ii) a decision made by a donee or deputy or by the Court of Protection.

*Before this certificate is given the registered medical practitioner concerned shall consult two other persons who have been professionally concerned with the patient's medical treatment but, of those persons–
(a) one shall be a nurse and the other shall be neither a nurse nor a registered medical practitioner; and

(b) neither shall be the responsible clinician (if there is one) or the approved clinician in charge of the treatment in question.

In 2002 a Broadmoor patient challenged the fact that he was given treatment under Section 58 and sought leave to seek judicial review of his treatment, which had been prescribed by his responsible medical officer (RMO) and supported by a second opinion appointed doctor (SOAD). The patient had expert opinion from an independent doctor that the treatment was not appropriate. The Court of Appeal (*R* v. *Broadmoor Hospital*) held that the court would have to consider the medical necessity of the proposed treatment and the capacity of the patient and any future forcible treatment in the light of the Articles of the European Convention and the three doctors should be called to give evidence. The Court of Appeal also held that Article 6 of the Convention required that the certification process by the SOAD should involve the making of an independent and primary judgment on the desirability and propriety of treatment and should not comprise merely a review of the RMO's decision.

Urgent treatment for longer term detained patients

In an emergency or where the patient has withdrawn his consent to treatment under section 58 and 58A, the provisions of sections 57, 58 and 58A do not apply, and Section 62 applies. Section 62 is shown in Box 25.3.

Box 25.3 Section 62 Mental Health Act 1983

Any treatment which is immediately	necessary	to save the patient's life
Treatment which is not irreversible	if it is immediately necessary	to prevent serious deterioration
Treatment which is not irreversible or hazardous	if it is immediately necessary	to alleviate serious suffering
Treatment which is not irreversible or hazardous	if it is immediately necessary and represents the minimum interference necessary	to prevent the patient from behaving violently or being a danger to himself or others

Section 62 enables different treatments to be given according to the degree of urgency and whether they are irreversible or hazardous.

Irreversible is defined as 'if it has unfavourable irreversible physical or psychological consequences' and hazardous is defined as 'if it entails significant physical hazard'.

Amendments have been made to Section 62 to cover ECT and other treatments specified under Section 58,

(1A) Section 58A above, in so far as it relates to electro-convulsive therapy by virtue of subsection (1)(a) of that section, shall not apply to any treatment which falls within paragraph (a) or (b) of subsection (1) above.

(1B) Section 58A above, in so far as it relates to a form of treatment specified by virtue of subsection (1)(b) of that section, shall not apply to any treatment which falls within such of paragraphs (a) to (d) of subsection (1) above as may be specified in regulations under that section.

In addition, regulations made under Section 58 A may

(a) may make different provision for different cases (and may, in particular, make different provision for different forms of treatment);
(b) may make provision which applies subject to specified exceptions; and
(c) may include transitional, consequential, incidental or supplemental provision.

Emergency treatment recall of a community patient or revocation of the community treatment order.

The 2007 Act introduced a community treatment order and a new Section 62A has been added to the 1983 Act to cover treatment for those on recall of a community treatment order or a revocation of the order which is shown in Box 25.4.

Section 63 treatments

It can be seen from Box 25.2 that those treatments which do not come under sections 57, 58 or 58A come under section 63 and can be given without the consent of the patient provided that the treatment is for mental disorder and is

Box 25.4 62A Treatment on recall of community patient or revocation of order

(1) This section applies where—
   (a) a community patient is recalled to hospital under section 17E above; or
   (b) a patient is liable to be detained under this Act following the revocation of a community treatment order under section 17F above in respect of him.
(2) For the purposes of section 58(1)(b) above, the patient is to be treated as if he had remained liable to be detained since the making of the community treatment order.
(3) But section 58 above does not apply to treatment given to the patient if—
   (a) the certificate requirement is met for the purposes of section 64C or 64E below; or
   (b) as a result of section 64B(4) or 64E(4) below, the certificate requirement would not apply (were the patient a community patient not recalled to hospital under section 17E above).
(4) Section 58A above does not apply to treatment given to the patient if there is authority to give the treatment, and the certificate require-ment is met, for the purposes of section 64C or 64E below.
(5) In a case where this section applies, the certificate requirement is met only in so far as—
   (a) the Part 4A certificate expressly provides that it is appropriate for one or more specified forms of treatment to be given to the patient in that case (subject to such conditions as may be specified); or
   (b) a notice having been given under subsection (4) of section 64H below, treatment is authorised by virtue of subsection (7) of that section.
(6) Subsection (4)(a) above shall not preclude the continuation of any treat-ment, or of treatment under any plan, pending compliance with section 58 or 58A above if the approved clinician in charge of the treatment considers that the discontinuance of the treatment, or of the treatment under the plan, would cause serious suffering to the patient.
(7) In a case where subsection (1)(b) above applies, subsection (3) above only applies pending compliance with section 58 above.
(8) In subsection (5) above—
   'Part 4A certificate' has the meaning given in section 64H below; and 'specified', in relation to a Part 4A certificate, means specified in the certificate.

given by or under the direction of the approved clinician in charge of the treatment . In the case of *B* v. *Croydon HA* [1995] the Court of Appeal held that treatment for mental disorder could include treatment to relieve the symptoms of the mental disorder as well as treatment ancillary to the core treatment. It could therefore cover compulsory feeding of a patient suffering from anorexia. (Force-feeding of anorexia patients was also permitted under section 63 in two other cases: *Riverside Mental Health NHS Trust* v. *Fox* [1994] and *Re KB* (1994). The definition of treatment for mental disorder was given an extended meaning in the case of *Tameside and Glossop Acute Services Trust* v. *CH* where the court held that a patient detained under the Mental Health Act could be given a caesarean section as treatment for her mental disorder (see Chapter 12). In the light of the decision of the Court of Appeal in St George's NHS Trust (1998), where a woman suffering from mental disorder is detained under the Mental Health Act 1983 and is refusing a caesarean, best practice would ensure that an application were made to court for a determination of her capacity and (if it is held that she lacks mental capacity) a determination of what is in her best interests.

Further information on the law relating to detained patients can be obtained from the Department of Health website. The Mental Health Acts can be accessed on the Office of Public Sector Information website (http://www.opsi. gov.uk/).

Patients not detained under the Mental Health Act

Where a patient is a detained patient under Mental Health legislation, the treatment for mental disorder is covered by the Mental Health Acts and not the Mental Capacity Act 2005. However, where the patient is not detained, then the patient may come under the Mental Capacity Act if the patient lacks the requisite mental capacity.

In the case of *R* v. *Bournewood Community and Mental Health NHS Trust* the House of Lords held that patients who did not have the capacity to consent to admission to psychiatric hospital could be detained under common law powers. The European Court of Justice however held that the use of common law powers to detain a person conflicted with article 5 rights. Concerns about the clash between this use of common law powers and Article 5 of the European Convention of Human Rights were taken account in the Mental Health Act 2007 which amended the Mental Capacity Act 2005 to provide safeguards for such persons. These safeguards are known as the Bournewood safeguards or Deprivation of Liberty Safeguards and are discussed below.

The Deprivation of Liberty (Bournewood) safeguards

Where a person is suffering from mental disorder and needs to be deprived of liberty for their own safety or to safeguard that of others, an application can be made by the managing authority (e.g. care home or hospital) to the supervisory authority for permission to detain that person. On receipt of the application the supervisory authority must ensure that they receive several assessments to ensure that the qualifying requirements of the deprivation of liberty safeguards are met. The safeguards came into force in April 2009.

The supervisory body has a legal responsibility to select assessors who are both suitable and eligible. Assessments must be completed within 21 days for a standard deprivation of liberty authorisation, or, where an urgent authorisation has been given, before the urgent authorisation expires. The assessments are:

- age assessment – the person must be over 18 years
- no refusals assessment – an advance decision or the appointment of an attorney under a LPA which conflicted with the deprivation of liberty would prevent the detention proceedings
- mental capacity assessment – to determine if the person lacks capacity as defined in the MCA
- mental health assessment – to determine if the person suffers from mental disorder as defined in the MHA 1983 (as amended by the 2007 Act)
- eligibility assessment – a person who is detained under the MHA or subject to recall under the MHA is not eligible for deprivation of liberty under these provisions
- best interests assessment – to determine if it is in the best interests of the relevant person to be deprived of liberty; if it is necessary for them to be deprived of liberty in order to prevent harm to themselves, and if the deprivation of liberty is a proportionate response to the likelihood of the relevant person suffering harm and the seriousness of that harm.

Standard forms are available for completion by each of the assessors.

An urgent authorisation can be given in specific circumstances where the need for the person to be deprived of their liberty is so urgent that deprivation needs to begin before the standard authorisation request is made, or it has made a request for a standard authorisation, but believes that the need for a person to be deprived of liberty has now become so urgent that deprivation of liberty needs to begin before the request is dealt with by the supervisory body. This means that an urgent authorisation can never be given without a request for a standard authorisation being made simultaneously.

The managing authority must decide the period for which the urgent authorisation is given, but this must not exceed seven days. The authorisation must be in writing and must state:

- the name of the relevant person
- the name of the relevant hospital or care home
- the period for which the authorisation is to be in force, and
- the purpose for which the authorisation is given.

A supplementary Code of Practice covering the deprivation of liberty safeguards has been published by the Lord Chancellor (Lord Chancellor (2008)) and can be down loaded from the Office of Public Guardian website (http://www.publicguardian.gov.uk/). The supplementary Code of Practice provides key points for care homes and hospitals (managing authorities); key points for local authorities and NHS bodies (supervisory bodies); and key points for managing authorities and supervisory bodies. Regulations can be accessed on the OPSI website (http://www.opsi.gov.uk/) (MCA, 2008).

Independent mental health advocates

The Mental Health Act 2007 also introduced into the 1983 Act provisions for the appointment of independent mental health advocates for qualifying patients. These arrangements and their functions are discussed in Chapter 17. The regulations relating to the appointment of independent mental health advocates can be found on the OPSI website (http://www.opsi.gov.uk/) (MHA, 2008).

Application of the law to the case scenario (Box 25.1)

As a consequence of the changes introduced by the Mental Health Act 2007, a patient over 18 years can only be given ECT if he consents to it and has the requisite mental capacity to give consent or if he lacks the requisite mental capacity and certain conditions are satisfied. These conditions are that an independent doctor has certified that:

(a) that the patient is not capable of understanding the nature, purpose and likely effects of the treatment; but
(b) that it is appropriate for the treatment to be given; and
(c) that giving him the treatment would not conflict with–

(i)   an advance decision which the registered medical practitioner concerned is satisfied is valid and applicable; or

(ii) a decision made by a donee or deputy or by the Court of Protection.

In this situation, even though Ashmed is no longer capable of understanding the nature, purpose and likely effects of the ECT and even though it may be an appropriate treatment clinically, it cannot be given to him contrary to his advance decision. It must be established that this advance decision is valid and applicable.

Conclusions

There have been significant changes to the law relating to compulsory treatment and detention in recent years. The amendments introduced by the Mental Health Act 2007 are only just being implemented and the Deprivation of Liberty (Bournewood) safeguards are very much in their infancy. It is hoped that there will be close monitoring of the situation to ascertain how successful these innovations and amendments are in providing protection for those who are incapable of giving consent to treatment as a result of mental disorder.

References

B v. *Croydon HA* [1995] 1 All ER 683.

Re KB (Adult) (Mental Patient: Medical Treatment) (1994) 19 B.M.L.R.144.

Lord Chancellor (2008) *Deprivation of Liberty Safeguards. Code of Practice to Supplement the Main Mental Capacity Act 2005 Code of Practice.* Stationery Office, London.

MCA (2008) *The Mental Capacity (Deprivation of Liberty: Standard Authorisation Assessment and Ordinary Residence) Regulations 2008* SI 2008 No 1858.

MHA (2008) *Mental Health Act 1983 (Independent Mental Health Advocates) (England) Regulations 2008* SI 2008 No 3166.

Riverside Mental Health NHS Trust v. *Fox* [1994] 1 F.L.R. 6614.

R v. *Bournewood Community and Mental Health NHS Trust Ex p L* [1999] 1 AC 458.

R v. *Broadmoor Hospital (and others)* [2002] Lloyd's reports Medical 41.

St George's Healthcare NHS Trust v. *S, R* v. *Collins ex parte S* (1998) 44 BMLR 160 CA; [1998] 3 All ER 673.

Tameside and Glossop Acute Services Trust v. *CH (A patient)* [1996] 1 F.L.R. 762.

CHAPTER 26

Overview

This final chapter, attempts, in the light of the relevant statutes, the common law and the Department of Health guidance, to draw out the main principles which have been explored in this book.

Consent as part of a process

The first point to emphasise is that consent is not simply a signature on a form: it is the outcome of a process of communication between clinician and patient over the nature of the treatment and investigations proposed and the risks and benefits which could occur. Communication should be a two-way process and the questions of the patient should be answered fully and honestly. The signature should be evidence that this process has been followed and that the patient consents. Consent can also be evidenced by word of mouth and by non-verbal communication, but in situations where there are risks or potential disagreement over whether consent was given, it is preferable to obtain the patient's signature.

Distinction between trespass to the person and breach of the duty of care to inform

If the patient understands what is proposed and gives consent to that invasion of his or her person, then the patient would not be successful in an action for trespass to the person (assault or battery). A trespass to the person is a civil wrong – one of a group known as 'torts' – and is actionable without the person proving that harm has been suffered. In contrast, failure to inform the patient of the significant risks of substantial harm arising would give rise to an action in negligence for breach of the duty to inform the patient according to the reasonable standard of care (i.e. the Bolam test: *Bolam* v. *Friern Hospital Management Committee* [1957]). In this latter action, harm must have occurred.

Capacity

In order to give a valid consent a person must have the mental capacity to understand the information which is being given to him or her. Under the Mental Capacity Act 2005, there is a statutory presumption in favour of the fact that a person over 16 years has the requisite mental capacity, but this can be displaced if evidence suggests a lack of capacity. In the case of *Re C (adult: refusal of medical treatment)* [1994], the judge held that where the capacity of the patient was in dispute or doubt, there were three tests which must be applied:

■ Could the patient comprehend and retain the necessary information?
■ Was he able to believe it?
■ Was he able to weigh the information, balancing risks and needs, so as to arrive at a choice?

In applying these tests to the patient before him, the judge decided that the Broadmoor patient (who was a chronic schizophrenic) did have the mental capacity to refuse a life-saving amputation.

These tests have now been placed on a statutory footing by the Mental Capacity Act 2005, which sets the following criteria to determine if a person is unable to make decisions as a result of an impairment of, or a disturbance in the functioning of, the mind or brain. A person is unable to make decisions if he is unable:

(a) to understand the information relevant to the decision,
(b) to retain that information,
(c) to use or weigh that information as part of the process of making the decision, or
(d) to communicate his decision (whether by talking, using sign language or any other means).

Voluntary and without fraud

The consent must also be given with the free will of the mentally competent adult and without any deception. The DoH guidance warns of the dangers of patients being pressurised by parents or family members as well as health or care professionals. Care should be taken to avoid coercion which invalidates consent, especially where the patient is under involuntary detention as in prison or a mental hospital (DoH, 2001a, paragraphs 3 and 3.1).

Withdrawal of consent

Consent can usually (there are exceptions under the Human Fertilisation and Embryology Act 1990 (see Chapter 24)) be withdrawn at any time, but checks should be made to ensure that the patient has the capacity to withdraw the consent. For example, a patient may as a result of pain or panic ask for the treatment to stop. In a situation where the patient, having given a valid consent, objects during the process of treatment and asks for the practitioner to stop, the DoH suggests that it is good practice for the practitioner to establish the patient's concerns and explain the consequences of not completing the procedure (DoH, 2001a, paragraphs 18 and 18.1).

Advance refusals (living wills)

Advance refusals or advance decisions are valid by statute, if at the time they were made the patient was mentally competent and the contents apply to the situation which has arisen and at this later time the patient lacks capacity. There are more stringent rules to follow if the refusal relates to life-sustaining treatment.

Adults lacking mental capacity

If mental incapacity has been established, healthcare professionals have a duty to act in the best interests of the patient following the steps set out in the Mental Capacity Act. Legislation providing for decision making on behalf of a mentally incapacitated adult has been enacted in the Mental Capacity Act 2005. If there is doubt over the validity of a living will, an application can be made to the newly established Court of Protection and the patient kept alive until the court has decided on its validity. Professionals withholding care on the basis of a valid living will would be acting lawfully. The Court of Appeal has issued guidelines on the action which should be taken if a person is refusing necessary care and treatment and there are reasonable doubts over the person's mental capacity to refuse (*Re MB (an adult: medical treatment)*, 1997).

Children and young persons

A young person of 16 or 17 years has a statutory right to give consent to treatment which includes medical, surgical and dental treatment, anaesthetic and diagnostic procedures (Family Law Reform Act 1969 – sections 8(1) and (2)). Parents of children below 18 years also have the right to give consent to treatment on the child provided it is in the best interests of the child. Children and young persons (i.e. persons under 18 years) do not have the right in law to refuse life-saving treatment if that is in their best interests (*Re W (a minor) (medical treatment)* [1992]). However, overruling a young person's refusal of treatment would not be lightly done. Children under 16 years, while they do not have a statutory right to give consent, are able at common law to give a valid consent, provided that they have sufficient understanding and intelligence to enable them to understand fully what is involved in a proposed intervention (i.e. they are considered to be Gillick-competent – *Gillick* v. *West Norfolk and Wisbech AHA* [1986]).

Withdrawing and withholding life-prolonging treatment

Life-saving treatment (including resuscitation) can be withdrawn or withheld for the reasons cited in Table 26.1. These principles were confirmed by the House of Lords in the case involving the Hillsborough victim Tony Bland

Table 26.1 Reasons for withdrawing and withholding life-saving treatment (including resuscitation).

- The patient refuses to have it and the patient is mentally competent
- The patient has drawn up a valid advance refusal which applies to the situation and complies with the statutory requirements for refusing life-sustaining treatment
- The treatment would not succeed
- The long-term prognosis of the patient is such that treatment is not in the best interests of a mentally incapacitated patient

(*Airedale NHS Trust* v. *Bland* [1993]). The DoH has issued guidance on 'not for resuscitation' instructions (NHS Executive, 2000). It recommends the guidance issued by the British Medical Association (BMA), the Resuscitation Council (UK) and the RCN which was issued in 1999 and recently updated (BMA, Resuscitation Council (UK), RCN, 2001 revised 2007). Withholding life-saving treatment from patients in a persistent vegetative state has been held not to be contrary to articles 2 or 3 of the European Convention on Human Rights (*NHS Trust A* v. *Mrs M* and *NHS Trust B* v. *Mrs H Family Division* [2001]).

Other situations

As this book has shown, there are many and varied situations where these basic principles have to be applied. Thus, the laws relating to consent and research, organ donation, and caesarean sections have all been considered in detail. The law relating to those compulsorily detained under the Mental Health Act 1983 (as amended by the 2007 Act) is considered in Chapter 25.

The NHS Constitution

At the time of writing there is being debated in Parliament a Health Bill 2009 which would place on a statutory footing an NHS Constitution, the finalised version of which was published in January 2009. It sets out rights (i.e legally enforceable obligations on others) and pledges (i.e aims which the NHS will strive to deliver).

In relation to consent it states the following:

Respect, consent and confidentiality:

You have the right to be treated with dignity and respect in accordance with your human rights.

You have the right to accept or refuse treatment that is offered to you, and not to be given any physical examination or treatment unless you have given valid consent. If you do not have the capacity to do so, consent must be obtained from a person legally able to act on your behalf, or the treatment must be in your best interests.

You have the right to be given information about your proposed treatment in advance, including any significant risks and any alternative treatments which may be available, and the risks involved in doing nothing.

You have the right to privacy and confidentiality and to expect the NHS to keep your confidential information safe and secure.

You have the right to access your own health records. These will always be used to manage your treatment in your best interests.

The NHS also commits:
- to share with you any letters sent between clinicians about your care (pledge).

Informed choice:

You have the right to choose your GP practice, and to be accepted by that practice unless there are reasonable grounds to refuse, in which case you will be informed of those reasons.

You have the right to express a preference for using a particular doctor within your GP practice, and for the practice to try to comply.

You have the right to make choices about your NHS care and to information to support those choices. The options available to you will develop over time and depend on your individual needs. Details are set out in the *Handbook to the NHS Constitution.*

The NHS also commits:
- to inform you about the healthcare services available to you, locally and nationally (pledge); and
- to offer you easily accessible information to enable you to participate fully in your own healthcare decisions and to support you in making choices. This will include information on the quality of clinical services where there is robust and accurate information available (pledge).

Involvement in your healthcare and in the NHS:

You have the right to be involved in discussions and decisions about your healthcare, and to be given information to enable you to do this.

You have the right to be involved, directly or through representatives, in the planning of healthcare services, the development and consideration of proposals for changes in the way those services are provided, and in decisions to be made affecting the operation of those services.

The NHS also commits:

- to provide you with the information you need to participate effectively to influence the planning and delivery of NHS services (pledge); and
- to work in partnership with you, your family, carers and representatives (pledge).

Conclusions

Inevitably decisions by the judges in interpreting the Mental Capacity Act 2005 and the other statutes relating to consent and in filling the gaps in statutory provisions covering the law on consent will add to the law outlined in this book. More guidance will be issued by professional registration bodies and other associations to assist healthcare professionals. In addition, at the time of writing, the Coroners and Justice Bill is making its way through Parliament and may lead to significant changes in the offences of manslaughter and assisted suicide. There may be more statutory provisions – for example to cover the amputation of healthy limbs – which may provide more clarity. It is hoped however that this second edition will provide a foundation of understanding upon which these future changes can be built.

References

Airedale NHS Trust v. *Bland* [1993] AC 789.

Bolam v. *Friern Hospital Management Committee* [1957] 1 WLR 582.

British Medical Association, Resuscitation Council (UK) and Royal College of Nursing (2001 revised 2007) *Decisions Relating to Cardiopulmonary Resuscitation: A Joint Statement from the BMA, Resuscitation Council (UK) and the RCN.* BMA, London.

Department of Health (1999) *Reform of the Mental Health Act 1983.* Stationery Office, London.

Department of Health (2002) *Draft Mental Health Bill.* Stationery Office, London.

Gillick v. *West Norfolk and Wisbech AHA* [1986] AC 112.

Lord Chancellor (1999) *Making Decisions on Behalf of Mentally Incapacitated Adults.* Lord Chancellor's Office, London.

NHS Executive (2000) *Executive Resuscitation Policy. HSC 2000/028.* NHS Executive, Leeds.

NHS Trust A v. *Mrs M* and *NHS Trust B* v. *Mrs H Family Division* [2001] Lloyd's Rep Med 27.

Re C (adult: refusal of medical treatment) [1994] 1 All ER 819.

Re F (mental patient: sterilisation) [1990] 2 AC 1.

Re MB (an adult: medical treatment) (1997) 38 BMLR 175; *St George's Healthcare NHS Trust v. S* [1998] 3 All ER 673.

Re W (a minor) (medical treatment) [1992] 4 All ER 627.

Further reading

Archbold (2007) *Criminal Pleadings, Evidence and Practice*, 55th rev edn (ed. P. J. Richardson). Sweet and Maxwell, London.

Atkinson, J. (2007) *Advance Directives in Mental Health – Theory, Practice and Ethics*. Jessica Kingsley, London.

Beauchamp, T. L. and Childres, J. F. (2001) *Principles of Biomedical Ethics*, 5th edn. Oxford University Press, Oxford.

Blackstone's *Civil Practice 2008* (ed. William Rose). Oxford University Press, Oxford.

Brazier, M. (2007) *Medicine, Patients and the Law*, 4th edn. Penguin, Harmondsworth.

British Medical Association (1998) *Medical Ethics Today*. BMJ Publishing, London.

Britton, A. *Health Care Law and Ethics*. W. Green, London.

Clerk, J. F. (2006) *Clerk and Lindsell on Torts*, 19th edn, Sweet & Maxwell, London.

Deakin, S., Johnston, A. and Markensinis, B. (2007) *Markensinis and Deakin's Tort Law*, 6th edn. Clarendon Press, Oxford.

Denis, I. H. (1999) *The Law of Evidence*, Sweet & Maxwell, London.

Dimond, B. C. (2002) *Legal Aspects of Pain Management*. Quay Publications/Mark Allen, London.

Dimond, B. C. (2008) *Legal Aspects of Death*. Quay Publications/Mark Allen, London.

Dimond, B. C. (2008) *Legal Aspects of Nursing*, 5th edn. Pearson Education, Harlow.

Dimond, B. C. (1999) *Patients' Rights, Responsibilities and the Nurse*, 2nd edn. Central Health Studies, Quay Publications, London.

Dimond, B. C. (2008) *Legal Aspects of Mental Capacity*. Wiley Blackwell, Chichester.

Eliot, C. (2007) *The English Legal System*, 8th edn. Pearson Education, Harlow.

Harris, D. J. (2005) *Cases and Materials on the European Convention on Human Rights*, 2nd edn. Butterworth, London.

Harris, P. (2007) *An Introduction to Law*, 7th edn. Butterworth, London.

Hendrick, J. (2006) *Law and Ethics in Nursing and Healthcare*, 2nd edn. Nelson Thornes, London.

Herring, J. (2006) *Medical Law and Ethics*. Oxford University Press, Oxford.

Hockton, A. (2002) *The Law on Consent to Treatment*. Sweet & Maxwell, London.

Hoggett, B. (2005) *Mental Health Law*, 5th edn. Sweet & Maxwell, London.

Hurwitz, B. and Paquita, Z. (2006) *Everyday Ethics in Primary Care*. BMJ, London.

Ingman, T. (2006) *The English Legal Process*, 11th edn. Blackstone Press, Oxford.

Jones, M. A. (2002) *Textbook on Torts*, 8th edn. Oxford University Press, Oxford.

Jones, M. A. (2003) *Medical Negligence*, 3rd edn. Sweet & Maxwell, London.

Jones, M. A. and Morris, A. E. (2005) *Blackstone's Statutes on Medical Law*, 4th edn. Oxford University Press, Oxford.

Jones, R. (2006) *Mental Health Act Manual*, 10th edn. Sweet & Maxwell, London.

Keenan, D. (2004) *Smith and Keenan's English Law*, 14th edn. Longman, Harlow.

Kennedy, I. and Grubb, A. (2000) *Medical Law*, 3rd edn. Butterworth, London.

Leach, P. (2005) *Taking a Case to the European Court of Human Rights*, 2nd edn. Blackstone Press, Oxford.

Mason, J. K., McCall-Smith, R. A. and Laurie, G. T. (2002) *Law and Medical Ethics*, 6th edn. Butterworth, London.

McHale, J. and Fox, M. (2007) *Health Care Law*, 2nd edn. Sweet & Maxwell, London.

McHale, J. and Tingle, J. (2007) *Law and Nursing*, 2nd edn. Elsevier Health Sciences, Oxford.

McLean, S. (2007) *Impairment and Disability: Law and Ethics At the Beginning and End of Life*. Routledge-Cavendish, London.

Montgomery, J. (2003) *Health Care Law*, 2nd edn. Oxford University Press, Oxford.

Murphy, J. (2006) *Street on Torts*, 12th edn. Butterworth, London.

Rogers, W. V. H. (2006) *Winfield and Jolowicz on Tort*, 17th edn. Thomson, Sweet & Maxwell, London.

Rowson, R. (1990) *An Introduction to Ethics for Nurses*. Scutari Press, London.

Rowson, R. (2006) *Working Ethics – How to Be Fair in a Culturally Complex World*. Jessica Kingsley, London.

Sime, S. (2006) *Practical Approach to Civil Procedure*, 9th edn. Blackstone Press, Oxford.

Skegg, P. D. G. (1998) *Law, Ethics and Medicine*, 2nd edn. Oxford University Press, Oxford.

Slapper, G. and Kelly, D. (2006) *The English Legal System*, 8th edn. Routledge-Cavendish, London.

Stauch, M. (2005) *Text and Materials on Medical Law*. 3rd edn. Cavendish, London.

Steiner, J. (2006) *Textbook on EC Law*, 9th edn. Oxford University Press, Oxford.

Storch, J. (2004) *Towards a Moral Horizon: Nursing Ethics for Leadership and Practice*. Pearson Education, Harlow.

Tingle, J. and Cribb, A. (2007) *Nursing Law and Ethics*, 3rd edn. Blackwell, Oxford.

Tingle, J. and Foster, C. (2002) *Clinical Guidelines: Law, Policy and Practice*. Cavendish, London.

Tschudin, V. (2002) *Ethics in Nursing: the Caring Relationship*, 3rd edn. Butterworth-Heinemann, London.

Vincent, C. (ed.) (1995) *Clinical Risk Management*. BMJ Publishing, London.

Wheeler, J. (2006) *The English Legal System*, 2nd edn. Pearson Education, Harlow.

White, R., Carr, P. and Lowe, N. (2002) *A Guide to the Children Act 1989*, 3rd edn. Butterworth, London.

Wilkinson, R. and Caul eld, H. (2000) *The Human Rights Act: A Practical Guide for Nurses*. Whurr Publishers, London.

Glossary

acceptance an agreement to the terms of an offer which leads to a binding legal obligation, i.e. a **contract**

accusatorial a system of court proceedings where the two sides contest the issue (contrast with **inquisitorial**)

Act of Parliament, **statute**

action legal proceedings

actionable *per se* a court action where claimant does not have to show loss, **damage** or harm to obtain compensation, e.g. an action for **trespass to the person**

actus reus essential element of a crime that must be proved to secure a conviction, as opposed to the mental state of the accused (***mens rea***)

advance decision occurs when someone who has mental capacity (is able to make and understand a decision) decides that they do not want a particular type of treatment if they lack capacity in the future. A doctor must respect this decision if it is valid and applicable. An advance decision must be about treatment a person wants to refuse and when that person wants to refuse it.

adversarial approach adopted in an **accusatorial** system

advocate a person who pleads for another: it could be paid and professional, such as a **barrister** or solicitor, or it could be a lay advocate either paid or unpaid; a witness is not an advocate

affidavit a statement given under oath

alternative dispute resolution methods to resolve a dispute without going to court such as mediation

approved social worker a social worker qualified for the purposes of the Mental Health Act 1983. The Mental Health Act 2007 replaces the ASW with an Approved Mental Health Professional

arrestable offence an offence defined in Section 24 of the Police and Criminal Evidence Act 1984 that gives to the citizen the power of arrest in certain circumstances without a warrant

assault a threat of unlawful contact (**trespass to the person**)

bailee A person to whom goods have been formally handed over, e.g. for safe-keeping or repair.

balance of probabilities standard of proof in **civil** proceedings

barrister a lawyer qualified to take a case in court

battery an unlawful touching (*see* **trespass to the person**)

bench magistrates, justices of the peace

best interests anything done for people without capacity must be in their best interests (there is no legal definition of best interests, but the criteria to be used are in section 4 of the Mental Capacity Act 2005). Best Interests means that thinking about what is best for the person, not about what anyone else wants.

Bolam Test test laid down by Judge McNair in the case of *Bolam* v. *Friern HMC* on the standard of care expected of a professional in cases of alleged **negligence**

burden of proof duty of a party to litigation to establish the facts or, in criminal proceedings, the duty of the prosecution to establish both *actus* **reus** and *mens* **rea**

case citation Each case is reported in an official series of cases according to the following symbols: *Re F* (i.e. in the matter of F) or *F* v. *West Berkshire Health Authority* 1989 2 All ER 545, which means the year 1989 volume 2 of the *All England Law Reports*, page 545. Each case can be cited by means of this reference system. In the case of *Whitehouse* v. *Jordan*, Whitehouse is the claimant, Jordan the defendant and 'v.' stands for versus, i.e. against. Other law reports include: AC *Appeals Court*; QB *Queens Bench Division* and WLR *Weekly Law Reports*

cause of action The facts that entitle a person to sue.

certiorari an **action** taken to challenge an administrative or judicial decision (literally: to make more certain)

civil action proceedings brought in the civil courts

civil wrong an act or omission which can be pursued in the civil courts by the person who has suffered the wrong (*see* **tort**)

claimant person bringing a civil **action** (originally **plaintiff**)

committal proceedings hearings before the **magistrates** to decide if a person should be sent for **trial** in the Crown Court

common law law derived from the decisions of judges, case law, judge made law

conditional fee system a system whereby client and lawyer can agree that payment of fees is dependent on the outcome of the court **action**; also known as 'no win, no fee'

conditions terms of a contract (*see* **warranties**)

constructive knowledge knowledge that can be obtained from the circumstances

continuous service length of service an employee must have served to be entitled to receive certain statutory or contractual rights

contract an agreement enforceable in law

contract for services an agreement enforceable in law whereby one party provides services, not being employment, in return for payment or other consideration from the other

contract of service a contract for employment

coroner a person appointed to hold an inquiry (inquest) into a death that occurred in unexpected or unusual circumstances

counter-offer a response to an offer that suggests different terms and is therefore counted as an offer, not an **acceptance**

criminal wrong an act or omission which can be pursued in the criminal courts

cross-examination questions asked of a witness by the lawyer for the opposing side: leading questions may be asked

damages a sum of money awarded by a court as compensation for a tort or breach of contract

declaration a ruling by the court setting out the legal situation

delegation When a health professional asks someone else, who could be a colleague, student, or support worker, to carry out a task or treatment on their behalf.

disclosure documents made available to the other party

discovery The process in a civil action whereby the parties each disclose to the other side all the relevant documents in their possession, whether or not they are prejudicial to their own case

dissenting judge a judge who disagrees with the decision of the majority of judges

distinguished (of cases) rules of precedent require judges to follow decisions of judges in previous cases, where these are binding on them. However, in some circumstances, it is possible to come to a different decision, because the facts of the earlier case are not comparable to the case now being heard and therefore the earlier decision can be 'distinguished'

examination in chief witness is asked questions in court by the lawyer of the party that has asked the witness to attend. Leading questions may not be asked

ex gratia as a matter of favour, e.g. without admission of **liability**, of payment offered to a claimant

ex parte An application made to the court (usually on an urgent matter) without the other side being present or represented

expert witness evidence given by a person whose general opinion, based on training or experience, is relevant to some of the issues in dispute (contrast with **witness of fact**)

fitness to practise when the HPC says that someone is 'fit to practise', it means that they have the skills, knowledge, character and health to do their job safely and effectively. The HPC also means that it trusts them to act legally

frustration (of contracts) ending of a contract by operation of law, because of the existence of an event not contemplated by the parties when they made the contract, e.g. imprisonment, death, blindness

guardian *ad litem* a person with a social work and child care background who is appointed to ensure that the court is fully informed of the relevant facts which relate to a child and that the wishes and feelings of the child are clearly established. The appointment is made from a panel set up by the local authority.

guilty a finding in a criminal court of responsibility for a criminal offence

habeas corpus the proceedings commenced by a writ whereby an organisation or official who has another person in their custody is required to produce that person

hearsay evidence that has been learnt from another person

hierarchy recognised status of courts that results in lower courts following the decisions of higher courts (see **precedent**). Thus decisions of the House of Lords must be followed by all lower courts unless they can be **distinguished**

indictment a written accusation against a person, charging him with a serious crime, triable by jury

informed consent When a patient/client/service user has all the necessary information in a form they can understand so that they can make an informed decision about whether they wish to have a particular treatment.

informal of a patient who has entered hospital without any statutory requirements

injunction an order of the court restraining a person

inquisitorial a system of justice whereby the truth is revealed by an inquiry into the facts conducted by the judge, e.g. **coroner's** court

invitation to treat early stages in negotiating a **contract**, e.g. an advertisement or letter expressing interest. An invitation to treat will often precede an **offer** that, when accepted, leads to the formation of an agreement that, if there is consideration and an intention to create legal relations, will be binding

judicial review an application to the High Court for a judicial or administrative decision to be reviewed and an appropriate order made, e.g. declaration

justice of the peace (JP) a lay **magistrate**, i.e. not legally qualified, who hears **summary** (minor) **offences** and sometimes indictable (serious) offences in the magistrates' court in a group of three (*see* bench)

liable/liability responsible for the wrong doing or harm in civil proceedings

litigation civil proceedings

magistrate a person (*see* **justice of the peace and stipendiary magistrate)** who hears summary (minor) offences or indictable offences that can be heard in the magistrates' court

mens rea mental element in a crime (contrast with *actus reus*)

negligence a civil action for compensation, also a failure to follow a reasonable standard of care

next friend a person who brings a court action on behalf of a minor

offer a proposal made by a party that, if accepted, can lead to a contract. It often follows an invitation to treat

ombudsman a commissioner (e.g. health, local government) appointed by the government to hear complaints

payment into court an offer to settle a dispute at a particular sum, which is paid into court. The claimant's failure to accept the offer means that the claimant is liable to pay costs, if the final award is the same or less than the payment made

pedagogic of the science of teaching

plaintiff term formerly used to describe one who brings an action in the civil courts. Now the term **claimant** is used

plea in mitigation a formal statement to the court aimed at reducing the sentence to be pronounced by the judge

practice direction guidance issued by the head of the court to which they relate on the procedure to be followed

pre-action protocol rules of the Supreme Court that provide guidance on action to be taken before legal proceedings commence

precedent a decision that may have to be followed in a subsequent court hearing (*see* **hierarchy**)

prima facie at first sight; sufficient evidence brought by one party to require the other party to provide a defence

privilege in relation to evidence, being able to refuse to disclose it to the court

privity relationship that exists between parties as the result of a legal agreement

professional misconduct conduct of a registered health practitioner that could lead to conduct and competence proceedings by the registration body

proof evidence that secures the establishment of a claimant's, prosecution's or defendant's case

prosecution pursuing of criminal offences in court

quantum amount of compensation, or the monetary value of a claim

Queen's Counsel (QC) a senior barrister, also known as a 'silk'

reasonable doubt to secure a conviction in criminal proceedings the prosecution must establish 'beyond reasonable doubt' the guilt of the accused

Re F ruling a professional who acts in the best interests of an incompetent person who is incapable of giving consent does not act unlawfully if he follows the accepted standard of care according to the **Bolam Test**

rescission where a **contract** is ended by the order of a court or by the cancellation of the contract by one party entitled in law to do so

scope of practice a health professional's scope of practice is the area or areas of their profession in which they have the knowledge, skills and experience to practise lawfully, safely and effectively

solicitor a lawyer who is qualified on the register held by the Law Society

standards for continuing professional development The standards for continuing professional development link a health professional's ongoing learning and development with their continued registration.

standards of proficiency These are the standards for safe and effective practice in each profession. Health professionals must meet these standards to become registered

statute law (statutory) law made by **Acts** of Parliament

stipendiary magistrate a legally qualified magistrate who is paid (i.e. has a stipend)

strict liability liability for a criminal act where the mental element does not have to be proved; in civil proceedings liability without establishing **negligence**

subpoena an order of the court requiring a person to appear as a witness (*subpoena ad testificandum*) or to bring records/documents (*subpoena duces tecum*)

summary judgment a procedure whereby the claimant can obtain judgment without the defendant being permitted to defend the action

summary offence a lesser offence that may only be heard by **magistrates**

tort a civil wrong excluding breach of contract. It includes: negligence, trespass (to the person, goods or land), nuisance, breach of statutory duty and defamation

trespass to the person a wrongful direct interference with another person. Harm does not have to be proved

trial a court hearing before a judge

ultra vires outside the powers given by law (e.g. of a statutory body or company)

vicarious liability liability of an employer for the wrongful acts of an employee committed while in the course of employment

volenti non fit injuria to the willing there is no wrong; voluntary assumption of risk

ward of court a minor placed under the protection of the High Court, which assumes responsibility for him or her and all decisions relating to his or her care must be made in accordance with the directions of the court

warranties terms of a **contract** that are considered to be less important than the terms described as **conditions**: breach of a condition entitles the innocent party to see the contract as ended, i.e. repudiated by the other party (breach of warranties entitles the innocent party to claim damages)

Wednesbury principle court will intervene to prevent or remedy abuses of power by public authorities if there is evidence of unreasonableness or perversity. Principle laid down by the Court of Appeal in the case of *Associated Provincial Picture House Ltd* v. *Wednesbury Corporation* [1948] 1 KB 233

without prejudice without detracting from or without disadvantage to. The use of the phrase prevents the other party using the information to the prejudice of the one providing it

witness of fact a person who gives evidence of what they saw, heard, did or failed to do (contrast with **expert witness**)

writ a form of written command, e.g. the document that used to commence civil proceedings. Now a claim form is served

Abbreviations

A&E	Accident and Emergency
AC	Appeals Court
ALL ER	All England Law Reports
AGM	Annual General Meeting
BMA	British Medical Association
BMLR	British Medical Law Reports
CA	Court of Appeal
CNST	Clinical Negligence Scheme for Trusts
CPR	Cardiopulmonary Resuscitation
CQC	Care Quality Commission
CSA	Child Support Agency
CSCI	Commission for Social Care Inspection
DH	Department of Health
DNR	Do Not Resuscitate
DPP	Director of Public Prosecutions
DoLS	Deprivation of Liberty Safeguards
EC	European Community
ECHR	European Court of Human Rights
ECT	Electro-convulsive therapy
EWCA	England and Wales Court of Appeal
FLR	Family Law Reports
GMC	General Medical Council
GP	General Practitioner
HFEA	Human Fertilisation and Embryology Authority
HTA	Human Tissue Act or Authority
ICAS	Independent Complaints Advocacy Service
IMCA	Independent Mental Capacity Advocate
IMHA	Independent Mental Health Advocate
LGR	Local Government Reports
LPA	Lasting Power of Attorney
LREC	Local Research Ethics Committee
MCA	Mental Capacity Act
MHA	Mental Health Act
MREC	Multicentre Research Ethics Committee
NICE	National Institute for Health and Clinical Excellence

NMC	Nursing and Midwifery Council
NFR	Not For Resuscitation
NSF	National Service Framework
OPG	Office of Public Guardian
OPSI	Office of Public Sector Information
PCT	Primary Care Trust
QBD	Queen's Bench Division
RCN	Royal College of Nursing
SHA	Strategic Health Authority
SOAD	Second Opinion Appointed Doctor
UKCC	United Kingdom Central Council for Nursing, Midwifery and Health Visiting
UKHL	United Kingdom House of Lords
WLR	Weekly Law Reports

Websites

Action for advocacy	www.actionforadvocacy.org
Action on Elder Abuse	www.elderabuse.org.uk
Advisory Conciliation and Arbitration Service	www.acas.org.uk
Age Concern	www.ageconcern.org.uk
Alert	www.donoharm.org.uk
Alzheimer's Research	www. Alzheimers-research.org.uk
Alzheimer's Society	www.alzheimers.org.uk
ASA Advice	www.advice.org.uk
Association of Contentious Trust and Probate Solicitors	www.actaps.com
Audit Commission	www.audit-commission.gov.uk
Bailii (case law resource)	www.bailii.org/ew/cases
CARERS UK	www.carersonline.org.uk; www.carersuk.org
Care Quality Commission	www.cqc.org.uk
Care Services Improvement Partnership	www.csip.org.uk
Citizens Advice Bureaux	www.citizensadvice.org.uk
Citizen Advocacy Information and Training	www.citizenadvocacy.rg.uk
Civil Procedure Rules	www.open.gov.uk/lcd/civil/procrules_fin/ crules.htm
Clinical Negligence Scheme for Trusts	www.nhsla.com/Claims/Schemes/CNST/
Equality and Human Rights Commission	www.equalityhumanrights.com.
Commission for Racial Equality	www.cre.gov.uk/
Community Legal Service Direct	www.clsdirect.org.uk
Complementary Healthcare Information Service	www.chisuk.org.uk
Contact the Elderly	www.contact-the-elderly.org
Convention on the International Protection of Adults	www.hcch.net/index_en.php
Council for Healthcare Regulatory Excellence	www.chre.org.uk
Commission for Patient and Public Involvement in Health	www.cppih.org
Counsel and Care	www.counselandcare.org.uk
Court Funds Office	www.hmcourts-service.gov.uk/infoabout/cfo/ index.htm
Court of Protection	via the Office of Public Guardian or HM Courts Services
Central Office for Research Ethics Committees	www.corec.org.uk
Dementia Care Trust	www.dct.org.uk
Department for Business Enterprise and Regulatory Reform	www.berr.gov.uk/employment

Department for Education and Skills	www.dfes.gov.uk
Department for Work and Pensions	www.dwp.gov.uk/
Department of Health	www.dh.gov.uk
Department of Trade and Industry	www.dti.gov.uk/
Disability Law Service	www.dls.org.uk/
Domestic Violence	www.domesticviolence.gov.uk
Down's Syndrome Association	ww.downs-syndrome.org.uk; www.dsa-uk.com
Family Carer Support Service	www.familycarers.org.uk
Family Mediation Helpline	www.familymediationhelpline.co.uk
Foundation for People with Learning Disabilities	www.learningdisabilities.org.uk
General Medical Council	www.gmc-uk.org
Headway – brain injury Association	www.headway.org.uk
Health and Safety Executive	www.hse.gov.uk
Help the Aged	www.helptheagedorg.uk
Help the Hospices	www.hospiceinformation.info
Health Professions Council	www.hpc-uk.org
HM Courts Service	www.hmcourts-service.gov.uk
Home Farm Trust	www.hft.org.uk
Human Fertilisation and Embryology Authority	www.hfea.gov.uk/
Human Genetics Commission	www.hgc.gov.uk
Human Rights	www.humanrights.gov.uk
Independent Mental Capacity Advocate	www.dh.gov.uk.imca
Information Commissioner's Office	www.ico.gov.uk
Law Centres Federation	www.lawcentres.org.uk
Law Society	www.lawsociety.org.uk/choosingandusing/ findasolicitor.law
Legal cases (England and Wales)	www.bailli.org/ew/cases
Legislation	www.opsi.gov.uk/legislation or www. legislation.hmso.gov.uk
Linacre Centre for Healthcare Ethics	www.linacre.org
Making Decisions Alliance	www.makingdecisions.org.uk
Manic Depression Fellowship	www.mdf.org.uk
MedicAlert Foundation	www.medicalert.org.uk
Medicines and Healthcare Products Regulatory Agency	www.mhra.gov.uk
MENCAP	www.mencap.org.uk
Mental Capacity Implementation Programme	www.dca.go.uk/legal-policy/mental-capacity/ index.htm
Mental Health Foundation	www.mentalhealth.org.uk
Mental Health Lawyers Assoc	www.mhla.co.uk
Mental Health Matters	www.mentalhealthmatters.com
Mind	www.mind.org.uk
Ministry of Justice	www.justice.gov.uk
Motor Neurone Disease Association	www.mndassociation.org.uk
National Audit Office	www.nao.gov.uk
National Autistic Society	www.nas.org.uk; www.autism.org.uk
National Care Association	www.nca.gb.com
National Family Carer Network	www.familycarers.org.uk

National Health Service Litigation Authority	www.nhsla.com
National Mediation Helpline,	www.nationalmediationhelpline.com
National Patient Safety Agency	www.npsa.gov.uk
National Perinatal Epidemiology Unit	www.npeu.ox.ac.uk
National Treatment Agency	www.nta.nhs.uk
NHS website	www.nhs.uk
NHS Direct	www.nhsdirect.nhs.uk
NHS Professionals	www.nhsprofessionals.nhs.uk
NICE	www.nice.org.uk
Nursing and Midwifery Council	www.nmc-uk.org
Office of Public Guardian	www.publicguardian.gov.uk
Office of Public Sector Information	www.opsi.gov.uk
Official Solicitor	www.officialsolicitor.gov.uk
Open Government	www.open.gov.uk
Pain website	www.pain-talk.co.uk
Patient's Association	www.patients-association.org.uk
Patient Concern	www.patientconcern.org.uk
People First	www.peoplefirst.org.uk
Prevention of Professional Abuse Network	www.popan.org.uk
Princess Royal Trust for Carers	www.carers.org
Relatives and Residents Association	www.releres.org
RESCARE (The National Society for mentally disabled people in residential care)	www.rescare.org.uk
Respond	www.respond.org.uk
Rethink (formerly the National Schizophrenia Fellowship)	www.rethink.org
Royal College of Nursing	www.rcn.org.uk
Royal College of Psychiatrists	www.rcpsych.ac.uk
SANE	www.sane.org.uk
Scope	www.scope.org.uk
Sense	www.sense.org.uk
Solicitors for the Elderly	www.solicitorsfortheelderly.com
Speaking Up	www.speakingup.org
Speakability	www.speakability.org.uk
Shipman Inquiry	www.the-shipman-inquiry.org.uk/reports.asp
Solicitors for the Elderly	www.solicitorsfortheelderly.com
Stroke Association	www.stroke.org.uk
Together: Working for Wellbeing	www.together-uk.org
Turning Point	www.turning-point.co.uk
UK Homecare Association	www.ukhca.co.uk
UK Parliament	www.parliament.uk
United Response	www.unitedresponse.org.uk
Values into Action	www.viauk.org
Veterans Agency	www.veteransagency.org.uk
VOICE UK	www.voiceuk.clara.net
Voluntary Euthanasia Society	www.ves.org.uk
Welsh Assembly Government	www.wales.gov.uk
World Medical Associsation	www.wma.net/e/policy/b3.htm

Schedule 1 to the Human Rights Act 1998

Schedule 1 to the Human Rights Act 1998
Articles of the European Convention on Human Rights

Part I
THE CONVENTION

RIGHTS AND FREEDOMS
Article 2
Right to life

1. Everyone's right to life shall be protected by law. No one shall be deprived of his life intentionally save in the execution of a sentence of a court following his conviction of a crime for which this penalty is provided by law.
2. Deprivation of life shall not be regarded as inflicted in contravention of this Article when it results from the use of force which is no more than absolutely necessary:
   (a) in defence of any person from unlawful violence;
   (b) in order to effect a lawful arrest or to prevent the escape of a person lawfully detained;
   (c) in action lawfully taken for the purpose of quelling a riot or insurrection.

Article 3
Prohibition of torture

No one shall be subjected to torture or to inhuman or degrading treatment or punishment.

Article 4
Prohibition of slavery and forced labour

1. No one shall be held in slavery or servitude.
2. No one shall be required to perform forced or compulsory labour.
3. For the purpose of this Article the term 'forced or compulsory labour' shall not include:

(a) any work required to be done in the ordinary course of detention imposed according to the provisions of Article 5 of this Convention or during conditional release from such detention;

(b) any service of a military character or, in case of conscientious objectors in countries where they are recognised, service exacted instead of compulsory military service;

(c) any service exacted in case of an emergency or calamity threatening the life or well-being of the community;

(d) any work or service which forms part of normal civic obligations.

Article 5
Right to liberty and security

1. Everyone has the right to liberty and security of person. No one shall be deprived of his liberty save in the following cases and in accordance with a procedure prescribed by law:

(a) the lawful detention of a person after conviction by a competent court;

(b) the lawful arrest or detention of a person for non-compliance with the lawful order of a court or in order to secure the fulfilment of any obligation prescribed by law;

(c) the lawful arrest or detention of a person effected for the purpose of bringing him before the competent legal authority on reasonable suspicion of having committed an offence or when it is reasonably considered necessary to prevent his committing an offence or fleeing after having done so;

(d) the detention of a minor by lawful order for the purpose of educational supervision or his lawful detention for the purpose of bringing him before the competent legal authority;

(e) the lawful detention of persons for the prevention of the spreading of infectious diseases, of persons of unsound mind alcoholics or drug addicts or vagrants;

(f) the lawful arrest or detention of a person to prevent his effecting an unauthorised entry into the country or of a person against whom action is being taken with a view to deportation or extradition.

2. Everyone who is arrested shall be informed promptly, in a language which he understands, of the reasons for his arrest and of any charge against him.

3. Everyone arrested or detained in accordance with the provisions of paragraph 1(c) of this Article shall be brought promptly before a judge or other officer authorised by law to exercise judicial power and shall be entitled to trial within a reasonable time or to release pending trial. Release may be conditioned by guarantees to appear for trial.

4. Everyone who is deprived of his liberty by arrest or detention shall be entitled to take proceedings by which the lawfulness of his detention shall be decided speedily by a court and his release ordered if the detention is not lawful.

5. Everyone who has been the victim of arrest or detention in contravention of the provisions of this Article shall have an enforceable right to compensation.

Article 6
Right to a fair trial

1. In the determination of his civil rights and obligations or of any criminal charge against him, everyone is entitled to a fair and public hearing within a reasonable time by an independent and impartial tribunal established by law. Judgment shall be pronounced publicly but the press and public may be excluded from all or part of the trial in the interest of morals, public order or national security in a democratic society, where the interests of juveniles or the protection of the private life of the parties so require, or to the extent strictly necessary in the opinion of the court in special circumstances where publicity would prejudice the interests of justice.

2. Everyone charged with a criminal offence shall be presumed innocent until proved guilty according to law.

3. Everyone charged with a criminal offence has the following minimum rights:
   (a) to be informed promptly, in a language which he understands and in detail, of the nature and cause of the accusation against him;
   (b) to have adequate time and facilities for the preparation of his defence;
   (c) to defend himself in person or through legal assistance of his own choosing or, if he has not sufficient means to pay for legal assistance, to be given it free when the interests of justice so require;
   (d) to examine or have examined witnesses against him and to obtain the attendance and examination of witnesses on his behalf under the same conditions as witnesses against him;
   (e) to have the free assistance of an interpreter if he cannot understand or speak the language used in court.

Article 7
No punishment without law

1. No one shall be held guilty of any criminal offence on account of any act or omission which did not constitute a criminal offence under national or international law at the time when it was committed. Nor shall a heavier

penalty be imposed than the one that was applicable at the time the criminal offence was committed.

2. This Article shall not prejudice the trial and punishment of any person for any act or omission which, at the time when it was committed, was criminal according to the general principles of law recognised by civilised nations.

Article 8
Right to respect for private and family life

1. Everyone has the right to respect for his private and family life, his home and his correspondence.
2. There shall be no interference by a public authority with the exercise of this right except such as is in accordance with the law and is necessary in a democratic society in the interests of national security, public safety or the economic wellbeing of the country, for the prevention of disorder or crime, for the protection of health or morals, or for the protection of the rights and freedoms of others.

Article 9
Freedom of thought, conscience and religion

1. Everyone has the right to freedom of thought, conscience and religion; this right includes freedom to change his religion or belief and freedom, either alone or in community with others and in public or private, to manifest his religion or belief, in worship, teaching, practice and observance.
2. Freedom to manifest one's religion or beliefs shall be subject only to such limitations as are prescribed by law and are necessary in a democratic society in the interests of public safety, for the protection of public order, health or morals, or for the protection of the rights and freedoms of others.

Article 10
Freedom of expression

1. Everyone has the right to freedom of expression. This right shall include freedom to hold opinions and to receive and impart information and ideas without interference by public authority and regardless of frontiers. This Article shall not prevent States from requiring the licensing of broadcasting, television or cinema enterprises.
2. The exercise of these freedoms, since it carries with it duties and responsibilities, may be subject to such formalities, conditions, restrictions or penalties as are prescribed by law and are necessary in a democratic society, in the interests of national security, territorial integrity or public safety, for the prevention of disorder or crime, for the protection of health or morals, for the protection of the reputation or rights of others, for preventing the

disclosure of information received 'in confidence, or for maintaining the authority and impartiality of the judiciary.

Article 11
Freedom of assembly and association

1. Everyone has the right to freedom of peaceful assembly and to freedom of association with others, including the right to form and to join trade unions for the protection of his interests.
2. No restrictions shall be placed on the exercise of these rights other than such as are prescribed by law and are necessary in a democratic society in the interests of national security or public safety, for the prevention of disorder or crime, for the protection of health or morals or for the protection of the rights and freedoms of others. This Article shall not prevent the imposition of lawful restrictions on the exercise of these rights by members of the armed forces, of the police or of the administration of the State.

Article 12
Right to marry

Men and women of marriageable age have the right to marry and to found a family, according to the national laws governing the exercise of this right.

Article 14
Prohibition of discrimination

The enjoyment of the rights and freedoms set forth in this Convention shall be secured without discrimination on any ground such as sex, race, colour, language, religion, political or other opinion, national or social origin, association with a national minority, property, birth or other status.

Article 16
Restrictions on political activity of aliens

Nothing in Articles 10, 11 and 14 shall be regarded as preventing the High Contracting Parties from imposing restrictions on the political activity of aliens.

Article 17
Prohibition of abuse of rights

Nothing in this Convention may be interpreted as implying for any State, group or person any right to engage in any activity or perform any act aimed at the destruction of any of the rights and freedoms set forth herein or at their limitation to a greater extent than is provided for in the Convention.

Article 18
Limitation on use of restrictions on rights

The restrictions permitted under this Convention to the said rights and freedoms shall not be applied for any purpose other than those for which they have been prescribed.

Part II
THE FIRST PROTOCOL

Article 1
Protection of property

Every natural or legal person is entitled to the peaceful enjoyment of his possessions. No one shall be deprived of his possessions except in the public interest and subject to the conditions provided for by law and by the general principles of international law.

The preceding provisions shall not, however, in any way impair the right of a State to enforce such laws as it deems necessary to control the use of property in accordance with the general interest or to secure the payment of taxes or other contributions or penalties.

Article 2
Right to education

No person shall be denied the right to education. In the exercise of any functions which it assumes in relation to education and to teaching, the State shall respect the right of parents to ensure such education and teaching in conformity with their own religious and philosophical convictions.

Article 3
Right to free elections

The High Contracting Parties undertake to hold free elections at reasonable intervals by secret ballot, under conditions which will ensure the free expression of the opinion of the people in the choice of the legislature.

Part III
THE SIXTH PROTOCOL

Article 1
Abolition of the death penalty

The death penalty shall be abolished. No one shall be condemned to such penalty or executed.

Article 2
Death penalty in time of war

A State may make provision in its law for the death penalty in respect of acts committed in time of war or of imminent threat of war; such penalty shall be applied only in the instances laid down in the law and in accordance with its provisions. The State shall communicate to the Secretary General of the Council of Europe the relevant provisions of that law.

Schedule 3 of the Human Fertilisation and Embryology Act

SCHEDULE 3 CONSENT TO USE OR STORAGE OF GAMETES,
EMBRYOS OR HUMAN ADMIXED EMBRYOS ETC.
(Bold indicates amendments made by the 2008 Act)

Section 12 etc Consent

1 (1) A consent under this Schedule, and any notice under paragraph 4 varying or withdrawing a consent under this Schedule, must be in writing and, subject to sub-paragraph (2), must be signed by the person giving it. (2) A consent under this Schedule by a person who is unable to sign because of illness, injury or physical disability (a "person unable to sign"), and any notice under paragraph 4 by a person unable to sign varying or withdrawing a consent under this Schedule, is to be taken to comply with the requirement of sub-paragraph (1) as to signature if it is signed at the direction of the person unable to sign, in the presence of the person unable to sign and in the presence of at least one witness who attests the signature. (3) In this Schedule "effective consent" means a consent under this Schedule which has not been withdrawn.

2 (1) A consent to the use of any embryo must specify one or more of the following purposes—
(a) use in providing treatment services to the person giving consent, or that person and another specified person together,
(b) use in providing treatment services to persons not including the person giving consent,
(ba) use for the purpose of training persons in embryo biopsy, embryo storage or other embryological techniques, or (c) use for the purposes of any project of research, and may specify conditions subject to which the embryo may be so used.

(1A) A consent to the use of any human admixed embryo must specify use for the purposes of any project of research and may specify conditions subject to which the human admixed embryo may be so used.

(2) **A consent to the storage of** any gametes, any embryo **or any human admixed embryo** must–

(a) **specify the maximum period of storage (if less than the statutory storage period),**

(b) **except in a case falling within paragraph (c), state what is to be done with the gametes, embryo or human admixed embryo if the person who gave the consent dies or is unable, because the person lacks capacity to do so, to vary the terms of the consent or to withdraw it, and**

(c) **where the consent is given by virtue of paragraph 8(2ZA) or 13(2), state what is to be done with the embryo or human admixed embryo if the person to whom the consent relates dies, and may (in any case) specify conditions subject to which the gametes, embryo or human admixed embryo may remain in storage.**

(2A) **A consent to the use of a person's human cells to bring about the creation *in vitro* of an embryo or human admixed embryo is to be taken unless otherwise stated to include consent to the use of the cells after the person's death.**

(2B) **In relation to Scotland, the reference in sub-paragraph (2)(b) to the person lacking capacity is to be read as a reference to the person–**

(a) **lacking capacity within the meaning of the Age of Legal Capacity (Scotland) Act 1991, or**

(b) **being incapable within the meaning of section 1(6) of the Adults with Incapacity (Scotland) Act 2000.**

(3) A consent under this Schedule must provide for such other matters as the Authority may specify in directions.

(4) **A consent under this Schedule may apply–**

(a) **to the use or storage of a particular embryo or human admixed embryo, or**

(b) **in the case of a person providing gametes or human cells, to the use or storage of–**

    (i)   **any embryo or human admixed embryo whose creation may be brought about using those gametes or those cells, and**

    (ii)   **any embryo or human admixed embryo whose creation may be brought about using such an embryo or human admixed embryo.**

(5) **In the case of a consent falling within sub-paragraph (4)(b), the terms of the consent may be varied, or the consent may be withdrawn, in accordance with this Schedule either generally or in relation to–**

(a) **a particular embryo or particular embryos, or**

(b) a particular human admixed embryo or particular human admixed embryos.

Procedure for giving consent
3 (1) Before a person gives consent under this Schedule–
(a) he must be given a suitable opportunity to receive proper counselling about the implications of taking the proposed steps, and
(b) he must be provided with such relevant information as is proper.

(2) Before a person gives consent under this Schedule he must be informed of the effect of paragraph 4 **and, if relevant, paragraph 4A** below.

Variation and withdrawal of consent
4 (1) The terms of any consent under this Schedule may from time to time be varied, and the consent may be withdrawn, by notice given by the person who gave the consent to the person keeping the gametes, **human cells**, **embryo or human admixed embryo** to which the consent is relevant.

(2) **Subject to sub-paragraph (3), the** terms of any consent to the use of any embryo cannot be varied, and such consent cannot be withdrawn, once the embryo has been used–
(a) in providing treatment services,
(aa) in training persons in embryo biopsy, embryo storage or other embryological techniques, or
(b) for the purposes of any project of research.

(3) Where the terms of any consent to the use of an embryo ("embryo A") include consent to the use of an embryo or human admixed embryo whose creation may be brought about *in vitro* using embryo A, that consent to the use of that subsequent embryo or human admixed embryo cannot be varied or withdrawn once embryo A has been used for one or more of the purposes mentioned in sub-paragraph (2)(a) or (b).

(4) Subject to sub-paragraph (5), the terms of any consent to the use of any human admixed embryo cannot be varied, and such consent cannot be withdrawn, once the human admixed embryo has been used for the purposes of any project of research.

(5) Where the terms of any consent to the use of a human admixed embryo ("human admixed embryo A") include consent to the use of a human admixed embryo or embryo whose creation may be brought about *in vitro* using human admixed embryo A, that consent to the use of that subsequent human admixed embryo or embryo cannot be varied or withdrawn

once human admixed embryo A has been used for the purposes of any project of research.

4A (1) This paragraph applies where–

(a) a permitted embryo, the creation of which was brought about *in vitro*, is in storage,

(b) it was created for use in providing treatment services,

(c) before it is used in providing treatment services, one of the persons whose gametes were used to bring about its creation ("P") gives the person keeping the embryo notice withdrawing P's consent to the storage of the embryo, and

(d) the embryo was not to be used in providing treatment services to P alone.

(2) The person keeping the embryo must as soon as possible take all reasonable steps to notify each interested person in relation to the embryo of P's withdrawal of consent.

(3) For the purposes of sub-paragraph (2), a person is an interested person in relation to an embryo if the embryo was to be used in providing treatment services to that person.

(4) Storage of the embryo remains lawful until–

(a) the end of the period of 12 months beginning with the day on which the notice mentioned in sub-paragraph (1) was received from P, or

(b) if, before the end of that period, the person keeping the embryo receives a notice from each person notified of P's withdrawal under sub-paragraph (2) stating that the person consents to the destruction of the embryo, the time at which the last of those notices is received.

(5) The reference in sub-paragraph (1)(a) to a permitted embryo is to be read in accordance with section 3ZA.

Use of gametes for treatment of others
5 (1) A person's gametes must not be used for the purposes of treatment services **or non-medical fertility services** unless there is an effective consent by that person to their being so used and they are used in accordance with the terms of the consent.

(2) A person's gametes must not be received for use for those purposes unless there is an effective consent by that person to their being so used.

(3) This paragraph does not apply to the use of a person's gametes for the purpose of that person, or that person and another together, receiving treatment services.

In vitro fertilisation and subsequent use of embryo

6 (1) A person's gametes **or human cells** must not be used to bring about the creation of any embryo *in vitro* unless there is an effective consent by that person to any embryo, the creation of which may be brought about with the use of those gametes **or human cells**, being used for one or more of the purposes mentioned in **paragraph 2(1)(a), (b) and (c)** above.

(2) An embryo the creation of which was brought about *in vitro* must not be received by any person unless there is an effective consent by **each relevant person in relation to** the embryo to the use for one or more of the purposes mentioned in **paragraph 2(1)(a), (b), (ba) and (c)** above of the embryo.

(3) An embryo the creation of which was brought about *in vitro* must not be used for any purpose unless there is an effective consent by each **relevant person in relation to** the embryo to the use for that purpose of the embryo and the embryo is used in accordance with those consents.

(3ZA) If the Authority is satisfied that the parental consent conditions in paragraph 15A are met in relation to the proposed use under a licence of the human cells of a person who has not attained the age of 18 years ("C"), the Authority may in the licence authorise the application of sub-paragraph (3ZB) in relation to C.

(3ZB) Where the licence authorises the application of this sub-paragraph, the effective consent of a person having parental responsibility for C–
(a) to the use of C's human cells to bring about the creation of an embryo *in vitro* for use for the purposes of a project of research, or
(b) to the use for those purposes of an embryo in relation to which C is a relevant person by reason only of the use of C's human cells, is to be treated for the purposes of sub-paragraphs (1) to (3) as the effective consent of C.

(3ZC) If C attains the age of 18 years or the condition in paragraph 15A(3) ceases to be met in relation to C, paragraph 4 has effect in relation to C as if any effective consent previously given under sub-paragraphs (1) to (3) by a person having parental responsibility for C had been given by C but, subject to that, sub-paragraph (3ZB) ceases to apply in relation to C.
(3ZD) Sub-paragraphs (1) to (3) have effect subject to paragraphs 15B and 15F.

(3A) For the purposes of sub-paragraphs (2), (3) and (3ZB) each of the following is a relevant person in relation to an embryo the creation of which was brought about *in vitro* **("embryo A")–**

(a) each person whose gametes or human cells were used to bring about the creation of embryo A,

(b) each person whose gametes or human cells were used to bring about the creation of any other embryo, the creation of which was brought about *in vitro***, which was used to bring about the creation of embryo A, and**

(c) each person whose gametes or human cells were used to bring about the creation of any human admixed embryo, the creation of which was brought about *in vitro***, which was used to bring about the creation of embryo A.**

(4) Any consent required by this paragraph is in addition to any consent that may be required by paragraph 5 above.

Embryos obtained by lavage, etc
7 (1) An embryo taken from a woman must not be used for any purpose unless there is an effective consent by her to the use of the embryo for that purpose and it is used in accordance with the consent.

(2) An embryo taken from a woman must not be received by any person for use for any purpose unless there is an effective consent by her to the use of the embryo for that purpose.

(3) **Sub-paragraphs (1) and (2) do** not apply to the use, for the purpose of providing a woman with treatment services, of an embryo taken from her.

(4) An embryo taken from a woman must not be used to bring about the creation of any embryo *in vitro* **or any human admixed embryo** *in vitro***.**

Storage of gametes and embryos
8 (1) A person's gametes must not be kept in storage unless there is an effective consent by that person to their storage and they are stored in accordance with the consent.

(2) An embryo the creation of which was brought about *in vitro* must not be kept in storage unless there is an effective consent, by each **relevant person in relation to** the embryo, to the storage of the embryo and the embryo is stored in accordance with those consents.

(2ZA) Where a licence authorises the application of paragraph 6(3ZB) in relation to a person who has not attained the age of 18 years ("C"), the

effective consent of a person having parental responsibility for C to the storage of an embryo in relation to which C is a relevant person by reason only of the use of C's human cells is to be treated for the purposes of sub-paragraph (2) as the effective consent of C.

(2ZB) If C attains the age of 18 years or the condition in paragraph 15A(3) ceases to be met in relation to C, paragraph 4 has effect in relation to C as if any effective consent previously given under sub-paragraph (2) by a person having parental responsibility for C had been given by C but, subject to that, sub-paragraph (2ZA) ceases to apply in relation to C.

(2A) For the purposes of sub-paragraphs (2) and (2ZA), each of the following is a relevant person in relation to an embryo the creation of which was brought about *in vitro* ("embryo A")–
(a) each person whose gametes or human cells were used to bring about the creation of embryo A,
(b) each person whose gametes or human cells were used to bring about the creation of any other embryo, the creation of which was brought about *in vitro*, which was used to bring about the creation of embryo A, and
(c) each person whose gametes or human cells were used to bring about the creation of any human admixed embryo, the creation of which was brought about *in vitro*, which was used to bring about the creation of embryo A.

(3) An embryo taken from a woman must not be kept in storage unless there is an effective consent by her to its storage and it is stored in accordance with the consent.

(4) Sub-paragraph (1) has effect subject to paragraphs 9 and 10; and sub-paragraph (2) has effect subject to paragraphs 4A(4), 15B and 15F.

Cases where consent not required for storage
9 (1) The gametes of a person ("C") may be kept in storage without C's consent if the following conditions are met.

(2) Condition A is that the gametes are lawfully taken from or provided by C before C attains the age of 18 years.

(3) Condition B is that, before the gametes are first stored, a registered medical practitioner certifies in writing that C is expected to undergo medical treatment and that in the opinion of the registered medical practitioner–

(a) the treatment is likely to cause a significant impairment of C's fertility, and

(b) the storage of the gametes is in C's best interests.

(4) Condition C is that, at the time when the gametes are first stored, either–

(a) C has not attained the age of 16 years and is not competent to deal with the issue of consent to the storage of the gametes, or

(b) C has attained that age but, although not lacking capacity to consent to the storage of the gametes, is not competent to deal with the issue of consent to their storage.

(5) Condition D is that C has not, since becoming competent to deal with the issue of consent to the storage of the gametes–

(a) given consent under this Schedule to the storage of the gametes, or

(b) given written notice to the person keeping the gametes that C does not wish them to continue to be stored.

(6) In relation to Scotland, sub-paragraphs (1) to (5) are to be read with the following modifications–

(a) for sub-paragraph (4), substitute- "(4) Condition C is that, at the time when the gametes are first stored, C does not have capacity (within the meaning of section 2(4) of the Age of Legal Capacity (Scotland) Act 1991) to consent to the storage of the gametes.", and

(b) in sub-paragraph (5), for "becoming competent to deal with the issue of consent to the storage of the gametes" substitute "acquiring such capacity".

10 (1) The gametes of a person ("P") may be kept in storage without P's consent if the following conditions are met.

(2) Condition A is that the gametes are lawfully taken from or provided by P after P has attained the age of 16 years.

(3) Condition B is that, before the gametes are first stored, a registered medical practitioner certifies in writing that P is expected to undergo medical treatment and that in the opinion of the registered medical practitioner–

(a) the treatment is likely to cause a significant impairment of P's fertility,

(b) P lacks capacity to consent to the storage of the gametes,

(c) P is likely at some time to have that capacity, and (d) the storage of the gametes is in P's best interests.

(4) Condition C is that, at the time when the gametes are first stored, P lacks capacity to consent to their storage.

(5) Condition D is that P has not subsequently, at a time when P has capacity to give a consent under this Schedule–
(a) given consent to the storage of the gametes, or
(b) given written notice to the person keeping the gametes that P does not wish them to continue to be stored.

(6) In relation to Scotland–
(a) references in sub-paragraphs (3) and (4) to P lacking capacity to consent are to be read as references to P being incapable, within the meaning of section 1(6) of the Adults with Incapacity (Scotland) Act 2000, of giving such consent,
(b) the references in sub-paragraphs (3) and (5) to P having capacity are to be read as references to P not being so incapable, and
(c) that Act applies to the storage of gametes under this paragraph to the extent specified in section 84A of that Act. 12 A person's gametes must not be kept in storage by virtue of paragraph 9 or 10 after the person's death.

Creation, use and storage of human admixed embryos
13 (1) A person's gametes or human cells must not be used to bring about the creation of any human admixed embryo *in vitro* unless there is an effective consent by that person to any human admixed embryo, the creation of which may be brought about with the use of those gametes or human cells, being used for the purposes of any project of research.

(2) A human admixed embryo the creation of which was brought about *in vitro* must not be received by any person unless there is an effective consent by each relevant person in relation to the human admixed embryo to the use of the human admixed embryo for the purposes of any project of research.

(3) A human admixed embryo the creation of which was brought about *in vitro* must not be used for the purposes of a project of research unless–
(a) there is an effective consent by each relevant person in relation to the human admixed embryo to the use of the human admixed embryo for that purpose, and
(b) the human admixed embryo is used in accordance with those consents.

(4) If the Authority is satisfied that the parental consent conditions in paragraph 15A are met in relation to the proposed use under a licence of the human cells of a person who has not attained the age of 18 years ("C"), the Authority may in the licence authorise the application of sub-paragraph (5) in relation to C.

(5) Where the licence authorises the application of this sub-paragraph, the effective consent of a person having parental responsibility for C–

(a) to the use of C's human cells to bring about the creation of a human admixed embryo *in vitro* for use for the purposes of a project of research, or

(b) to the use for those purposes of a human admixed embryo in relation to which C is a relevant person by reason only of the use of C's human cells, is to be treated for the purposes of sub-paragraphs (1) to (3) as the effective consent of C.

(6) If C attains the age of 18 years or the condition in paragraph 15A(3) ceases to be met in relation to C, paragraph 4 has effect in relation to C as if any effective consent previously given under sub-paragraphs (1) to (3) by a person having parental responsibility for C had been given by C but, subject to that, sub-paragraph (5) ceases to apply in relation to C.

(7) Sub-paragraphs (1) to (3) have effect subject to paragraphs 16 and 20.

(1) A human admixed embryo the creation of which was brought about *in vitro* must not be kept in storage unless–

(a) there is an effective consent by each relevant person in relation to the human admixed embryo to the storage of the human admixed embryo, and

(b) the human admixed embryo is stored in accordance with those consents.

(2) Where a licence authorises the application of paragraph 13(5) in relation to a person who has not attained the age of 18 years ("C"), the effective consent of a person having parental responsibility for C to the storage of a human admixed embryo in relation to which C is a relevant person by reason only of the use of C's human cells is to be treated for the purposes of sub-paragraph (1) as the effective consent of C.

(3) If C attains the age of 18 years or the condition in paragraph 15A(3) ceases to be met in relation to C, paragraph 4 has effect in relation to C as if any effective consent previously given under sub-paragraph (1) by a person having parental responsibility for C had been given by C but, subject to that, sub-paragraph (2) ceases to apply in relation to C. (4) Sub-paragraph (1) has effect subject to paragraphs 15B and 15F.

14 For the purposes of paragraphs 12 and 13, each of the following is a relevant person in relation to a human admixed embryo the creation of which was brought about *in vitro* ("human admixed embryo A")–
(a) each person whose gametes or human cells were used to bring about the creation of human admixed embryo A,
(b) each person whose gametes or human cells were used to bring about the creation of any embryo, the creation of which was brought about *in vitro*, which was used to bring about the creation of human admixed embryo A, and
(c) each person whose gametes or human cells were used to bring about the creation of any other human admixed embryo, the creation of which was brought about *in vitro*, which was used to bring about the creation of human admixed embryo A.

Parental consent conditions
15A (1) In relation to a person who has not attained the age of 18 years ("C"), the parental consent conditions referred to in paragraphs 6(3ZA) and 13(4) are as follows.

(2) Condition A is that C suffers from, or is likely to develop, a serious disease, a serious physical or mental disability or any other serious medical condition.

(3) Condition B is that either–
(a) C is not competent to deal with the issue of consent to the use of C's human cells to bring about the creation *in vitro* of an embryo or human admixed embryo for use for the purposes of a project of research, or
(b) C has attained the age of 16 years but lacks capacity to consent to such use of C's human cells.

(4) Condition C is that any embryo or human admixed embryo to be created *in vitro* is to be used for the purposes of a project of research which is intended to increase knowledge about–
(a) the disease, disability or medical condition mentioned in sub-paragraph (2) or any similar disease, disability or medical condition, or
(b) the treatment of, or care of persons affected by, that disease, disability or medical condition or any similar disease, disability or medical condition.

(5) Condition D is that there are reasonable grounds for believing that research of comparable effectiveness cannot be carried out if the only human cells that can be used to bring about the creation *in vitro* of embryos or human admixed embryos for use for the purposes of the project are the human cells of persons who–

(a) have attained the age of 18 years and have capacity to consent to the use of their human cells to bring about the creation *in vitro* of an embryo or human admixed embryo for use for the purposes of the project, or

(b) have not attained that age but are competent to deal with the issue of consent to such use of their human cells.

(6) In relation to Scotland, sub-paragraphs (1) to (5) are to be read with the following modifications–

(a) for sub-paragraph (3) substitute– "(3) Condition B is that C does not have capacity (within the meaning of section 2(4ZB) of the Age of Legal Capacity (Scotland) Act 1991) to consent to the use of C's human cells to bring about the creation *in vitro* of an embryo or human admixed embryo for use for the purposes of a project of research.",

(b) in sub-paragraph (5)(a), for "have capacity to consent" substitute "are not incapable (within the meaning of section 1(6) of the Adults with Incapacity (Scotland) Act 2000) of giving consent", and

(c) in sub-paragraph (5)(b), for "are competent to deal with the issue of" substitute "have capacity (within the meaning of section 2(4ZB) of the Age of Legal Capacity (Scotland) Act 1991) to".

Adults lacking capacity: exemption relating to use of human cells etc.
15B (1) If, in relation to the proposed use under a licence of the human cells of a person who has attained the age of 18 years ("P"), the Authority is satisfied–

(a) that the conditions in paragraph 15C are met,

(b) that paragraphs (1) to (4) of paragraph 15D have been complied with, and

(c) that the condition in paragraph 15D(5) is met, the Authority may in the licence authorise the application of this paragraph in relation to P.

(2) Where a licence authorises the application of this paragraph, this Schedule does not require the consent of P–

(a) to the use (whether during P's life or after P's death) of P's human cells to bring about the creation *in vitro* of an embryo or human admixed embryo for use for the purposes of a project of research,

(b) to the storage or the use for those purposes (whether during P's life or after P's death) of an embryo or human admixed embryo in relation to which P is a relevant person by reason only of the use of P's human cells.

(3) This paragraph has effect subject to paragraph 15E.

Consent to use of human cells etc. not required: adult lacking capacity
15C (1) The conditions referred to in paragraph 15B(1)(a) are as follows.

(2) Condition A is that P suffers from, or is likely to develop, a serious disease, a serious physical or mental disability or any other serious medical condition.

(3) Condition B is that P lacks capacity to consent to the use of P's human cells to bring about the creation *in vitro* of an embryo or human admixed embryo for use for the purposes of a project of research.

(4) Condition C is that the person responsible under the licence has no reason to believe that P had refused such consent at a time when P had that capacity.

(5) Condition D is that it appears unlikely that P will at some time have that capacity.

(6) Condition E is that any embryo or human admixed embryo to be created *in vitro* is to be used for the purposes of a project of research which is intended to increase knowledge about–
(a) the disease, disability or medical condition mentioned in sub-paragraph (2) or any similar disease, disability or medical condition, or
(b) the treatment of, or care of persons affected by, that disease, disability or medical condition or any similar disease, disability or medical condition.

(7) Condition F is that there are reasonable grounds for believing that research of comparable effectiveness cannot be carried out if the only human cells that can be used to bring about the creation *in vitro* of embryos or human admixed embryos for use for the purposes of the project are the human cells of persons who–
(a) have attained the age of 18 years and have capacity to consent to the use of their human cells to bring about the creation *in vitro* of an embryo or human admixed embryo for use for the purposes of the project, or
(b) have not attained that age but are competent to deal with the issue of consent to such use of their human cells. (8) In this paragraph and paragraph 15D references to the person responsible under the licence

are to be read, in a case where an application for a licence is being made, as references to the person who is to be the person responsible.

(9) In relation to Scotland

(a) references in sub-paragraphs (3) to (5) to P lacking, or having, capacity to consent are to be read respectively as references to P being, or not being, incapable (within the meaning of section 1(6) of the Adults with Incapacity (Scotland) Act 2000) of giving such consent, and

(b) sub-paragraph (7) is to be read with the following modifications–

    (i)   in paragraph (a), for "have capacity to consent" substitute "are not incapable (within the meaning of section 1(6) of the Adults with Incapacity (Scotland) Act 2000) of giving consent", and

    (ii) in paragraph (b), for "are competent to deal with the issue of" substitute "have capacity (within the meaning of section 2(4ZB) of the Age of Legal Capacity (Scotland) Act 1991) to".

Consulting carers etc. in case of adult lacking capacity

15D (1) This paragraph applies in relation to a person who has attained the age of 18 years ("P") where the person responsible under the licence ("R") wishes to use P's human cells to bring about the creation *in vitro* of an embryo or human admixed embryo for use for the purposes of a project of research, in a case where P lacks capacity to consent to their use.

(2) R must take reasonable steps to identify a person who–

(a) otherwise than in a professional capacity or for remuneration, is engaged in caring for P or is interested in P's welfare, and

(b) is prepared to be consulted by R under this paragraph of this Schedule.

(3) If R is unable to identify such a person R must nominate a person who–

(a) is prepared to be consulted by R under this paragraph of this Schedule, but

(b) has no connection with the project.

(4) R must provide the person identified under sub-paragraph (2) or nominated under sub-paragraph (3) ("F") with information about the proposed use of human cells to bring about the creation *in vitro* of embryos or human admixed embryos for use for the purposes of the project and ask F what, in F's opinion, P's wishes and feelings about the use of P's human cells for that purpose would be likely to be if P had capacity in relation to the matter.

(5) The condition referred to in paragraph 15B(1)(c) is that, on being consulted, F has not advised R that in F's opinion P's wishes and feelings would be likely to lead P to decline to consent to the use of P's human cells for that purpose.

(6) In relation to Scotland, the references in sub-paragraphs (1) and (4) to P lacking, or having, capacity to consent are to be read respectively as references to P being, or not being, incapable (within the meaning of section 1(6) of the Adults with Incapacity (Scotland) Act 2000) of giving such consent.

Effect of acquiring capacity
15E (1) Paragraph 15B does not apply to the use of P's human cells to bring about the creation *in vitro* of an embryo or human admixed embryo if, at a time before the human cells are used for that purpose, P–
(a) has capacity to consent to their use, and
(b) gives written notice to the person keeping the human cells that P does not wish them to be used for that purpose.

(2) Paragraph 15B does not apply to the storage or use of an embryo or human admixed embryo whose creation *in vitro* was brought about with the use of P's human cells if, at a time before the embryo or human admixed embryo is used for the purposes of the project of research, P–
(a) has capacity to consent to the storage or use, and
(b) gives written notice to the person keeping the human cells that P does not wish them to be used for that purpose.

(3) In relation to Scotland, the references in sub-paragraphs (1)(a) and (2)(a) to P having capacity to consent are to be read as references to P not being incapable (within the meaning of section 1(6) of the Adults with Incapacity (Scotland) Act 2000) of giving such consent.

Use of cells or cell lines
15F (1) Where a licence authorises the application of this paragraph in relation to qualifying cells, this Schedule does not require the consent of a person ("P")–
(a) to the use of qualifying cells of P to bring about the creation *in vitro* of an embryo or human admixed embryo for use for the purposes of a project of research, or
(b) to the storage or the use for those purposes of an embryo or human admixed embryo in relation to which P is a relevant person by reason only of the use of qualifying cells of P.

(2) "Qualifying cells" are human cells which–

(a) were lawfully stored for research purposes immediately before the commencement date, or

(b) are derived from human cells which were lawfully stored for those purposes at that time.

(3) The "commencement date" is the date on which paragraph 9(2)(a) of Schedule 3 to the Human Fertilisation and Embryology Act 2008 (requirement for consent to use of human cells to create an embryo) comes into force.

Conditions for grant of exemption in paragraph 20

15G (1) A licence may not authorise the application of paragraph 15F unless the Authority is satisfied–

(a) that there are reasonable grounds for believing that scientific research will be adversely affected to a significant extent if the only human cells that can be used to bring about the creation *in vitro* of embryos or human admixed embryos for use for the purposes of the project of research are–

    (i) human cells in respect of which there is an effective consent to their use to bring about the creation *in vitro* of embryos or human admixed embryos for use for those purposes, or

    (ii) human cells which by virtue of paragraph 15B can be used without such consent, and

(b) that any of the following conditions is met in relation to each of the persons whose human cells are qualifying cells which are to be used for the purposes of the project of research.

(2) Condition A is that–

(a) it is not reasonably possible for the person responsible under the licence ("R") to identify the person falling within sub-paragraph (1)(b) ("P"), and

(b) where any information that relates to P (without identifying P or enabling P to be identified) is available to R, that information does not suggest that P would have objected to the use of P's human cells to bring about the creation *in vitro* of an embryo or human admixed embryo for use for the purposes of the project.

(3) Condition B is that–

(a) the person falling within sub-paragraph (1)(b) ("P") is dead or the person responsible under the licence ("R") believes on reasonable grounds that P is dead. (b) the information relating to P that is available to R does not suggest that P would have objected to the use of P's human cells to bring about the creation *in vitro* of an embryo or human admixed embryo for use for the purposes of the project, and

(c) a person who stood in a qualifying relationship to P immediately before P died (or is believed to have died) has given consent in writing to the use of P's human cells to bring about the creation *in vitro* of an embryo or human admixed embryo for use for the purposes of the project.

(4) Condition C is that–

(a) the person responsible under the licence ("R") has taken all reasonable steps to contact–
  (i)   the person falling within sub-paragraph (1) (b) ("P"), or
  (ii) in a case where P is dead or R believes on reasonable grounds that P is dead, persons who could give consent for the purposes of sub-paragraph (3)(c) but has been unable to do so, and

(b) the information relating to P that is available to R does not suggest that P would have objected to the use of P's human cells to bring about the creation *in vitro* of an embryo or human admixed embryo for use for the purposes of the project.

(5) The HTA consent provisions apply in relation to consent for the purposes of sub-paragraph (3)(c) as they apply in relation to consent for the purposes of section 3(6)(c) of the Human Tissue Act 2004; and for the purposes of this sub-paragraph the HTA consent provisions are to be treated as if they extended to Scotland.

(6) In sub-paragraph (5) "the HTA consent provisions" means subsections (4), (5), (6), (7) and (8)(a) and (b) of section 27 of the Human Tissue Act 2004.

(7) In this paragraph references to the person responsible under the licence are to be read, in a case where an application for a licence is being made, as references to the person who is to be the person responsible.

(8) Paragraphs 1 to 4 of this Schedule do not apply in relation to a consent given for the purposes of sub-paragraph (3)(c).

Interpretation
16 (1) In this Schedule references to human cells are to human cells which are not–
(a) cells of the female or male germ line, or
(b) cells of an embryo.

(2) References in this Schedule to an embryo or a human admixed embryo which was used to bring about the creation of an embryo ("embryo A")

or a human admixed embryo ("human admixed embryo A") include an embryo or, as the case may be, a human admixed embryo which was used to bring about the creation of–

(a) an embryo or human admixed embryo which was used to bring about the creation of embryo A or human admixed embryo A, and

(b) the predecessor of that embryo or human admixed embryo mentioned in paragraph (a), and

(c) the predecessor of that predecessor, and so on.

(3) Reference in this Schedule to an embryo or a human admixed embryo whose creation may be brought about using an embryo or a human admixed embryo are to be read in accordance with sub-paragraph (2).

(4) Reference in this Schedule (however expressed) to the use of human cells to bring about the creation of an embryo or a human admixed embryo include the use of human cells to alter the embryo or, as the case may be, the human admixed embryo. (5) References in this Schedule to parental responsibility are–

(a) in relation to England and Wales, to be read in accordance with the Children Act 1989,

(b) in relation to Northern Ireland, to be read in accordance with the Children (Northern Ireland) Order 1995, and

(c) in relation to Scotland, to be read as references to parental responsibilities and parental rights within the meaning of the Children (Scotland) Act 1995.

(6) References in this Schedule to capacity are, in relation to England and Wales, to be read in accordance with the Mental Capacity Act 2005.

(7) References in this Schedule to the age of 18 years are, in relation to Scotland, to be read as references to the age of 16 years.

Schedule 3ZA of the Human Fertilisation and Embryology Act

SCHEDULE 3ZA CIRCUMSTANCES IN WHICH OFFER OF
COUNSELLING REQUIRED AS CONDITION OF LICENCE FOR
TREATMENT

Part 1
KINDS OF TREATMENT IN RELATION TO WHICH COUNSELLING
MUST BE OFFERED

1   The treatment services involve the use of the gametes of any person and
    that person's consent is required under paragraph 5 of Schedule 3 for the
    use in question.
2   The treatment services involve the use of any embryo the creation of which
    was brought about *in vitro*.
3   The treatment services involve the use of an embryo taken from a woman
    and the consent of the woman from whom the embryo was taken was
    required under paragraph 7 of Schedule 3 for the use in question.

Part 2
EVENTS IN CONNECTION WITH WHICH COUNSELLING MUST BE
OFFERED

4   A man gives the person responsible a notice under paragraph (a) of subsec-
    tion (1) of section 37 of the Human Fertilisation and Embryology Act 2008
    (agreed fatherhood conditions) in a case where the woman for whom the
    treatment services are provided has previously given a notice under para-
    graph (b) of that subsection referring to the man.
5   The woman for whom the treatment services are provided gives the person
    responsible a notice under paragraph (b) of that subsection in a case where
    the man to whom the notice relates has previously given a notice under
    paragraph (a) of that subsection.
6   A woman gives the person responsible notice under paragraph (a) of sub-
    section (1) of section 44 of that Act (agreed female parenthood conditions)
    in a case where the woman for whom the treatment services are provided

has previously given a notice under paragraph (b) of that subsection referring to her.

7   The woman for whom the treatment services are provided gives the person
responsible a notice under paragraph (b) of that subsection in a case where
the other woman to whom the notice relates has previously given a notice
under paragraph (a) of that subsection.

Index of cases

Index of statutes

Index